Weapons and Warfare
in
Anglo-Saxon England

Members of The Dark Ages Society in action with sword and shield. St. Cross College Garden, January 1987.
(Photo: Janet Wakeley)

Oxford University Committee for Archaeology
Monograph No. 21

Weapons and Warfare
in
Anglo-Saxon England

edited by
Sonia Chadwick Hawkes

Oxford University Committee for Archaeology
1989

Published by
Oxford University Committee for Archaeology
Institute of Archaeology
Beaumont Street
Oxford

Distributed by
Oxbow Books
Park End Place, Oxford OX1 1HN

ISBN 0 947816 21 6

Typeset by Oxbow Books
at Oxford University Computing Service

Printed in Great Britain
at the Short Run Press, Exeter

Contents

Acknowledgements

Many institutions and individuals have contributed to the making of this book. First, I should like to acknowledge the contribution of Regent's Park College, Oxford, which hosted the Conference in January 1987 and kept us warm, well-fed and comfortable in bitter cold weather, and to thank St Cross College, Oxford, for the use of the garden where we held our affray-at-arms on a sharp, frosty Saturday afternoon. I am particularly indebted to the members of the Dark Ages Society, Alan Baxter, Neil Bell, Peter Bone and David Gale, who enlivened and informed our proceedings by their practical experience of re-enacting Anglo-Saxon warfare. It was highly instructive to be allowed to handle and study their replica weapons, which made a grand display when piled on the dais of the College lecture-room, and most educational of all to watch, and take part in, their realistic demonstrations of combat.

I am grateful to David Brown of Oxbow Books, and his team, who have produced this book for us using the University Lasercomp, and for his help with the illustration on the cover. Marion Cox has fair-copied the drawings for most of the contributions and Seamus Ross has dramatically improved the computer graphics for Heinrich Härke's paper. The photograph used as a frontispiece is by courtesy of Janet Wakeley. Marion Cox's drawing of the Repton Rider Stone is adapted from the version published by Martin and Birthe Kjølbye-Biddle, with their consent.

Sonia Chadwick Hawkes
20 November 1988

Chapter 1

Weapons and Warfare in Anglo-Saxon England: An Introduction

Sonia Chadwick Hawkes

This book is the outcome of a particularly successful conference held in Oxford in January 1987. It was the fourth of a series of *Oxford Seminars in Anglo-Saxon Studies*, weekend conferences restricted by invitation to small numbers of contributing scholars, and priding themselves on their interdisciplinary character and composition.

Previous such Seminars during the 1980's, on the themes of *East Anglia, Arts and Crafts* and *Mercia*, had been immensely enjoyable and stimulating but had not, for various reasons, lent themselves to publication in any systematic way. A few contributions from them have been published in the Oxford-based occasional series *Anglo-Saxon Studies in Archaeology and History*, or *ASSAH*, the fifth volume of which should appear more or less simultaneously with the present book. However, the conference on *Weapons and Warfare in Anglo-Saxon England* seemed from its very inception to be breaking new ground: the contributions were mostly fresh and new, not weary restatements of old views or rehashes of existing publications, and though there were some enjoyable 'rehashes' of known views on the lecture platform, notably those especially requested by myself, as organizer, from such redoubtable protagonists as Professors Nicholas Brooks and R. Allen Brown, on the warlike abilities of English and Norman respectively, these speakers wisely declined to contribute what would inevitably have been derivative material to any publication in the present book. On a more detailed scale, the contributions from Martin Biddle on the Repton Rider Stone (which we do however figure, p. 81, fig. 6.15.2, with his permission) and Dominic Tweddle on the helmet from Coppergate, York, while good in the context of the conference, have either been fully published already or are destined to appear elsewhere.

At the conference itself, however, there was a general feeling that, these already familiar contributions notwithstanding, the whole topic of Anglo-Saxon warfare and weapons had been greatly neglected in modern literature, and a book on the subject was badly needed. This is an astonishing admission to have to make about the current state of research into a society which prided itself on its prowess in war, to the extent that its recorded annals, history and literature, are dominated by references to battles. But it is a fact that modern research has tended to sheer away from this fundamental aspect of life in Anglo-Saxon England, probably for modern sociological reasons, and that modern viewpoints have tended to obscure some fundamental truths about our Anglo-Saxon forefathers. One hopes that the present book of essays may help correct the imbalance, and restore to our enfeebled imagination some concept of the paramount importance of martial training and martial prowess amongst the male population of Anglo-Saxon England. Without the protection of the kings and other great magnates with their retinues of highly-trained warriors, Anglo-Saxon society could not have afforded conditions under which the talented craftsmen, poets and writers, through whom it is best known to us today, could have functioned at all, let alone survived for any length of time.

In this connexion, it must be stressed that the warrior class was composed of an élite that was physically as well as socially supreme. Boys with any major physical handicaps, and common sense should suggest to us that they must have been at least as common then as now, would obviously have been totally unsuited to the tough disciplines of serious training for war, however well connected they may have been socially. A cripple, a blind or very short-sighted boy, or even a child who suffered severely from asthma, would have been disqualified as potential warriors either from the outset or as time went by and their disabilities became apparent. However, recent work on Anglo-Saxon skeletons from pagan cemeteries is making it increasingly clear that this was a society that valued its children and kept them alive even when grossly handicapped. There are known cases of severe *spina bifida*, for example, and even a case of a congenitally deformed man, born with only one arm, who was yet allowed to live out what was then a not abnormally short life-span of about thirty years (Hawkes and Wells 1976; 1983, 9). Evidence such as this suggests that there was a place even in pagan Anglo-Saxon society for the physically handicapped. We do not know enough about the workings of class structure to tell how such basic disadvantages could affect the individual's social status and whether a handicapped child born to a good family could descend to the status of the slave or servant, such as the one-armed man, from his lack of grave-goods and general condition, seems to have been. But clearly for the physically handicapped child of good birth who was intelligent and otherwise talented there must have been alternative career-prospects in the arts. These will have existed already in pagan times, for it is surely no coincidence that different Indo-European societies have common traditions of blind bards and lame smiths. To these we may certainly add the near-sighted jeweller, for no man without a short focal length of vision could have produced such minutely detailed masterpieces as the jewellery from Sutton Hoo. But opportunities must have increased dramatically with the coming of Christianity, when there was both a proliferation of sheltered accommodation in monasteries and a greatly increased range of quiet skills to be practised, from gardening to calligraphy and manuscript illumination. One wonders, indeed, whether we may owe our first English history to the chance that the seven-year old Bede proved unable to hit a barn door at five yards.

But to digress in such a way into considering the fate of the handicapped child in Anglo-Saxon society, which could offer not the simplest of artificial aids to alleviate its lot, fascinating though it can be, should not distract our minds from the paramount importance of the physically fit to the survival of that society. Even today the handicapped require immense amounts of help from the fit members of our community. And in Anglo-Saxon society the fittest males were the fighting men who ensured its survival.

It seems appropriate, therefore, that one of the most important topics to emerge at the Conference, and this reaffirms itself in the book, is how Anglo-Saxon boys were trained for their military role. There is no contemporary manual on the subject, nor much in the literature of direct relevance, but in the first paper, 'On the Training of Warriors', Hilda Ellis Davidson draws widely on Anglo-Saxon, Celtic and Norse literary sources to give a convincing account of how such training must have been carried out, and Nicholas Hooper reverts to the topic in his own paper, 'The Anglo-Saxons at War', which closes the book. Boys of the aristocratic warrior class were separated at the early age of seven, primarily through fosterage, into segregated peer-groups which were intensively trained in martial skills and hunting into a warrior élite, in small bands such as might have been fostered together in a royal or otherwise aristocratic household with veteran warriors as trainers. The modern equivalent, though of course less martial, would be the English boys' Prep School. One of the most important things for the boys was to acquire a group-identity and loyalty which would carry them through into the next stage of graduation into the category of 'young warriors'.

One of the most difficult things for us to come to terms with today is the short absolute time-scale of their lives: boys became young warriors as early as fourteen or even twelve and could expect to be rewarded with land for their services by their middle twenties. But in a society where the average life expectancy of a man, once he had survived the hazards of childhood, did not exceed forty years, and a woman had even less chance of reaching what we now consider to be the prime of life, of course people grew up faster and had to take on serious responsibilities much younger than we do today. After all, nowadays we can expect twice the life-span of an Anglo-Saxon. No wonder, then, that in studying pagan cemeteries we find small boys buried with small weapons and boys in their early and middle teens buried with the weapons of adults. The archaeological evidence in this respect is simply reflecting what can be culled from the literary sources. And no wonder that Calvin Wells has been able to detect, from their skeletons, the signs that Anglo-Saxons were subjected to heavy physical stresses of one form or another from their early teens (Hawkes and Wells 1983, 14).

There has been much discussion about the actual numbers of fighting men engaged in the invasion of Britain and the early battles. Modern cemetery and settlement evidence from this country begins seriously to suggest that Anglo-Saxon numbers were initially small, and John Hines's new study of the ritual weapon-deposits in the lakes and graves of the English homelands in south Jutland and North Germany reinforces that impression. His conclusion is that the rich weapon-deposits in several such sacred lakes, belonging to different regions within the northern homelands, represent armies of not more than two hundred men who had been raised from 'tribal' or regional populations of many thousands. From the paucity of weapon-graves in the homelands he infers a 'thinly spread military élite..within which even the non-sword bearers could be counted. Warfare would seem to have been the business of this élite and few others.' Against such a background we could expect the 'invasion' of Britain to have been carried out by warrior groups of anything from two-hundred downwards, but scarcely more. Given such a scenario, the Anglo-Saxon Chronicler's much maligned record of land-takings by two, three or five ship-loads of men, far from being merely formulaic, must represent something approximating to the truth. Allowing crews of about forty apiece, such as had manned the ship at Sutton Hoo, the warbands in those early invasion ships conform in numbers to what we should now begin to accept as the norm for the period. Traditional leaders such as Hengest, Stuf/Wihtgar, Baeda/Maegla and Cerdic may have led armies numbering between about eighty and two hundred men. This makes the best recorded opposing army from the British side, the much discussed three hundred of the Gododdin, a far less insignificant force than some historians have suggested (Jackson 1969, 13–18).

The evidence from individual Germanic cemeteries established in the fifth century suggests that land could be taken and held in Britain by Anglo-Saxon communities with just one or two major weapon-bearing families in charge. I have suggested elsewhere that at a local level a very few armed men must have sufficed to intimidate and contain the British population, which will have been mostly civilian and untrained to arms (Hawkes 1986, 74). However, even given their absolutely small numbers, Hines notes that the percentage of weapon-burials in Germanic cemeteries in England is higher than in Scandinavia or North Germany. This is not unnatural: obviously the success of the land-takings in England will have depended on the presence and protection of more weapon-bearing males than were needed to maintain the *status quo* at home. Obviously the whole venture will have attracted the warrior classes, who probably organised the shipment and movement of the farming families who must have made up the bulk of the 'invaders'. Young warriors especially will have seen the success of the migration to Britain as an irresistible opportunity to acquire land for themselves at an earlier age than at home. Though many of the settlers came as refugees from the destruction of their native environments, by the flooding of the coastlands of Saxony and Friesland, for example, many of the earliest and most warrior-like Germanic settlers of England came from regions not so directly or disastrously affected by deteriorating ecological conditions. Angles, Jutes and Franks may have joined the movement out of sheer opportunism. And some of their leaders were indeed young. The young Frank with decorated sword and lyre in grave 42 at Abingdon, for example, who seems to have been the dominant male there in the period just after the middle of the fifth century (Hawkes 1986, 78), died while still biologically adolescent, ie. before he was eighteen (Leeds & Harden 1936, 38). Two generations later in the more stable and prosperous kingdom of Kent, *c.* 525, the aristocrat who founded the Finglesham cemetery, having presumably been granted his estate after serving successfully in the warband of the Kentish king of the day, died at about age twenty-five (Hawkes 1982, 25).

Where the incoming Anglo-Saxons were heavily outnumbered by existing and resisting British, as in Northumbria or Southern Wessex, it is not surprising to find that the numbers of weapon-bearing males exceeded the norm for Anglo-Saxon England as a whole (Alcock 1981). Härke's paper, 'Early Anglo-Saxon Weapon Burials', while qualifying the whole concept of weapon-sets in burials as true statements about status (in other words, economies were being practised in the funeral-rite), nonetheless stresses the numerical and social differences in the armaments represented in the various regions.

Hilda Ellis Davidson concludes that as few as a hundred men made up an army and within the army there were individual units of about ten men who, having trained together, formed individual warbands who could combine with each other at need. The importance of training as a band and maintaining group-identity was well demonstrated by the members of the Dark Ages Society who attended the Conference. Not only did they enrich our discussions by their experience of what Anglo-Saxon warfare must have been like in practice, but they also contributed almost realistic and certainly frightening demonstrations of individual combat with sword, spear and shield. To those of us who became involved with them as inexperienced recruits to either shield-wall or melée, it at once became clear that you not only needed to have lightning reflexes, which could only have been produced by incessant training, but also the security of being able to rely on and instantly recognise the other members of your team. A well-trained unit of about ten young men would have been just about the ideal number to belong to. They would probably have been familiar with every detail of each other's clothing, equipment and individual styles of fighting, so when raiding together would have needed no other recognition-symbols. But a warband made up of several such smaller units must have needed easy means of recognition in the heat of battle. One cannot overstress the likelihood that the different sides wore team colours of some sort, feathers perhaps or bright sprigs of broom, and distinctively coloured shields, plus instantly identifiable devices, such as individualistic helmets on the heads, and horse-tail plumes in the standards, of their leaders.

Personally I have never understood why some scholars should have been incredulous about the human reality of the traditional co-founders of the Kentish royal house, Hengest and Horsa, to the extent of calling them 'twin horse-deities' (Turville-Petre 1956–7). Anglo-Saxons enjoyed a robust if primitive sense of humour, as their Riddles, their human- and place-names all witness. They used pet-names even for their leaders. For a pair of leaders whose totem is likely to have been the horse, the giving of nick-names such as 'stallion' and 'horse' must have been perfectly natural to their following, as it was to be later amongst the warbands of the North American Indians.

To return to more practical matters, the members of the Dark Ages Society have researched and reproduced their weapons with great care and accuracy. Two of them, Peter Bone and David Gale, contribute articles to this book which usefully summarise the developments of the two-edged long sword and single-edged seax respectively. David Gale's argument that the seax was primarily a hunting knife rather than a weapon of war was brilliantly illustrated at the Conference, by a practical demonstration of its total ineffectiveness against both spear and sword. Other replicas made by the Society proved equally instructive to handle. Even for an archaeologist familiar with the remains of weapons from rivers or graves, it comes as something of a shock to experience the heavy weight of a long sword and of a properly constructed plank-built wooden shield in pristine condition. With their prominent hand-protecting iron bosses, shields were used actively, not just to parry blows but to inflict them on the body of the opponent, so a man fighting with spear and shield, or sword and shield, will have needed much strength and stamina as well as ambidextrous skills.

Sword-hilts, and very probably shield-grips too, seem to have been tailored to fit the hands of their owners very tightly, with the result that the fingers of the fighting man would very quickly have become numbed and would 'freeze' on to the weapon, so as to prevent it being dropped from exhaustion. One has to imagine how trained reflexes must have taken charge after a prolonged stand in the shield-wall, as exemplified at Hastings, or in the sort of running fight that must have been characteristic of many a raid and probably most regular battles in the early period. The small size of shields in the pagan period (average diameter about 50 cm) suggests that battle tactics then favoured not the shield-wall so much as the melée. In the melée the outcome will have been dictated by the results of a series of duels amongst the protagonists, such as described in the poem *The Battle of Maldon*, which consisted of bouts of furious activity – twenty minutes being a maximum for the Dark Ages Society re-enactment group – in which blows were exchanged, interspersed with pauses in which to draw breath and exchange insults or jokes, before resuming the action. There must have been rules to this type of warfare, to prevent exhausted protagonists being stabbed in the back by outsiders, or the major combatants were perhaps guarded.

This type of question is addressed by Guy Halsall in his important paper on 'The Ritual war in Anglo-Saxon England'. He draws on anthropological models to adduce that there must have been different levels of warfare in Anglo-Saxon England, which ranged from the local feud or cattle-raid scale of action through to the serious emergency involving outright war with another kingdom. All these levels of war, from ritual play-war to the real thing, were necessary to the welfare of the society involved, in preserving group-identity and, not least, exercising and testing the talents of the warrior class and the success of the king as leader. This is another of the topics studied by Nicholas Hooper, who concludes 'that successful war was essential to stable kingship and society'.

The most prestigious weapon throughout the Anglo-Saxon period was of course the long sword, the weapon of the aristocrat, which is most honoured in heroic poetry; the weapon which could acquire its own mystique and even bear a name of its own (Davidson 1962). When one excavates a sword after it has been more than a thousand years underground one tends first to look at the hilt-fittings to estimate its date and the social quality of its owner, but of course the really important thing about a sword is its blade. The quality of the blade was what made a sword famous, or not as the case may be, the ideal sword being razor-sharp and both strong and flexible. Assessing the original composition and quality of that yard of rusty iron after such a lapse of time is not generally possible without X-Raying it. The importance of radiographs in the study of ancient ironwork is now well understood: indeed these days X-Rays are used routinely as a first step in the work of conservation. Yet, despite a preliminary essay by the writer in 1960 (admittedly unpublished), there has been no systematic large-scale study of Anglo-Saxon swords by this essential method until very recently. The important paper by Janet Lang and Barry Ager in this volume, 'Swords of the Anglo-Saxon and Viking Periods in the British Museum; a Radiographic Study', gives us the results of radiographing nearly 150 swords. The high percentage of composite blades, produced by the process known as pattern-welding, in the sixth and seventh centuries, especially in the wealthy kingdom of Kent, highlights the loving attention given by sword-smiths to the blade. The core of the blade could consist of from two to ten bundles of iron rods, which would be welded together, hammered, ground, etched and polished, to give a fine decorative finish. It is a pity that this study could not determine whether the pattern-welding technique was used primarily for strength and flexibility, as one had hitherto been led to suppose (France-Lanord 1949; Anstee and Biek 1961) and not just for decorative effect. But from Anstee's practical estimate of the time and materials a fine pattern-welded sword would take to make – at least 200 hours and 2–3 cwt of charcoal – I myself feel that he was right to favour the functional role of pattern-welding. Assuredly, 'the patterned surface of a sword...did provide the customer with a guarantee of quality' (Anstee and Biek 1961, 85) and it can be no accident that Lang and Ager's radiographic study demonstrates clearly that the grander the sword's context and fittings the more complex the blade structure is likely to be. Thus the princes at Sutton Hoo and Taplow were buried with very elaborately constructed blades indeed.

The lethal results of sword-wounds are vividly brought home to us by Sarah Wenham, at the time of the Conference a medical student at Leicester University, in her paper 'Anatomical interpretations of Anglo-Saxon weapon injuries'. She had made a special study of weapon-injuries on skeletons from a Middle to Late Saxon cemetery at Eccles, on the River Medway, in Kent. In Anglo-Saxon cemeteries generally it is unusual to find the skeletons of people who have been killed in combat. This is probably because battles took place away from home and the dead could not be brought back for burial. Exceptional cases such as the man impaled by a spear in the cemetery at Harwell, Oxon (Brown 1967) and the man in grave 94 in my own cemetery at Finglesham, Kent, who had suffered a fatal sword-cut to the head that had lifted a whole disc of scalp and bone, can probably be interpreted as the victims of local outbursts of violence, such as the blood feud must often have provoked. However, the situation at Eccles where no less than six men were killed at one time and buried in one small community's cemetery, looks far more serious. Most of the able-bodied men seem to have been wiped out, all by sword-cuts to the head, and one of them, perhaps the leader, was also brutally chopped up by savage cuts to arms and abdomen. Such a scene of carnage is so exceptional that one looks outside the immediate locality for a cause. The date of this massacre is likely to have been in the ninth or tenth centuries when the Vikings were active around the coasts of Kent and up the Medway. Here perhaps we have an illustration of the frightful impact professionally trained warrior-raiders might have had on a normally peaceful farm or village whose less well-trained and armed menfolk had the courage to resist them. Unfortunately, given the date of these slaughtered men, they were not buried with the weapons which would have told us about their social and martial status.

The Vikings terrorized England for nearly two centuries, during which they established settlements which have left surprisingly little trace archaeologically, created dialects which have enriched the English language without supplanting it, and imposed short-term kingship which was in its turn to be succeeded by English and Norman. The strength of the English economy, which was able to buy them off many times by the payment of Danegeld, to prevent their harrying the land to destruction, is discussed by Michael Metcalf in his masterly article on 'Danegelds in relation to War and History'.

Wherever they landed their longships and went ravaging across the land of England, the Vikings found horses to ride. The availability of horses capable of being ridden over long distances raises questions about the extent to which horses were being bred for war in Anglo-Saxon England. This question is addressed in 'Did the Anglo-Saxons have warhorses?', by R.H.C. Davis. He makes a good case for the existence of royal studs in the later Saxon period and for the beginning of specialized breeding, but, as Jennifer Bourdillon told us at the Conference, there is no archaeological evidence for the existence of anything larger than what we would nowadays call ponies. But then what did people in Anglo-Saxon England do with thorough-bred riding horses once they were dead? In these days traditionally the huntsman feeds them to the dogs: they are not recycled into human consumption, in this country at any rate. So in Anglo-Saxon times probably they would not appear at all in the midden of a town such as Southampton (Bourdillon 1988): they would surely have been too much esteemed to have been eaten except on great ritual occasions, if then. According to the written evidence (Mcaney forthcoming) the eating of horseflesh was anyway taboo in Christian Anglo-Saxon England, presumably because it had pagan associations. This seems to be one area where the documentary evidence is more reliable than the archaeological.

Finally, 'In the Anglo-Saxons at War', Nicholas Hooper sums up the whole question of the competence of the Anglo-Saxons to meet the Normans in war. In a wide-ranging, thoughtful study, he reviews the evidence for all aspects of Anglo-Saxon warfare, from the motivation, the training, through to mobility, tactics and supply.

By the eleventh century it was possible for Harold Godwinson, like Alfred before him, to raise a large army quickly and to maintain it for months on end, as indeed he did during the summer of 1066, when threatened by the long wind-delayed invasion from Normandy. But, as everyone knows, from the vivid account in the *Anglo-Saxon Chronicle*, the fates were against Harold. It was his misfortune to be faced with the treachery of his brother Tostig, who had allied himself with another potent invader, Harald king of Norway, and after having been forced to disband his fleet and army in the south because it was out of provisions by 8th September, to have to take an army north overland, moving fast 'by day and night as quickly as he could assemble his force', eventually to meet and defeat the combined forces of the enemy at Stamford Bridge in Yorkshire, on 25th September.

Just three days later, the adverse winds which had kept William on the other side of the Channel for weeks having changed with impeccable timing for the Normans, William was able to land his own army at Pevensey on 28th September. He had sunk his teeth into the land which had been the heart of the Godwinson patrimony in Harold's own earldom of Wessex, and his ravaging of his adversary's home territory is thought to have been a major factor in driving Harold to retaliate as quickly as he did (William of Poitiers, 170). The news that William had finally landed in the south will have reached Harold on about 1st October, just when he was relaxing and celebrating his victory in the north.

Thereafter he moved with decisive, some say reckless, speed (Brown 1985, 137) in an attempt to dislodge William before he had established too strong a foothold and done too much damage. By 13th October, having ridden with such force as could keep up with him over the 190 miles from York to London, having stayed a mere six days in London to assemble an army in the south, he moved with all speed towards William's fortified position at Hastings, in the hope of taking William by surprise. He arrived with his army on the evening of 13th October, but 'William seized the initiative.. the Norman army advanced from Hastings against Harold, and imposed on him a defensive action, hastily prepared, in a position something less than ideal, with an army weaker in numbers than it need have been, and already worn out by its own exertions' (Brown 1985, 138–9). Harold was forced to take station on the hill where Battle Abbey now stands. According to the D and E versions of the *Anglo-Saxon Chronicle*, William surprised Harold by forcing him to fight before all his army was drawn up and in position; Florence of Worcester (i, 227) says there was not room for all the potential fighting men on Harold's confined hill-top position and that many deserted on that account; while William of Malmesbury tells us that Harold had chiefly professional soldiers in his army and few members of the provincial levies. As to Harold's army as a whole, he says (*Gesta Regum*, i, 282) 'They were indeed few in number and exceedingly brave: they spared not their bodies and gave up their lives for their country'.

Such courage notwithstanding, by the evening of the day following, 14th October, Harold, his brothers and most of his army lay dead on the battlefield. They had fought on foot behind the shield wall, with spear, sword and battle-axe, exposed to attacks not just by comparable foot-soldiers, but by the massed archery and heavy cavalry which were the special tactical weapons of the Normans. The whole tragic tale is portrayed vividly and with amazing accuracy and detail in that most splendid of all archaeological documents for the period, The Bayeux Tapestry (Stenton 1957 & 1965; Wilson 1985). Considering all the odds against Harold, it is astonishing that William did not have an easier victory. And yet Hastings was a hard-fought battle, lasting a whole day, with heavy losses on both sides. It is a proud testimony to the trained martial skills and tough discipline of Harold's housecarls and other professional warriors, and to their loyalty to their king, that they were not overwhelmed by the more varied and flexible tactics, above all the cavalry charges, of the

Normans, but stood their ground. In the end it was the death of Harold which finally broke their resistance and gave William the victory but, as Hooper says, had William been killed or gravely wounded, 'the outcome might well have been different.'

References

Alcock, L. 1981: Quantity or quality: the Anglian graves of Bernicia, *Angles, Saxons and Jutes: Studies presented to J.N.L. Myres*, ed. V.I. Evison (Oxford), 168–86.

Anstee, J.W. and Biek, L. 1961: A study of pattern-welding, *Medieval Archaeology* 5, 71–93.

Bourdillon, J. 1988: Countryside and Town: the animal resources of Saxon Southampton, *Anglo-Saxon Settlements*, ed. Della Hooke (Oxford).

Brown, P.D.C. 1967: The Anglo-Saxon cemetery at Harwell, grave 7, *Oxoniensia* 32, 73–4.

Brown, R.A. 1985: *The Normans and the Norman Conquest* (2nd ed. Bury St Edmunds).

Florence of Worcester: *Chronicon ex Chronicis*, ed. B. Thorpe, 2 vols. (London. 1848–9).

France-Lanord, A. 1949: La fabrication des épées damassées aux époques mérovingiennes et carolingiennes, *Pays gaumais* 10.

Hawkes, S.C. 1982: Finglesham a cemetery in East Kent, *The Anglo-Saxons*, ed. J. Campbell (Oxford), 24–5.

Hawkes, S.C. 1986: The early Saxon period, *The Archaeology of the Oxford Region*, ed. G. Briggs *et al.* (Oxford), 64–114.

Hawkes, S.C. and Wells, C. 1976: Absence of the left upper limb and pectoral girdle in a unique Anglo-Saxon burial, *Bulletin of the New York Academy of Medicine* 2 ser. 2, no. 10, 1229–1235.

Hawkes, S.C. and Wells, C. 1983: The inhumed skeletal material from an early Anglo-Saxon cemetery in Worthy Park, Kingsworthy, Hampshire, *Paleobios* 1, 3–36.

Jackson, K.H. 1969: *The Gododdin* (Edinburgh).

Leeds, E.T. and Harden, D.H. 1936: *The Anglo-Saxon Cemetery at Abingdon, Berkshire* (Oxford).

Meaney, A.L. forthcoming: Anglo-Saxon ecclesiasts and idolators, *Anglo-Saxon Studies in Archaeology and History 5*.

Stenton, F.M. (ed) 1957, 2 ed. 1965: *The Bayeux Tapestry* (London).

Turville-Petre, J.E. 1956–7: Hengest and Horsa, *Viking Society for Northern Research..Saga Book* 14, part 4, 273–90.

William of Malmesbury: *Gesta Regum Anglorum*, ed. William Stubbs. Rolls Series 90. 2 vols. (London. 1887, 1889).

William of Poitiers: *Gesta Guilelmi Ducis Normannorum et Regis Anglorum*, ed. R. Foreville (Paris. 1952).

Wilson, D.M. (ed.) 1985: *The Bayeux Tapestry* (London).

Chapter 2

The Training of Warriors

Hilda Ellis Davidson

In a book called *The Art of War*, Christian Feest (1980) examines patterns of life in tribal societies where warfare had been an essential factor within recent times, using material from various African peoples, Polynesians and Melanesians in the Pacific Islands, and the North American Indians. Much of what he records is directly applicable to the world of the Celts and Germans as we see it reflected in medieval literature. His approach helps to reveal practices and symbols associated with warfare, reminding us of its importance in the lives of men and women in the early medieval period. Admittedly much of our literary material is derived from Iceland, where there was no need of a standing army to guard the borders, and such fighting as took place seems to have been on a tiny scale, with the numbers killed usually in single figures. Nevertheless the heroic background of warfare has left an indelible mark on Icelandic poetry and saga, while in Scandinavia, the British Isles and the Germanic areas of the Continent, warrior bands long continued to play an important part, impinging on the lives of the ruling classes and of the people in general.

From the Iron Age onwards, warfare permeated the social structure of north-western Europe, influencing art, symbolism and literature; it played an important part in the pre-Christian religion and left its mark on popular beliefs and customs. While the doings of the ruthless Vikings and the martial exploits of heroes like CúChulainn are widely known, the importance of warfare for understanding early literature can be easily underestimated, as armchair scholars concentrate on bookish elements and the influences of Christian learning. Ignorance of the techniques of weapon-play and of battle tactics may mean that much that is significant remains undetected in both art and literature. Since a warrior society depends for its survival on the efficient training of its youth, this aspect of life was an important one. Young men growing to manhood had to be able to defend themselves, while those destined to be leaders had need of many specialised skills. When a kingdom was under a strong central authority, as was usual in the early medieval period – Iceland again being an exception – training of special bodies of élite warriors was essential for the security and prestige of the ruler. He would need border or palace guards and expert fighters to lead the attack in time of war, or organise the equivalent of commando raids. Some men served as warriors in their youth and later retired to their estates, returning to serve the king when needed; others earned a living as mercenaries in a war-band, and others remained professional warriors until too old to fight. For these various careers a good and thorough training in boyhood was needed if they were to play an effective part in a warrior's world.

Not many youths, however, led a specialised life devoted solely to warfare. Feest makes it clear that the normal method of training was for bands of boys to live together away from home, practising the skills of warfare and hunting side by side, and in the societies which he studied he found little distinction between the weapons of war and those used by the hunter. Julius Caesar in *The Gallic War* (VI, 21) couples hunting and warfare together in describing the life of the Germans, and adds: 'they devote themselves from childhood to fatigue and hardships'. We hear of communities of young fighting men in both Norse and Irish literature. One well known group is that of the berserks in Scandinavian tradition, figures around which a wealth of folklore and wild legend prolificated, so that in the saga literature they appear as monstrous creatures, almost ogres, seizing wealth and women as they chose and impervious to ordinary weapons. In the ninth-century *Hrafnsmál*, however, a poem known also as *Haraldskvæði*, concerned with the fame of Harald Fairhair of Vestfold and attributed to one of his court poets (Kershaw 1922; Turville-Petre 1976), they became more credible figures. After mention of the leaders, champions and poets at the king's court, all of whom receive generous recompense from Harald, a question is asked about the berserks, to which comes the reply:

> Wolfcoats are they called, those who bear
> bloodstained swords to battle;
> they redden spears when they come to the slaughter,
> acting together as one.

It is in such fierce fighters, comments the poet, that a wise king puts his trust in time of battle. The reputation of the berserks depended on the wild fury with which they fought, cutting down all in their path and ignoring danger and the pain of wounds.

The name *berserkr* is generally taken to mean 'bearshirt', implying that these warriors wore the skins of bears as well as those of wolves, as indicated by the name 'Wolfcoats' (Davidson 1978, 132–3). An alternate interpretation of *berserkr* is 'bare shirt', based on the custom of fighting semi-naked, as in the modern expression 'birthday suit', and this is favoured in a recent article by Kim McCone (1987), an important study on the significance of Dog and Wolf names applied to early warriors to which I shall be making further reference. The berserks were reputed to fight without defensive armour, and the explanation of 'running berserk' (*berserksgangr*) given in *Heimskringla* (*Ynglinga Saga* 6), emphasises this:

> His (i.e. Odin's) men went without mailcoats and were as mad as dogs or wolves; they
> bit their shields and were as strong as bears or boars. They slew men, but neither fire
> nor iron had any effect on them. This is called 'running berserk'.

Outside observers of battles in which Germans or Celts took part report that some barbarian warriors fought naked except for a belt, and such figures are depicted both in Roman art and on Scandinavian helmet plates of about the sixth century AD. The little man shown on a buckle plate from grave 95 in the Anglo-Saxon cemetery at Finglesham, Kent, is a warrior of this kind, wearing only a belt and helmet (Hawkes, Davidson and Hawkes 1965). The belt would be convenient to hold a sword or knife, but might also have a symbolic significance if the skin of bear or wolf was used for it. In later Scandinavian folklore, men who changed into wolves at night were said to put on a belt of wolfskin before leaving the house, and this evidently represented the skin of the beast as a whole (Davidson 1978, 133; Lid 1950, 91f.). While there is evidently a close connection between berserks and wolves, confirmed by the name Wolfcoats given to them in the ninth century, the association with bears also seems important for Scandinavian warriors. The bear fights alone and not in a pack, and while in dreams in the Icelandic Sagas a band of enemies is often represented by a pack of wolves, a hero and leader, like Gunnar in *Brennu-Njáls Saga*, may be seen as a powerful bear (Davidson 1978, 137). It may be noted that in a number of tales in the sagas, such as *Víga-Glums Saga* and *Grettis Saga*, a young man proves his strength and courage by tackling a fierce bear single-handed (Danielli 1945). In one of these tales the youth wears a bearskin cloak, and brings back the snout of the bear to prove he has killed it; in another a bearskin cloak is thrown at the bear by the leader of a band of youths who are taunting the young man, and he has to get it back, and also prove that he has overcome the bear by cutting off one of its paws. In the second case the leader of the band is called Bjǫrn (bear). Another example of an encounter with a bear at the beginning of a young man's career as a warrior is found in the Latin account of the life of Hereward the Wake, *De Gestis Herwardi Saxonis* (3): the young Hereward joins a company of youths at the house of his godfather, Gisebritus, and at Christmas asks if he may be allowed to fight with a ferocious bear kept in a cage. He is told he is too young, but next day the bear gets loose and Hereward encounters it and kills it by cleaving its head with his sword, after which he holds up the dead beast to display it to the company. We are told that this deed made him envied and hated by the other boys, but that he won position and honour with the knights and was praised in the countryside, where women and girls made songs about him for their dances.

Both Bjǫrn and Ulf were popular elements in personal names. The famous Danish hero, Boðvar Bjarki, was originally named *Bjarki* (Little Bear), his first name being a nickname meaning 'warlike'; this may be the reason why the widespread folktale of the Bear's Son came to be attached to him in *Hrólfs Saga kraka*. In the sixth book of the *History* of Saxo Grammaticus (trans. Fisher 1979, 173, pp. 162ff.; commentary by Davidson 1980, 95f.), he has a tale of twelve fierce warriors in possession of an almost impregnable fortress on an island, and gives some of their names, all of which include the element *bjǫrn*, while Bjǫrn is given as the name of their leader. A puzzling statement in the preface to the *Prose Edda* of Snorri Sturluson implies an association between bearskins and young warriors, since Thor, here represented as a human hero afterwards deified, is said to have proved his strength in his youth by lifting twelve bearskins from the ground. Traces of bearskins have been found in men's graves in Norway and parts of Sweden from the period before the Viking Age (Vierck 1970, 385).

Thus there is evidence in support of the term *berserkr* meaning 'bear-shirt', although there is no doubt that the berserks were also associated with wolves. Figures on helmet-plates from Sweden and on scabbards and buckles from Alamannic graves appear to be men wearing animal skins and animal heads; some of these resemble bears and others wolves (Davidson 1965, 23f). They are sometimes shown in company with dancing naked warriors like the one on the Finglesham buckle. The emphasis on wild animals in warrior tradition is in keeping with the link between warfare and hunting made by Feest in his account of bands of young men undergoing training, and the test of manhood by killing a wild animal seems well-established. According to Julius Caesar, *Gallic War* VI, 28, the German youths proved themselves by trapping an aurochs, the great bull then found in central Europe, in a pit and going down to overcome it single-handed, and such a scene is illustrated on the base of the Gundestrup bowl. They are said to produce the horns in public as evidence of their achievement.

Wolves and dogs are closely linked, and both frequently associated with youthful warriors, as McCone has shown; the use of personal names derived from Wolf, Bear and Hound is well-established among Germans, Scandinavians and Celts in western Europe. We have an example in one of Saxo's tales of two boys who were hiding because of the hostility of their uncle, who had killed their father; wolves' claws were fastened to the boys' feet so that they left what seemed to be wolf-tracks, and they were then given the names of dogs, Hopp and Ho, according to *Hrólfs Saga kraka*, which includes the same story (Saxo Grammaticus 1979, VII, 182, p. 202). McCone gives many 'dog' names from Irish literature, of which the best known is that of CúChulainn (Hound of Culann) (Strachan 1944; Ganz 1981, 138f.). His original name was Sétanta, but he acquired the new one after overcoming the fierce hound which guarded the lands of King Conchobar, his mother's brother according to one tradition. The hound, which belonged to Culann the Smith, was so powerful that three men were needed to hold it, and the young boy encountered it after it had been loosed to guard the cattle during the night, but he was unafraid and overcame it with his bare hands. When the smith lamented the loss of his dog, which secured the lives and honour of the Ulstermen and was, he declared 'the man of the family', Sétanta offered to take its place:

> I will rear you a whelp from the same litter, and until it is grown and capable of action
> I will be the hound that protects your cattle and yourself.

In a number of Irish tales, young men belong to the *fiana*, the roving bands associated with the hero Finn MacCumaill (O'Grady 1892, vol. 2, 100; Sjoestadt 1982, 101f.; Nagy 1985, 41f.). They had no fixed abode and lived in the forest in the summer, occupied with hunting and warfare, independent of families and friends. For a youth to gain entry meant undergoing rigorous tests, such as being buried up to the waist in the earth and defending himself with a shield and a hazel-stick while the rest hurled javelins at him, or moving noiselessly through the forest without stirring a twig or ruffling his braided hair while pursued by armed warriors. The bands were divided into separate groups of nine or twelve, and in winter they supported themselves by foraging and robbery, and it was recognised that they might steal, and seize women. Sjoestedt suggests that they were tolerated, so long as they kept within certain bounds, because they were accounted 'among the institutions necessary to the prosperity of the tribe', and they waged war on its enemies. Caesar notes in *The Gallic War* (VI, 23) that German youths were not punished for robberies committed outside the boundaries of their own kingdom, since they claim that these are carried out for the purpose of discipling their youth and preventing sloth. These youths were associated with deer and hounds; one of Finn's wives was said to be a doe, and his sister's sons were hounds. He said that he preferred them so: 'If I were their father, I would prefer that they be as they are rather than be human.' Finn himself was said to appear as deer or dog according to how he wore his hood. There are such close resemblances between the traditions of bands of warriors in Irish and Norse sources that earlier scholars like Zimmer thought that the *fiana* were modelled on memories of Viking bands of raiders. However the cycle of tales goes back earlier than the Scandinavian invasion, as Sjoestedt pointed out, and she perceived the true nature of the parallel (Sjoestedt 1982, 106):

> It is not by comparison with the Vikings who invaded Ireland in the ninth century
> that Fenian mythology can be explained, but by comparison with the myths of the

Einherjar, the chosen of Odin, or with the savage *Berserkir*, the 'bearskin warriors'. On both sides we find the same violent life on the margin of ordered society, the same fury, the same personalities with animal components, and the same type of warrior fraternities.

The young warrior was clearly required to learn the skills of the hunter and to identify himself with the fierce animals of the wild. We are often told of the berserks fighting like wild beasts, howling as they went on their destructive path, killing all before them in the ecstasy of battle. Ability to lose oneself in such battle-fury was regarded as a gift of Odin, along with the inspiration which he granted to poets and orators. Parallels may be seen in the fantastic excesses attributed to Arthur's warriors in the Welsh *Mabinogion*, in Culhwch and Olwen (see also Davidson 1982), one of whom was covered with hair like a stag, while another emitted such heat from the soles of his feet that he could burn down any obstacle, and a third could drink up part of the sea; such descriptions convey something of the wild fury and heat of battle possessing these warriors. On one occasion CúChulainn had to be plunged into several buckets of cold water to restore him to a normal state of mind and release him from a destructive fury like that of a rogue elephant or maddened bull. Such traditions may account for one element in the many tales of shape-changing in the early literature, belonging to a different world from that of the fairytale or the cunning magician and reflecting the particular method of training which young men were required to undergo, emphasising a link with the wild animals of mountain and forest.

A tale which illustrates this is that of the training of young Sinfjǫtli, Sigmund's son, in *Vǫlsunga Saga* (8), when he and his father were preparing to take vengeance on the slayer of their kinsmen. They lived like outlaws in the forest, and one day came across two men asleep in a hut with gold rings on their arms, and two wolfskins hanging on the wall:

> They could take off the skins every tenth day, and they were kings' sons. Sigmund and Sinfjǫtli put on the wolfskins and were unable to take them off. With the wearing of them went the same nature as belonged to the skins: they spoke with the voice of wolves, and yet each understood what was uttered. They stayed out in the wilds, each going his own way; they made an agreement that each would take on as many as seven men but no more, and that he who was attacked first should cry out as a wolf does, 'We must not depart from this', said Sigmund, 'for you are young and full of reckless courage, and men will want to hunt you down'.

Accordingly when a band of men attacked Sigmund, he howled, and Sinfjǫtli came to his aid, but when the boy was alone, he met eleven men and managed to kill them all. However he got no praise for this: Sigmund was so angry with him for not summoning help that he leapt upon him and bit him in the throat. Sinfjǫtli would have died had his father not found a healing herb which cured the wound. Finally we are told that when the time came they took off the skins and forsook this way of life. Similar rules about fighting are found in the Icelandic sagas applied to bands of warriors living together, the most famous being the tradition of the Jómsberg vikings (Blake 1962). A parallel may be found in Irish literature, when the hero Cormac was asked what were his deeds as a young man (Meyer 1909, 8; McCone 1987, 111). 'Not hard to tell', he replied. 'When I was alone I would slay a bear, I would follow a track; when I was one of five I would march against a troop of five; when I was one of ten, I was ready to slay and wreck; when I was one of twenty I was ready for a raid; when I was one of a hundred, I was ready to give battle. These were my deeds'.

In the first century AD Tacitus in his *Germania* 31 describes certain picked warriors among the Chatti living the same kind of life as that of the berserks:

> None of them has home, land or business of his own. To whatever host they choose to go, they get their keep from him, wasting the goods of others while despising their own, until old age drains their blood and incapacitates them for so exacting a form of heroism.

Here we have what seems to be an extension of the temporary life lived by adolescents, a special troop of fighting men freed from the restrictions laid on normal members of the community, and yet under their own stern discipline. A picture of this type of warrior in old age is given by Saxo in his character of Starkad the Old, to whom he devotes a good deal of attention in books VI and VIII of his *History of the Danes* (see Davidson 1980, vol. 2 98f., 134f.). Starkad was an unflinching follower of Odin, a veteran of countless battle in which he suffered many horrible wounds; he despised all human weakness and had no time whatsoever for women, even refusing to accept help from one when severely hurt. He loathed comfort and merrymaking, and roundly condemned kings who entertained at splendid banquets and their wives who wore ornaments. In language reminiscent of the Roman satirists, whom Saxo was probably imitating here, or the sterner prophets of Ancient Israel, he makes plain the austere ideals of dedicated warriors. If men like him helped train the young, the heroic life must have been demanding indeed.

But it may be safely assumed that his ideas about women were not shared by most young warriors in training. In studies of tribal age-groups from various warrior societies, it is clear that dealings with girls were by no means condemned, and that sexual adventures formed a recognised part of the growing-up process. F.H. Stewart noted that members of adolescent age-groups among the Prairie Indians of North America not only pursued martial skills but also spent a good deal of time singing love-songs and performing dances to attract the girls. He points out that it is somewhat misleading to describe such groups as 'military associations' (Stewart 1971, 267):

> ... there is scarcely more justification for this than there would be for calling them 'erotic associations'. War, like love, was one of the dominating interests of the young Mandan or Hidatsa men, and it is not surprising that this interest finds its reflection in the age organisation ... But the age society did not normally, if ever, act as a military unit.

Evidently we must distinguish between such bands of young men learning warrior skills and special groups of committed men of the Starkad type. Most of the ruling class, having proved themselves and served as fighting men for a period, married and settled down as rulers of halls, probably with a grant of land from the king, as suggested by the term 'Land-right' (*lond-riht*) as used in *Beowulf*. Dorothy Whitelock pointed out the distinction made in the poem between *duguð* and *geoguð*, tried warriors and young retainers, in the retinue of King Hrothgar of Denmark; the king also relied on *folctogan*, chiefs of the people, who were ruling their own estates but prepared to give support and counsel when required (Whitelock 1951, 89f.). Similarly Saxo refers to the two classes of young men and veterans when describing the plan of the army in Book VII (Fisher 1979, 227). The young warriors were to fight with javelins behind the leading men who formed the wedge at the forefront of the battle, and behind the young men a company of older warriors 'to reinforce their comrades, if their strength waned, with their own brand of seasoned courage'.

The part played by women in these warrior societies is something about which we know little. There is a recurring tradition of the shieldmaid, the girl who fights along with men, in Old Norse literature, and this has become confused with the supernatural figures of valkyries, maids of Odin who decided the course of battle according to his commands and conducted dead heroes to his hall, and also with guardian spirits attached to certain families. In Irish tales of the *fiana* we find women living with the men in their war-bands and even fighting along with them, and Feest has found this in some tribal societies. He mentions women not only providing food for the warriors and nursing the wounded, but also dancing to support them, and sometimes sharing the fighting, while they may mutilate dead men after battle (Feest 1980, 18–19). Such possibilities may help to explain the vigour of the valkyrie tradition in Norse literature.

One wonders also what was the fate of children born of unions between women of the community and the men in camps and strongholds. A suggestion made by Kim McCone (1987, 104) may throw light on the puzzling Anglo-Saxon poem known as 'Wulf and Eadwacer', which has baffled its editors (Hamer 1970, 82f.) In this poem the speaker is a woman, who refers to her lover as Wulf; she speaks of him being on a separate island in the fens inhabited by men 'fierce in slaughter' (*wælreowe*), apparently not far away, but visiting her only rarely. If he comes with a troop, her people will try and capture him. She has either borne a child or is expecting one, but this brings no happiness: Wulf (or 'a wolf') will 'carry off our wretched whelp to the woods'. She laments that there can be no true marriage with her lover, and at the close she appeals directly not to Wulf but to Eadwacer. The idea that the father of her child is one of a band of young men living outside the community seems the most satisfactory one made up to now, and more probable than Richard Hamer's suggestion that Wulf is an enemy Viking. It would also explain the use of two names: Eadwacer could be the family name, and Wulf the young man's name as a member or leader of the war-band. There is a parallel, possibly, in the story of the childhood of the Zulu champion Shaka (Ritter 1978, 25f.). His father was a young chief belonging to a band of adolescent warriors, who were allowed sexual relationships with girls of the tribe, even those whom they were forbidden to marry, but were expected to take certain precautions so that no children would be born of such temporary unions. However Shaka's mother, a chief's daughter, gave birth to a son, to the amazement and strong disapproval of the community; the marriage could not be officially celebrated, and she and her son Shaka lived in dishonour. His position as a rejected and despised child may account for his extreme ruthlessness in later life. It is conceivable that some of those trained as berscrks may have been children of such unions with girls in the community. Another possible parallel here is that of the training of the Janissaries, the crack warriors of the Ottoman Empire (Prescott 1855; Bradford 1961, 86f.). These men fought with the skill, dedication and fearlessness of the berserks, and were trained for such a life from the age of seven. They were the children of Christian parents within the Empire who were thought to show special promise, and were taken away for tests and severe training at this early age.

The warrior groups do not appear to have included boys of all classes of society, but only sons of men of some standing. In *Rigsþula*, an Icelandic poem thought to show Irish influence, the bringing up of children of various classes is briefly described. This poem is usually included with poems of the *Codex Regius* in editions of the *Poetic Edda*, but is found only in the *Codex Wormius*, one of the MSS of Snorri's *Prose Edda*, where the end is now missing. The sons of thralls were taught to work with animals and in the fields, while those of the free farmers learned to build houses and run a farm. A Jarl's son, however, received special training as a warrior and hunter:

> There Jarl grew up in the halls;
> he swung the shield and fitted the bowstring,
> bent the bow and shafted the arrow,
> let fly the dart and wielded the spear,
> rode horses and loosed hounds,
> drew swords and swam the stream . . .

This can be compared with the list of accomplishments claimed by Jarl Rǫgnvald in the twelfth century, in a poem said to have been composed in his youth, before he became ruler of Orkney (Gordon 1957, 16(L), 155, 249). It was imitated from a poem of the Norwegian king Harald Hardradi, over a century earlier, of which unfortunately only two lines survive, and runs as follows:

> I am skilled at the board game,
> and have nine accomplishments.
> I can remember runes,
> I am busied with books and building,
> I can travel on skis,
> I can shoot and row if needed,
> I am skilled at the harp and at poetry-making.

Books and building may indicate the new demands of a Christian age and sword and spear are omitted, but on the whole Rǫgnvald appears to be following the traditional pattern of the skills of a young ruler to be. Knowledge of runes, harp-playing, composition of poetry and skill at board games had long been associated with kingship, and were more than mere amusements in the hall. Playing pieces and harps as well as weapons have been found in some of the richest Anglo-Saxon graves, most notably at Sutton Hoo and Taplow, and their inclusion may be due to the fact that they represented special knowledge and power which a ruler should possess. In *Rígsþula* the youngest son of Jarl is given the name of King (*Konr ungr*), and he is the only one to learn runes among the brothers. He also learned how to protect his men, and was taught magic spells to use in warfare; thus he could blunt the swords of enemies, calm a troubled sea, and understand the speech of birds, which could warn him of danger and bring him the knowledge to make right decisions. Emphasis on the training needed by a king's son is found again in the Edda poems concerned with the youth of Sigurd the Volsung, a hero very popular in Scandinavian tradition from the tenth century onwards. He appears in the poems *Reginsmál*, *Fáfnismál* and *Sigrdrífumál*, which are included in the *Codex Regius* with no divisions between them, and also in the *Vǫlsunga Saga*. Sigurd received a full if unconventional education. The god Odin instructed him in runic lore and battle strategy; the smith Regin acted as fosterfather and teacher, and reforged his father's broken sword; and a valkyrie, identified with Brynhild in later sources, gave him instruction on runes and battle-spells and moral counsel, warning him to keep solemn oaths, to avoid foolish brawls and entanglements with women, and the vengeance of the wolf. The last might be a reference to the threats offered by members of warrior fraternities sworn to avenge one another whatever the cost.

The Irish champion CúChulainn also had a series of teachers, some of whom were from the supernatural world. In childhood he forced his way into the troop of small boys associated with the royal hall, without first asking for their protection as a new arrival should have done. Then he became the king's 'guard dog', defending the boundaries of the land against attack, one of those young men 'strolling about the border', as Conchobar put it in the tale of 'Macc Da Thó's Pig'. CúChulainn received instruction from Cathub the druid, who taught a hundred young men at a time, dispensing the kind of wisdom which seems roughly equivalent to the runes and spells in the Sigurd poems. He then learned that a certain day would be fortunate for anyone receiving arms, since he would win unending fame, and so begged the king to grant him weapons. But he broke all he was given, until at last Conchobar gave him his own, presumably family heirlooms, and on the following day his own chariot, since ordinary chariots were too fragile for the powerful young hero. Next CúChulainn had to learn to use the weapons he had received. He went to a skilled fighter, Domnall the Warlike, who taught him many feats of skill and agility; then he sought out a supernatural woman warrior, Scáthach, who was reputed to have trained the greatest warriors in Ireland (Meyer 1892; Cross and Glover 1936, 163f.).

CúChulainn became famous for his feats, and they are listed more than once in the tales. A literal translation of these in one list, obviously difficult to interpret, was offered by Henderson (1899, 37) as follows:

> Over-breath feat, apple-feat, sprite-feat, screw-feat, cat-feat, valiant-champion's whirling-feat, barbed spear, quick stroke, mad roar, heroes' fury, wheel-feat, sword-edge-feat, climbing against spike-pointed things and straightening his body on each of them.

The feats of heroes in the tales and of CúChulainn in particular become increasingly fantastic, so that he may stand poised on a spearpoint, or make a 'salmon's leap' over a great distance to come down on his enemies from above. However those familiar with the martial arts or yoga will recognise that such names are not improbable for physical exercises such as might form a regular part of a young warrior's training. Other skills had to do with physical endurance, and one feat was to dance above the furnace in the forge until the soles of his feet were blackened and discoloured. Another example of the ability to endure heat is found in the tale of the Danish king Hrolf *kraki*, who, with his warriors suffered the heat from the fires in the royal hall at Uppsala without flinching (*Hrólfs Saga kraka*, 28), while Odin himself underwent a similar test, according to the prose introduction to *Grímnismál*. Another test was to endure extreme cold. CúChulainn once sat naked in the snow, and Starkad was nearly buried in snow when waiting for his opponent to arrive for a duel (Fisher 1979, VI, 181). In Anglo-Saxon and Norse literature we have occasional glimpses of the demands of the sword-duel, for which long practice and skill were required. This was not only important for self-defence, but also essential in battle, since this often depended on a series of duels between the leading warriors. One of the kings in Saxo's *History* is said to have set exacting standards of sword-play for his warriors (Fisher 1979, VII, 228):

Some of them became so adroit in this remarkable exercise of duelling that they could graze their opponent's eyebrow with unerring aim. If anyone at the receiving end so much as blinked an eyelid through fear, he was shortly discharged of his duties and dismissed from court.

The receiving of weapons was obviously a turning-point in the development of the young warrior, and once more CúChulainn's career provides us with a pattern, in spite of the excesses and fantasies of the narrative. As a small boy, he had wooden weapons, which could be used as a test of dexterity, and with considerable effect against other boys. His exploit in protecting himself with his thin wooden shield from their throwing sticks reads like a parody of the heroes of the *fían* warding off javelins with shield and hazel-stick. Entry into the boy troop seems to have been at about seven years of age, although of course exceptional heroes might make a premature appearance. In Bede's *Life* of St. Cuthbert, we are told that he joined the boys' company in his eighth year, 'the first year of boyhood succeeding from infancy', and that he took part in jumping, running, wrestling and other exercises, including some in which the boys performed various gymnastics naked, executing what are described as 'various unnatural contortions' (Colgrave 1940, 154–6). The next stage in training came at about fourteen; by the time he was fifteen, Guthlac seems to have become an active fighter, devastating the towns and residences of the enemy, collecting booty, and engaging in 'pillage, slaughter and rapine' at the head of a band of youths (Colgrave 1936, XVIII–XIX). St. Wilfrid likewise obtained arms and horses at the age of fourteen, although he made the decision to enter a monastery instead of engaging in military service (Colgrave 1927, II, 7). In the account of CúChulainn's youth, it seems that real but inferior weapons were available for boys ready to receive them, but in his case they were contemptuously broken, so that he was finally supplied with family weapons by his kinsman the king. Later he won splendid weapons in single combat, and brought these, together with the heads of the vanquished, to Conchobar. His special weapon of terrible potency, the *gai bulga*, a kind of barbed spear which could be sent through water, was supposed to have been received from his supernatural teacher, the woman warrior Scathach. There are also examples of Norwegian and Danish heroes receiving a special sword from the valkyrie who is bride and guardian to the young warrior, and sometimes being given a name at the same time; in such cases it seems that the sword is a family heirloom, handed to the young warrior (Davidson 1960).

In Germanic heroic tradition it seems that arms and armour could be won in a duel, received as gifts from the heads of the family, or from another king in return for some exploit. In Paul the Deacon's *History of the Lombards* (24) it is said that a prince had to receive his first set of arms from some ruler other than his father. When the young Alboin won a victory for his people by killing the son of the king of the Gepids in battle, he had still not officially received his own arms, and therefore was not permitted to sit beside his father at the feast to celebrate the victory. Alboin thereupon went to the king of the Gepids and formally requested the arms of the dead man. This was a foolhardy act, and the young warriors at the court would have killed him, but the king prevented this, acknowledging the justice of Alboin's request, and gave him the arms which brought him recognition as a mature warrior. It may be noted that in *Beowulf* the hero received many splendid gifts from the king of the Danes when he had overcome Grendel; these consisted of a standard, helmet, mailcoat, sword and eight fully equipped horses. Beowulf later presented sword, armour and four of the horses to his own king and kinsman, Hygelac; three more of the horses were given to Hygelac's queen, together with a breast-ornament which had been presented to Beowulf by the Danish queen, and presumably he kept the last horse for his own use. On receiving these rich gifts, Hygelac in turn presented Beowulf with a gold-adorned sword, a family heirloom which had belonged to Beowulf's grandfather, and also gave him a hall and lands. It seems as though the young hero had no special sword up to that time, since he overcame Grendel with his bare hands, and borrowed a sword for the encounter with Grendel's mother. The gifts received from Hygelac mark recognition of Beowulf as a fully established warrior and prince, though he still owed allegiance to the reigning king and only later took over the kingdom.

Weapons were apparently kept in the family armoury until it was time to hand them over to a youth who had proved his right to hold them. According to Tacitus (*Germania* 18), women played an important part in this, keeping the weapons until their sons grew up, and a bride received a gift of weapons from her husband's family to hold in trust for her sons:

> She is receiving something which she must hand over unspoilt and treasured to her children, for her son's wives to receive in their turn, and pass on to the grandchildren.

Some commentators refuse to accept this, thinking that Tacitus has misunderstood the nature of the dowry given by the bride's father, but other scholars have accepted it as genuine tradition, and the statement is clear enough. Echoes in later literature tend to confirm such a tradition. The mother of Sigurd the Volsung kept her husband's broken sword and gave it to Sigurd when he was ready to use it (*Vǫlsunga Saga*, 12, 15). The Norwegian king, Olaf Haraldson, known as St. Olaf, had a sword waiting for him from the time of his birth, said to have been taken from the burial mound of an earlier king (*Flateyjarbók* (1860–68), II, 12, 12). One day the boy asked his mother what the bright thing was he saw gleaming in a chest, and she replied 'It is the hilt of a sword'. He asked whose it was, and she replied that it was the sword Basing, which belonged to an earlier king Olaf. 'I want to have it', said the prince, who is said to have been eight years of age, 'and to wear it', and Asta then gave him the sword which he carried until his death in battle. Such heroic traditions often find their way into the Icelandic sagas, and there is a striking example in *Grettis Saga*. The young Grettir had so angered his father by his rebellious and destructive behaviour that he sent him away from home and refused to give him any weapon: 'You have not been dutiful towards me, and I don't intend to give you any.' His mother however went to see him off, and said as she bade him farewell:

> 'You are not being sent from home, my son, in the way that I would have wished for a man so well-born as you are. The worst lack, it seems to me, is that of a weapon fit to use, and my mind tells me that you will need one'. Then she took from under her cloak an ornamented sword, a very fine treasure, and said: 'This sword belonged to my grandfather Jǫkull, and to the men of Vatnsdale in former days, and brought them good fortune and victory. This sword I am going to give to you, and you must make good use of it'. (17)

The tale of this sword and of the outstanding luck of Jǫkull and his brothers is told in *Vatnsdæla Saga*, where it bears the name Ættartangi, but in *Grettis Saga* it is called the 'Gift of Jǫkull', as the sword given to Beowulf is referred to as the 'Heirloom of Hrethel' (Davidson 1962, 171–2). Those familiar with the sagas would recognise the allusion and realise

Grettir's folly in not keeping so lucky a weapon, for he took over another sword taken from a burial mound and let the family weapon pass into his brother's possession. The tales of heroes receiving swords from some guardian spirit or valkyrie connected with the family also emphasise their importance as heirlooms and symbols of the luck of their forbears. A parallel in Irish tradition is the goddess who becomes the bride of a king and represents sovereignty (MacCana 1955), and such traditions originally belonged to ruling families, both in Scandinavia and Ireland. There were many young men with claims to royal descent in the numerous small kingdoms of the Viking Age and earlier, and it was from such aristocratic circles that such traditions came.

Indeed the importance of royal and aristocratic tradition in the tales of young warriors needs to be emphasised. In the family sagas of Iceland such traditions have been used against a different background, and many have passed into popular tales and folklore, but we must not be misled by this. Heroic literature had a practical function in the training of the young, and was more than mere entertainment or even propaganda to enhance the glory of the ruler and his champions. It was part of the instruction for boys of good family, emphasising the ideals of courage, loyalty, endurance and skill with weapons, as well as the need to win fame by heroic deeds as quickly as possible, since life might well be short. There is much more about which we know little in the training of warriors, dancing, for example, seems to have been important, and is mentioned by Tacitus and confirmed by dancing figures shown on weapons. We need more information also concerning the methods by which youths with natural gifts for fighting but from a humbler background could succeed as warriors without family backing; possibly folktales preserve some memory of these. Certainly the heroic tradition has left a mark on popular tales, thus becoming part of the literary heritage of those never destined for leadership. But on the whole we are dealing with the training of a privileged class, like that of the knights of the Middle Ages, and this was of such importance for the community that it has widely affected both literature and art.

References

Blake, N.F. (ed. and trans.) 1962: *Jómsvíkinga Saga (Icelandic Texts)*.

Bradford, E. 1964: *The Great Siege* (London).

Colgrave, B. (ed. and trans.) 1927: *Life of Bishop Wilfred* (Cambridge).

Colgrave, B. (trans.) 1936: *Felix's Life of St Guthlac* (Cambridge).

Colgrave, B. (trans.) 1940: *Two Lives of St Cuthbert* (Cambridge).

Cross, T.P. and Glover, C.H. 1936: *Ancient Irish Tales* (London).

Danielli, M. 1945: Initiation ceremonial from Norse literature, *Folklore* 56, 229–45.

Davidson, H.R.E. 1960: The sword at the wedding, *Folklore* 71, 1–18.

Davidson, H.R.E. 1962: *The Sword in Anglo-Saxon England* (Oxford).

Davidson, H.R.E. 1978: Shape-changing in the Old Norse Sagas, *Animals in Folklore*, ed. J.R. Porter and W.M.S. Russell, *Mistletoe Books* 14 (folklore Society), 126–42.

Davidson, H.R.E. 1980: *Commentary* on Saxo Grammaticus, *History of the Danes*, Vol. 2 (Cambridge).

Davidson, H.R.E. 1982: The hero as a fool, *The Hero in Tradition and Folklore*, ed. H.R.E. Davidson, *Mistletoe Books* 19 (Folklore Society).

Feest, C. 1980: *The Art of War* (London).

Fisher, P. (trans.) 1979: Saxo Grammaticus, *History of the Danes*, Vol. 1 (Cambridge).

Ganz, J. 1981: *Early Irish Myths and Sagas* (Harmondsworth).

Gordon, E.V. 1957: *Introduction to Old Norse* (2nd ed. revised A.R. Taylor. Oxford).

Hamer, R. (trans.) 1970: *A Choice of Anglo-Saxon Verse* (London).

Hawkes, S.C., Davidson H.R.E. and Hawkes, C.F.C. 1965: The Finglesham Man, *Antiquity* 39, 17–32.

Henderson, G. 1899: *Fled Bricrend* (Bricriu's Feast) (Dublin).

Kershaw, N. (trans.). 1922: *Anglo-Saxon and Norse Poems* (Cambridge).

Lid, N. 1950: Til Varulvens Historie, *Trolldom* (Oslo) 82–108.

MacCana, P. 1955: Aspects of the theme of king and goddess in Irish literature, *Études Celtiques* 7, 76–114.

McCone, K. 1987: Hund, Wolf und Krieger bei den Indogermanen, *Studien zum indogermanischen Wortschatz*, ed. W. Meid (*Innsbrucker Beiträge zur Sprachwissenschaft* 52, 101–154.

Meyer, K. (trans.) 1892: The wooing of Emer, included in Cross and Glover 1936.

Meyer, K. (ed.) 1909: *Tecosca Cormaic* (Todd Lecture Series 15. Dublin).

Nagy, J.F. 1985: *The Wisdom of the Outlaw* (Berkeley, California).

O'Grady, S.H. 1892: *Silva Gadelica* (2 vols., London).

Prescott, W.H. 1855: *History of the Reign of Philip II*.

Ritter, E.A. 1978: *Shaka Zulu* (Harmondsworth).

Sjoestedt, M. 1982: *Gods and Heroes of the Celts* (Berkeley, California).

Stewart, F.H. 1971: *Fundamentals of Age-Group Systems* (New York).

Strachan J. (ed.) 1944: *Stories from the Táin*, 3rd ed. (Royal Irish Acad. Dublin).

Turville-Petre, E.O.G. 1976: *Scaldic Poetry* (Oxford).

Vierck, H. 1970: Zur nörrländischen Pelzwirtschaft..., K. Hauck, *Goldbrakteatern aus Sievern* (Munich) 380–90.

Whitelock, D. 1951: *The Audience of Beowulf* (Oxford).

Chapter 3

The Military Context of the *adventus Saxonum*: some continental evidence

John Hines

My aim in preparing this paper has been to investigate the parameters for the scope and character of organised military activity by the Germanic invaders of Britain, the Angles and Jutes in particular, as determined by the situation in the continental homelands of these peoples. This is a little explored aspect of the *adventus Saxonum*. Studies of the military character of the Germanic settlement of Britain in the 5th century – more fancifully in the 4th – have been concentrated very much on the receiving end. Several historians and archaeologists have sought to fit the colonists as barbarian troops or peoples within a late- or sub-Roman British defensive system as auxiliary *numeri* or *laeti*, or as *foederati*. Any pre-existent degree of military organisation amongst these Germanic barbarians is usually only indirectly implied by noting them as groups attached to a leader given the Latin title *rex*. How far Germanic folk in Britain did adapt themselves to the Roman system in any of these formally recognised modes has been a contentious issue for more than two decades now, and will probably remain so for some time in the future. The question of how readily different groups of Germanic folk may have been capable of adapting themselves to these modes seems an essential supplementary to any attempt to test these various theories in what has proved to be the unyielding and certainly inconclusive archaeological evidence representing the earliest Germanic phase in Britain. Behind this question lies a more fundamental problem with which military history and archaeology must be concerned, and which emerges as the crucial issue amongst the military aspects of the *adventus*: how far traditional military organisation may determine military activity or alternatively be adaptable – even radically transformable – to meet new circumstances or opportunities.

Questions concerning military organisation are also questions concerning social organisation. The size of armies that could be or were turned out is a function of the proportion of the population that could go under arms. Armies need leadership, leadership which may in varying degrees be a traditional, inherited role for some individuals, or the subject of *ad hoc* election when need arose, both of which models are implicit within Tacitus's generalized account of 1st-century Germanic practices (*Germania* 7 and 13–14). In our area of interest we must also be essentially concerned with the relationship of armies to political structures and entities. In *Germania* Tacitus refers to the selection of groups of a hundred men from (?)fixed districts, *centeni ex singulis pagis*, to make up a Germanic army (*ibid*. 6). Other historians too have contrived to give impressions of Germanic tribes acting like more modern nation-states, each with its national army, as, for instance, when Salway treats of the assault by Saxons and Franks on areas of Gaul as part of an integrated, presumably diplomatically organised 'barbarian conspiracy' which also involved the attacks of the Picts and Scots on Britain in 367 reported by Ammianus Marcellinus (Salway 1981, 374–83). Such issues can at least be probed historically and archaeologically to assess how far they appear true, constant, probable or possible.

It is no particular fault of either archaeologists or historians concerned with the early Anglo-Saxon period that these are as yet questions without substantive answers which might significantly influence our picture of the origins of the English nation. Some impression of the military face of the Germanic communities concerned is to be gained from the burial of weapons in a number of graves, but the deceased in weapon-graves in early Anglo-Saxon England and in northern *Germania* in the relevant periods would appear to be those who did not die on the battlefield, and their weapons, to judge by the criterion of cuts, seem normally to have been unused. It is not an acceptable assumption that the possibly symbolic military structure of grave-finds – particularly the configurations of 'weapon-sets' and the proportions of different classes of armament found – can be translated directly into the practical structure of an actual army on campaign. Battlefield burials would be an archaeological source giving a much more immediate vision of such an army, but as far as I know there are none of these reliably identified relating to early Anglo-Saxon England.

Historical sources offer very little reliable or contemporary insight into the size and structure of Germanic armies in our period, particularly as they are always liable to embellish battle scenes by the exaggeration of numbers. Some attention may be paid to the relatively small numbers of ships – two, three and five – in which early groups of invading Germanic folk are said to have arrived, as recorded by Anglo-Saxon tradition emerging in the Chronicle. But even if one playfully assumes that these numbers have any authentic historical value they immediately beg the questions of the size and form of these ships – imperfectly answerable from archaeological material – and whether the newcomers' ships first arrived with pioneering military men alone or complete with women, children, the elderly, and domestic possessions and animals. An exemplary study is provided by Alcock in *Arthur's Britain* (Alcock 1971, 335–6), allowing certain sources to say what they will through the filter of an unusual mixture of critical judgement and optimistic faith. From this emerges an image of warbands of this period consisting of a few hundred men, a point which does harmonize to a degree with archaeological evidence, as will appear. It must be strongly emphasized, however, that our concept of the military organisation of the earliest Anglo-Saxon folk is only hampered by unduly creative readings of sparse historical sources: for instance by involving the Saxons in a grand barbarian conspiracy in 367 (the word *conspiratio*, incidentally, need mean no more than 'simultaneous action'), or by regarding the siege of Mons Badonicus simplistically as a battle that halted advancing and conquering Saxons in their tracks for a couple of generations. Gildas's account very clearly tells a story of the reversion of Saxon expansion, plausibly to consolidate their territorial holdings in Britain, *before* a whole series of battles, instigated by Aurelius Ambrosianus, leading up to Mons Badonicus, which thus seems to be no more than the final military act in the recognition of a situation of stalemate (*de Excidio*, 24–26).

A well-known additional body of archaeological material relating to this topic has been found in the relevant overseas areas of southern Scandinavia and Schleswig-Holstein, in the form of great bog-finds with massive deposits of weapons. Most of the weapons in these deposits have very clearly been used: indeed by studying the angles and incidence of cuts on weapons from the Nydam bog, Michael Gebühr has succeeded in reconstructing certain thoroughly credible modes of weapon play, particularly with the lance (a spear with a relatively large head without barbs) used as a form of pikestaff and with the sword (Gebühr 1980). The established view of these weapon deposits is that they represent the equipment of defeated armies, plundered from the battlefield and sacrificed to war deities in sacred lakes or pools. Early literary evidence sufficiently supporting the case both for the sacrifice to war deities of plunder and prisoners from a defeated army and for the Germanic treatment of lakes and pools as sacred cult sites is conveniently collected by Hagberg in his discussion of the bog-find at Skedemose on Öland (*Skedemose II*, 65–9; see further below).

These bog deposits do not consistently offer direct answers to the basic questions of the size and structure of the defeated armies, whence they came and who defeated them, or with what frequency battles were fought, simply by the process of counting up different weapon-types, comparing and processing statistically their gross numbers and proportions from site to site, or by indentifying regionally or chronologically diagnostic types. If they could, such answers would have been abstracted long ago. There are manifold obstacles. For the most part the major finds are largely but still incompletely excavated, and they are almost uniformly incompletely published, either because they were excavated too long ago, such as in Conrad Engelhardt's campaign of the 1850's and 60's, disrupted by the Dano-German war of 1864, or because their excavation is very recent, as is the case at Illerup (cf. Engelhardt 1863, 1865, 1867 and 1869; Brøndsted 1960, 208–227; Ilkjær & Lønstrup 1975, 1977 and 1983; *JDA* 3, 235; see Postscript). The preservation of wood and iron in the bogs is usually good but not always so: the substantial loss of iron on account of the acidity of the peat has diminished the evidence from the most important sites of Torsbjerg and Skedemose. In the published accounts of the finds the use of vague expressions like 'large numbers' or 'several hundred' to enumerate the examples of certain weapon types is frustratingly frequent, expressions which as far as one could tell could refer to anything between about 300 and 900 examples. The establishment of a more precise statistical data base would require work in several museums, as Raddatz's list of five collections now holding material from Torsbjerg indicates (Raddatz 1957, 13–4; cf. Postscript). It has been appreciated for a long time that the major finds probably comprise more than a single deposit of military gear, but without published plans or any more than selective drawings of the objects found there arises an inevitable doubt over the structure of individual deposits and as to whether we have a series of occasional relatively large individual deposits on the sites or the effectively continuous deposition of single items during the period of functioning as a cult site. This is to say nothing of the general problems of both close and relative dating of material – particularly some weapon-types – from the Roman Iron Age and early Migration Period.

Bog or lake deposits of weapons or other military equipment (including a few examples containing no more than horse gear) dating up to *circa* 500 have been recorded at nearly thirty sites in Schleswig-Holstein and southern Scandinavia (Fig. 3.1). Some of these contain as little as a single recorded weapon. With the exception of an apparently voluminous but unfortunately much decayed deposit at Skedemose on Öland in the Baltic, all of the major finds, and some two-thirds of the total number of sites, lie on the eastern side of the Jutish peninsula and on Fyn. The remaining Danish islands and Skåne have each produced four sites, five of which qualify here only by including horse-gear, and one site is recorded from the northern part of Gotland. Neither further north in Scandinavia nor to

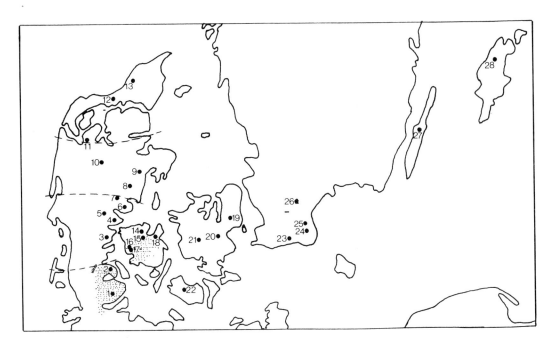

Fig. 3.1 Sketch map showing distribution of bog or lake deposits of weapons and associable military gear between the late 2nd century A.D. and circa 500. The Anglian culture-province is marked by stippling, and the Jutlandic cultural zones and Olgerdiget. *Key to sites: 1, Torsbjerg; 2, Nydam; 3, Ejsbøl; 4, Tranebær; 5, Vingsted; 6, Dallerup Sø; 7, Porskær; 8, Illerup; 9, Hedeliskær; 10, Vallerbæk; 11, Tværmosen; 12, Trinnemose; 13, Manna enge; 14, Vimose; 15, Pårup; 16, Kragehul; 17, Voldtofte; 18, Illemose; 19, Ballerup; 20, Eiby mose; 21, Grøbæksgård; 22, Sørup; 23, Sjörup; 24, Onslunda; 25, Fågeltofta; 26, Sösdala; 27, Skedemose; 28, Stora Hammars.*

the south in continental Europe does there appear to be any evidence of bog deposits of weapons although there is evidence of the contemporary deliberate deposition of other artefacts, such as dress-accessories, in lakes or pools which have subsequently become bogs (*Skedemose II*, 63–4).

The deliberate deposition of artefacts of any category in such lakes or pools has a long history in the area of the weapon deposits, and there is additionally evidence of the lengthy functioning – recurrently or continuously – of certain sites in this way. A very early example of the deposition of material interpretable as the sacrifice of plunder taken from a defeated war-band is that of the Hjortspring boat and weapons on the island of Als off the eastern coast of South Jutland, dated to the very beginning of the pre-Roman Iron Age in the area, perhaps early in the 3rd century B.C. (Brøndsted 1960, 31–9). Pre-Roman Iron-Age bog-finds also include individual dress-accessories such as brooches and pins. The longest lasting tradition of bog deposits – if indeed tradition it is – is that of the so-called 'bog pots'. A comprehensive corpus of this material was collected by Becker in the late 1940's, the subject of a fresh survey by himself published in 1971, and has more recently been partially supplemented by Manfred Rech (Becker 1971; Rech 1979). The sequence begins in the Neolithic period, and although the thread of continuity seems to be spun very thin in the late Neolithic and Bronze Ages there is a considerable upsurge of deposition of pots in the pre-Roman Iron Age, reaching a peak in the early Roman Iron Age. Where one finds pots deposited in such contexts containing animal bones, and capped with stones, one is faced with archaeological finds which are almost unique in connection with pagan Germanic folk in apparently being most plausibly interpreted, without the aid of historical evidence, as the products of religious ritual on the grounds that no less mystical explanation appears equally good if not better. As the material of bog deposits, however, the pots are quite abruptly superseded by deposits of military gear around the beginning of the late Roman Iron Age, probably around the end of the 2nd century A.D. From here up to the end of the Roman Iron Age we find a number of deposits, of varying sizes, of a full range of weapons – swords, spears, shields, bows and arrows, axes – and other material plausibly associated with military activity such as riding gear and belt fittings. A partial but significant shift in the character of bog deposits appears about the beginning of the Migration Period, probably around the beginning of the 5th century, when besides finding comprehensive collections of military gear we also find deposits apparently made on a principle of *pars pro toto*: in particular concentrations of scabbard fittings as at Ejsbøl-South, Nydam II and Porskær. A subsequent shift in ritual deposition – apparently at least partly away from deposition in water – is presumably represented by the numerous gold and silver hoards of southern Scandinavia of the later 5th and 6th centuries, from which so many of our known bracteates have come (cf. Mackeprang 1952, 96).

It is neither a particularly new nor a particularly surprising suggestion that this variation and shift between deposits of a military character and deposits of a peaceful character could represent the contrast between military and fertility cults. In particular this would suggest a major burgeoning of the cult of war gods in southern Scandinavia at the expense of fertility cults about the beginning of the late Roman Iron Age. What is most important to emphasize in the present context is that several sites, including the majority of those with the most voluminous weapon deposits, show a recurrence of use as sacrificial sites which may be the result of continuity of status despite this change in the character of the cult. Bog pots of the pre- or early Roman Iron Age occur below the weapon finds at the major sites of Ejsbøl, Kragehul and Vimose and the minor site at Tværmosen (cf. Becker 1971, 31–2). It is also frequently the case that some material from the sites of the major weapon finds, broadly contemporary with the weapon deposits at least in being of the same period, does not have a particularly military character. There are for instance dress-accessories which are most frequently encountered in women's graves such as armrings, pendants and beads at Torsbjerg, Vimose, Nydam I, Kragehul and Porskær. Alongside these we may note a sewing-needle from Vimose and a spindle-whorl from Nydam I. Agricultural tools, such as scythes, spades and rakes, are also reported amongst the weapon finds of Torsbjerg, Nydam I and Illemose, but are not yet dated in themselves. While it must be accepted that some unmilitary articles, for instance certain tools such as the plane, possibly for fashioning spear- and arrow-shafts, remains of wagons and boats, belt fittings, gaming-pieces and men's toilet articles are not out of place in a military assemblage, the search for apparently men's graves containing what are normally female dress accessories, to make the point that all these items could belong to an army, visibly approaches the category of special pleading (cf. Raddatz 1957, 117–20 and 135–42). It seems considerably easier to accept the principle that the totality of offerings could maintain a mixed character in the late Roman Iron Age.

Several sites seem also to have received more than one deposit of weapons, thus maintaining a continuity of function within the late Roman Iron Age and early Migration Period. The most recently excavated and most satisfactorily published example of this (although still leaving much to be looked for in the future) is the site at Illerup in central Jutland. Descriptions of this site published so far give the impression of three or four separate deposits of relatively substantial collections of military gear, the earliest, site 2, dated to *circa* 200 possibly preceded by or contemporary with deposition on Site 3, a later deposit, site 1, dated towards the end of the 4th century, and a more recently found place of deposition dated at *circa* 500 (Ilkjær & Lønstrup and *JDA* 3 as above, plus Andersen 1951 and 1956). Three separate areas of deposition dating between the later 4th and probably the earlier 6th centuries are now known from Nydam (Nydam I–III), and two deposits, of the 4th and 5th centuries respectively, at Ejsbøl, Ejsbøl-North and -South. The case for the integral deposition of substantial individual collections of military gear in the bog-finds is most easily made when plans showing the discrete distribution of such collections in the bog are available. Such evidence is reported, but not diagrammatically published, for Torsbjerg, where it is argued that more than 95% of the objects found represent a large deposit of plunder made about the very beginning of the 3rd century, distributed over the whole excavated area, while small discrete deposits of material from the latter half of the early Roman Iron Age and towards the close of the late Roman Iron Age represent an earlier and a later deposit of the same character. Some degree of sorting of weapons enhances the case for large simultaneous deposits: in the major Torsbjerg deposit it appears that all the shield bosses were collected together and dumped in a concentrated area while their separated grips were scattered more widely (Ilkjær & Lønstrup 1982).

Despite the positive results of a painstaking study by Ilkjær of variables of possible chronological significance on spearhead-types in connection with a bundle of spearheads from Vimose, and his confident conclusion that the possible longevity of individual weapons before being buried does not significantly diminish the possibility of particular forms being relatively closely dated on the basis of grave associations (Ilkjær 1975), weapon typology is only reliable to us for indicating the relative-chronological date-range of depositions on a bog-site, not the precise numbers and frequency of individual deposits. It is clear, on the basis of standard typological study, that for the most part the large bog deposit at Vimose on Fyn is of the same phase as the major deposit at Torsbjerg, while most material at Nydam I is of the same phase as the latest finds from Torsbjerg. However, parallels in various artefact-types give a strong impression of probable overlap between Vimose and Nydam I, by an earlier deposit or deposits within Nydam I and conceivably some later deposition at Vimose (Engelhardt/Ørsnes 1970a, xi–xiii; Figs. 3.2–5). It is important to note that Kragehul, in south-western Fyn, indicated by Brøndsted to be a Migration-period deposit, contains so many varied types in common with Nydam I that it is impossible to escape the conclusion that they are at least in part closely contemporary (Figs. 3.6–17; Brøndsted 1960, 287–8; Engelhardt 1865 and 1867; Engelhardt/Ørsnes 1970b, xiv–xv). Kragehul also contained pre- and early Roman Iron-age pots, a wrist-clasp, probably a female dress-accessory in this area, that should date to the later 5th or early 6th century, and, in common with Nydam III, spear-shafts engraved with an interlace pattern with occasional zoomorphic elements which it is very difficult to justify a date for stylistically significantly earlier than the 6th century (Figs. 3.18–19;

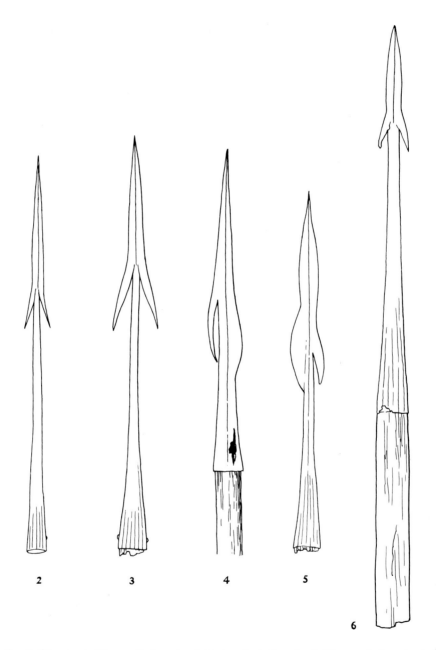

Figs. 3.2–6: 2, Spearhead, Vimose; 3, Spearhead, Nydam I; 4, Spearhead, Vimose; 5, Spearhead, Nydam I; 6, Spearhead, Kragehul.

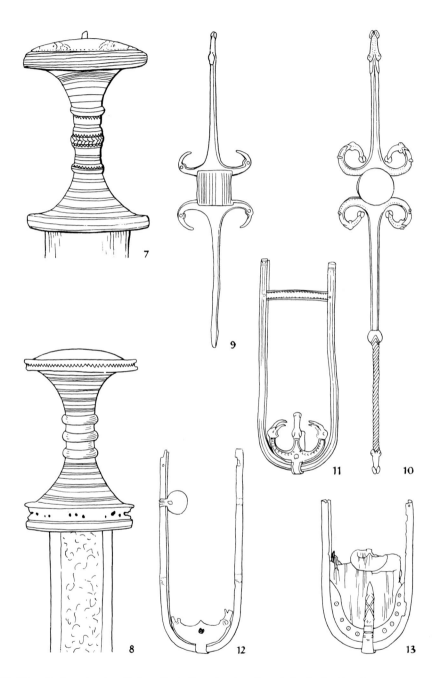

Figs. 3.7–13: 7, Sword grip, Nydam I; 8, Sword grip, Kragehul; 9, Scabbard mount, Nydam I; 10, Scabbard mount, Kragehul; 11, Scabbard chape, Nydam I; 12, Scabbard chape, Kragehul; 13, Scabbard chape, Kragehul.

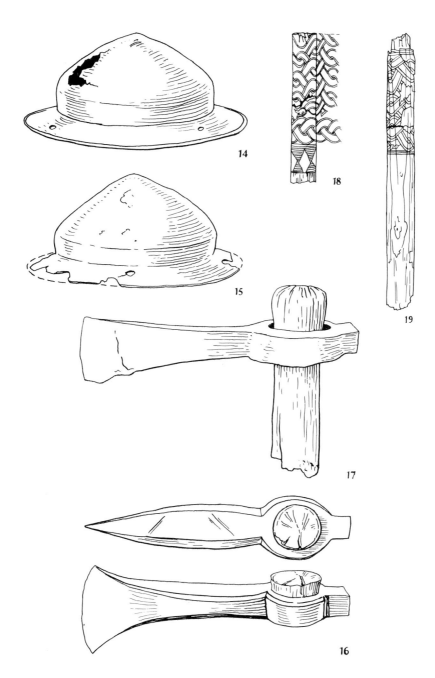

Figs. 3.14–19:   14, Shield boss, Nydam I; 15, Shield boss, Kragehul; 16, Axehead, Nydam I; 17, Axehead, Kragehul; 18, Decorated spearshaft, Kragehul; 19, Decorated spearshaft, Nydam III.

Engelhardt/Ørsnes 1970b, xv–xvii; *JDA* 4, 219). The possibility of regular rather than occasional deposition during at least some periods on some of these sites must still be allowed to remain open.

Both the greater and lesser deposits of weapons thus seem frequently to have been made at established sacrificial cult-sites, not at randomly selected *ad hoc* locations. The idea that these sites may have been the established cult-sites of specific groups of folk within definable territories has particularly been developed by Jankuhn in his study of the early history of the Angles, suggesting that Torsbjerg may have – indeed probably – constituted "ein zentrales Stammesheiligtum" for the Anglian folk (Jankuhn 1966, 50; see also Jankuhn 1977). It is a suggestion that can of course only be made tentatively, but it would be timorous to evade giving it the credit of consideration. Early historical sources, placenames and the limits of archaeological culture-provinces generally provide us only with most uncertain images of the bounds and location of different groups of Germanic folk in the late Roman Iron Age and Migration Period. All three of these sources do however combine to give us a moderately trustworthy map of the territory of the Angles in the 3rd to 5th centuries, within a culture-province centring on *Angeln* in Schleswig-Holstein and extending beyond the present West German border into the southern, western and central parts of Fyn and to the northern shore of the Flensborg Fjord, south-east of a long pallisaded ditch and bank of late 2nd-century origin, *Olgerdiget*, plausibly interpreted by Neumann as marking the boundary between the Angles and the Jutes (Fig. 3.1; cf. Genrich 1954; Neumann 1982). Within this area, however, we in fact have three major and one minor military bog-deposit sites of the 2nd to 5th centuries, Torsbjerg and Nydam I–III on the mainland, and the neighbouring Kragehul and Voldtofte in western Fyn. To the north and east of this area in southern Scandinavia group territories are not to be identified with such confidence. However for Jutland and the Danish islands, at least in the late Roman Iron Age, fairly clear culture provinces are distinguishable in South, Mid and North Jutland, and on the remainder of Fyn and the Sjælland-Lolland-Falster group. In central Fyn there is in fact a considerable area where culture provinces connected with Anglian Schleswig-Holstein and the Sjælland island group overlap (cf. Genrich 1954 and Lund Hansen 1976). The three remaining *major* bog-finds, Ejsbøl, Illerup and Vimose, are distributed to separate zones of this type, Ejsbøl in southern Jutland, Illerup in Mid Jutland and Vimose on northern Fyn. The smaller bog deposits are distributed relatively evenly across eastern and northern Jutland, Fyn, Sjælland and Lolland. Neither the evidence from the Anglian territory nor that from the remainder of Scandinavia particularly supports the thesis of such sites consistently representing a unique, central, national cult-site, but their distribution and recurrent use at least supports the notion of some group at a lower level in the social hierarchy expressing its cohesion by the repeated use of these sites. It is noteworthy that the three major sites in the supposedly Anglian area are in three geographically distinct districts.

Whatever sort of groups they were who were responsible for these bog-deposits, how strong is the evidence that what was placed there was the plunder taken from defeated armies? As has been stated, the literary evidence for this practice is reasonably satisfactory, although it could have been treated rather more circumspectly in many studies of the subject. Little distinction is often made, for instance, of the fact that some sources treat of comparable practices amongst Celts rather than Germans (e.g. Caesar, *dBG* VI.17 and Strabo, *Geographia* IV.I,13), and little account taken of the possible force of literary tradition: Orosius's account of the destruction of plunder and prisoners by the Cimbri and Teutones after the battle of Arausio (105 B.C.) is conceivably an embellishment, drawing on sources such as the above, of Livy's account of the death of thousands of Roman soldiers and camp followers at this place, including one named prisoner, M. Aurelius Scaurus (Orosius, *HaP* V.XVI,5; Livy, *aUC* LXVII). Nevertheless with Tacitus's tales in the *Annales* and *Germania* of Germanic folk dedicating war booty to their gods and the use of sacred lakes, and perhaps too Jordanes' description of similar practices amongst the Goths (Tacitus, *Annales* I.59 & 61 and *Germania* 40; Jordanes, *dOAG* 5), there is no need for obstructive scepticism particularly as it is usually the case that the weapons in the bog-deposits have been used in comprehensible ways. It can only be taken on trust as *a priori* a greater probability that such sacrifices will usually represent plunder from the defeated rather than the tried and proven weapons of the victorious. With regard to the question of the location of battles, we must bear in mind that battles were unlikely to take place consistently in the immediate vicinity of cult-places and so some transportation of the material from the battlefield is probable. It would not be inconceivable for material for sacrifice to be brought back from some quite distant campaign, if such a thing ever took place.

It is also undeniably the case that a military victory provides an appropriate occasion for a single, coherently structured weapon deposit, although obviously it would be a circular argument to take the apparent coherency of a single deposit as proof that it represents the plunder taken from a defeated army. One find stands out as almost unique in the attempt to reconstruct theoretically a Germanic war-band on campaign shortly before the Migration Period: Ejsbøl-North, relatively recently and fully excavated, although still only the subject of summary publication (Ørsnes 1964 and 1970; see Postscript). The material here appears to have been sorted into categories before deposition – something which may very plausibly have been done on the battlefield before transporting to the site – and all the material is consistently datable relatively late in the late Roman Iron Age, about the middle of the 4th century. The numerical coherency of this deposit appears most strikingly in the evidence of swords and belt sets, and of riding gear. *Circa* 60 swords are reported (the doubt, presumably, is accounted for by fragmentary examples), 60 buckles and 62 knives, implying the deposition of about 60 belt sets with swords. The swords have very clearly been used. Nine mounted men are indicated by nine bridles, nine sets of saddle-fittings, and eight or nine sets of spurs. One would presume that the nine riders were amongst the 60 or so swordsmen (but cf. Tacitus, *Germania* 6), and presume too that no man would go into battle with more than one sword. So far as I have been able to discover no weapon graves of this period and region contain more than one sword.

The number of shields is more problematic. The total represented is most likely to lie somewhere around 150–175, with 123 complete shield bosses and fragments of up to 52 more found. Ørsnes in his publication of the find has suggested a total army of about 200 men, a figure dictated primarily by the spear totals: 203 barbed throwing-spear heads plus 191 lanceheads. Ørsnes presumes here the arming of virtually every man in the army with a two-spear set, made up of a throwing-spear, intended primarily to pierce and weigh down the shield of an opponent, and a lance which might be used either one-handed as a prodding, stabbing weapon or two-handed as a form of pikestaff (see below). The two-spear set of this kind is certainly familiar in grave-finds of both the late Roman Iron Age and the Migration Period. There are five examples from late Roman Iron-age graves in

Fyn and Jutland (Albrectsen 1968 and 1971; Mackeprang 1943, 93–131; Brøndsted 1960, 415–9; Hedeager 1980, 81–104). Four of the five weapon graves of this period at Simris in Skåne have this combination, and a futher four are recorded in central Västergötland by Särlvik (Stjernquist 1955; Särlvik 1982, 68). The combination appears in graves from the early and the late Roman Iron Age on Gotland, and in no less than 100 Migration-period Norwegian graves recorded by Fett in the late 1930's (Almgren & Nerman 1923; Fett 1938–40). I know, however, of just one example from Schleswig-Holstein, from Krummensee/Pötterberg grave 105, and none from across the Elbe in northern Germany and the Rhineland (cf. Genrich 1954, Böhme 1974 and Raddatz 1981). Also known, though less frequent, is the combination of two lances, which could be used in the same way as the barbed spear plus lance: there are one or two examples from Fyn, one from Jutland, two in rather early graves on Gotland, and five, combined with barbed spears, from Fett's Norwegian graves. It should be stressed, however, that the majority of grave-finds with spears in Denmark, southern mainland Sweden and Schleswig-Holstein contain just one spear, sometimes barbed, sometimes not.

In interpreting the Ejsbøl-North spear totals we have to bear in mind the practicality of weapon sets in conditions of battle, and that grave assemblages may well represent symbolic rather than practicable weapon assemblages. The two weapons we can suppose to have been intended for close, face-to-face fighting are the sword and the lance. The sword, in the hand of a competent swordsman, should have been a substantial advantage in one-to-one combat, although that should not be supposed to be always the case in the *mêlée* of a battle. Such is this advantage that the combination of a sword and a lance in an individual's weaponry might appear an improbable one. Gebühr similarly argues that the combination of a lance and a shield is an awkward one if the lance is used two-handed, as his interpretation of the cuts on a substantial number of the Nydam I lanceheads indicates. Concurrently he points out the low ratio of shields to lances represented in this deposit, a ratio of less than 25%.

The tactical situation in which the lance should be of particular use to a man armed with a sword is the formation of a shield wall, or some variation of this such as the wedge. In this same situation the shield is of importance to the spearmen, and Tacitus bears clear witness of the knowledge and use of such tactics by some 1st-century Germanic folk (*Germania* 6). A limited number of variants on the combination of the throwing spear, lance, shield and occasional sword are, however, perfectly plausible. A combination of sword, shield and throwing spear, effectively equivalent to the standard armament of *gladius* plus *pilum* of the Roman infantryman, would be appropriate for men ranging behind the shield wall to deal with any enemies who might break through and threaten havoc from the rear. A relatively small number of men may have been armed with spears alone as Gebühr suggests. The ratio of shields to lances at Ejsbøl-North is considerably higher than at Nydam I, varying potentially between 75 and 90%. The initial formation of a shield wall in battle looks to have been considerably more important than Gebühr indicates. There is no particular contradiction between this and his evidence for the two-handed use of lances: it is not necessarily the case that a small, light shield would have been so awkward in this mode that its disadvantages outweighed its advantages, and a spearmen initially armed with a shield would presumably throw down that shield if it became encumbered by arrows or a throwing spear and fight with his lance alone. A late 2nd-century sculpted sarcophagus from Portonaccio near Rome shows barbarian, presumably Germanic, and Roman troops in the chaos of battle thrusting and wielding spears one-handed, with shields in their left hands (Andreae 1973 no. 504).

Recourse was taken to the evidence of grave-assemblages to support the hypothesis that a man would go into battle armed with no more than one sword, but grave finds must be treated most cautiously as a guide to the armanent of soldiers in battle. No small number of grave finds produce impractical sets of armament. A shield alone is obviously not a practicable weapon set, but is not uncommon in late Roman Iron-Age graves from Jutland, Fyn and occasionally southern Sweden. In the Anglian cemeteries of Schleswig-Holstein and to some degree in Saxon cemeteries across the Elbe, at Westerwanna in particular (Zimmer-Linnfeld 1960), the deposition of single arrowheads, and sword- or scabbard-fittings such as grips or chapes and even fragments of mailcoats in the cremation urns very plausibly represents the same process of *pars pro toto*. The interpretation of graves containing other single weapons, such as an axe or spear alone, is more problematic. It is relevant to Gebühr's discussion of the likelihood of a lanceman carrying a shield to note that ten recorded 3rd to 5th-century graves in Fyn, Jutland and Schleswig-Holstein contained a spear alone, against eight with a spear and a shield alone (and fourteen with a shield alone), but it is impossible to determine how far the occurrence of the spear alone represents actual military practice or is the result of selection. Problematic too is the possibility of the opposite process of creating excessively large weapon assemblages. In view of the discussion above, a familiar 'maximal' set of a sword, a shield and two spears, usually one barbed and one lance, is a practical one. This we have at Krummensee/Pötterberg grave 105, at Vils and Hjortbro in Jutland, combined with a set of spurs at Ellerup on Fyn (where there is also something similar in Fraugde grave 77), and most interestingly this whole set, with spurs, in a cremation urn at Skeltofte on Lolland. The set occurs in similar numbers in southern mainland Sweden, but occurs rather more frequently on the islands of Bornholm and Gotland and in 4th- to 6th-century Norway. However as the Migration Period progresses in Norway the set is increasingly likely to be extended in a militarily impractical direction by the addition of arrows and/or an axe, which may be a symbolic representation of the magnitude of military power but might alternatively be the incipient symbolisation of hunting as a distinguished pastime, something which becomes familiar in the culture of the succeeding Vendel Period (Sjösvard et al. 1983).

Ørsnes failed to find a place for archery in the postulated defeated army represented at Ejsbøl. There is no record of bows being found, but a total of 675 arrowheads is reported from the find. The role of the bow as a military weapon is probably underrepresented in southern Scandinavian grave-finds, where arrows turn up very infrequently indeed. I have records of one grave from Jutland, one from Sjælland, one from Skåne and two from Gotland of the late Roman Iron Age. Archery is rather better represented as we move southwards and westwards towards and into Saxon territory, at Hammoor and Westerwanna in particular, although still remaining in a minority to other weapon types. The proportion of arrows found in relation to other weapons is the most unstable statistic between the bog deposits. Besides the 675 arrowheads at Ejsbøl-North it is useful to note the 36 bows and 'several hundred' arrows recorded from Nydam I. A number of bogs have also produced cylindrical artefacts plausibly interpreted as quivers, and by simple calculation it appears that a full quiver could usually carry some 20–25 arrows. There is good reason to suppose that the bow and arrow was accorded low status, as an indecorous military weapon, being primarily a utilitarian hunting 'tool' used secondarily in warfare. An effective hunting bow does not necessarily make an effective war bow, although there is evidence that the arrows used were feathered (Raddatz 1963). Arrows on a battlefield are particularly obviously likely to be scattered and mixed, and so we cannot simply take the 675 arrowheads at Ejsbøl-North to represent the weaponry of the defeated army. Nevertheless the combination of this figure with the number of arrows an archer could be expected to carry and the data from Nydam I indicates that there were unlikely to be more than two or three dozen archers on either – possibly even both – sides in these cases. There is little evidence to suggest that these archers would have carried any other weaponry, although as we move into Frankish areas in western Europe the combination of the axe (not the *francisca* type) and arrows in grave assemblages becomes a familiar one. There is no record of axes having been found at Ejsbøl, although figures varying between 'a few' and 27 are recorded from Torsbjerg, Vimose, Illerup and Skedemose.

Before finally summarizing the evidence of Ejsbøl-North, we must be quite aware of the uncertainties in any image of a Germanic war-band we can derive from it. We can only treat the figures pertaining to the deposit as a sample of a defeated army. There can be no assumption of 100% deposition and recovery of the armament of a single army. It has been suggested that on the basis of casualty rates established for later Medieval warfare the Ejsbøl-North figures could be multiplied by two to five times to find the size of the army represented. To follow such a process however requires assumptions that the analogy is reliable and applicable and that the weapons deposited represent only battlefield casualties rather than captives too (cf. Keen 1984, 221–3; Vale 1981, 156–61). One could, alternatively, reduce the figures by postulating the provision of spare arms for the combatants. Obviously the sample would be confused by the loss, seizure and re-use of weapons on the battlefield. Despite all this there is a consistency in the figures for separate parts of sword and belt sets and riding gear at Ejsbøl-North which implies that those responsible for the deposit at least had in mind the size of army they wished to represent there. There is also a degree of similarity in size and structure between various bog-deposits that suggests that it is worth investigating the structure of such samples, even if it is impossible to estimate statistically from these samples the appurtenant population parameters to a determinable degree of probability.

The equipment at Ejsbøl-North thus represents about 60 swordsmen, nine of whom came to the battle mounted and who may have fought at least initially from horseback. If all of these had a two-spear set this leaves 131 spearmen all of whom could have carried a throwing spear and a lance. This leaves a slight surplus of twelve throwing spears found, which need not have any interpretable significance but could be accounted for by a few men carrying more than one throwing spear or by depriving a dozen swordsmen of lances and supposing a further dozen spearmen. Under such considerations the attestable number of spearmen might have been as many as 191. Approximately 15 to 30 archers may be postulated. The sum of fighting men represented may thus range from slightly more than 200 to about 280, with the balance of probability inclining markedly towards the lower figure. The possible grounds for considering that such a figure was intended to represent the defeated army rather than the total battle detritus have already been noted.

The image of armies of a few hundred men at most fits all the other major bog deposits, even Nydam I and Vimose, with totals of 106 swords and about 1,000 spears respectively, which may be more than one deposit each, and Torsbjerg where Ilkær and Lønstrup attribute some 95% of the recovered material to a single defeated army. The figures from

Ejsbøl-North may be compared with the closely contemporary Illerup site 1, also fully excavated, where Ilkjær and Lønstrup record 60+ swords, 50+ shield bosses, *circa* 60 spearheads, 90 lanceheads, and 100+ arrowheads, and Illerup site 2 where the equipment of more than 200 warriors is reported to have been found so far (Ilkær & Lønstrup 1983). A series of deposits however are very much smaller in scale, such as Kragehul, with 10–11 swords and about 80 spears, Vallerbæk, 6–8 swords and about 70 spears, and Hedeliskær, 5–6 swords, about 6 shields and 14 spears. If Ilkjær and Lønstrup are right about the size of the central deposit at Torsbjerg, the earlier and later deposits there can represent armed bands only attestably numbered in tens rather than hundreds. Such consistency as there is in armament profiles in the bog finds, and in broadly contemporary weapon graves in given regions, lies in the fact that swords are consistently less numerous than spears (except in 4th- and 5th-century weapon graves in Saxony and Frisia where they are in a small majority), and that shields too are consistently less numerous than spears, although the proportion is often less than 1:2, so that it is difficult to assess how typical it would be for a spearman not to carry a shield, as Gebühr predicts and as a number of the Ejsbøl-North army would appear to have done.

This seems to be as much as one can say on the size and structure of armies in this area without substantial new programmes of research and excavation, but there remains for consideration the issue of who was fighting whom. Recurrence of use of sites for military deposits indicates that those responsible for the bog deposits were local to these cult sites. Ilkjær and Lønstrup have put forward various arguments for the distinctly non-local origin of material in some of the major bog finds. Their case is based largely on the study of the geographical distribution in grave finds of artefact-types represented in the bog-deposits. The most positive characterization of the source of a defeated army comes from their study of the major Torsbjerg deposit. This deposit appears to have included some 50 or so brooches of types whose distribution in grave finds points to an origin around or to the west of the Elbe, from East Holstein as far as the Rhine, rather than in the Schleswig area itself or southern Scandinavia (Ilkjær & Lønstrup 1982). Ilkjær and Lønstrup also suggest that spear- and lancehead-types represented in Vimose and at Illerup site 2 belong to southern Norway or mainland Sweden rather than the present area of Denmark (Ilkjær 1975; Ilkjær & Lønstrup 1983, 113–6). There is greater room for doubt in relation to this argument in that it is scantly presented: the figures and proportions published for the number of graves containing the relevant types in the relevant areas, and the quantity of these types in the bog-deposits, are either markedly small or numerically imprecise. Even if we accept that alternative spear- and lancehead-types were characteristic of contemporary grave-groups in Jutland and Fyn it is contentious to presume any knowledge of the range and proportion of types available in the Sjælland island group where weapon graves are extremely few (see below). Finally Ilkjær and Lønstrup also suggest that the one boat of the three found at Nydam I, which is built of pinewood, is built in a material not then naturally available in Denmark, and therefore probably represents the transport of an invading army (Ilkjær & Lønstrup 1982, 100). A study of the one surviving boat from this find suggests that it could carry about 45 armed men, but would not then be a stable craft. This does not take account of the possible need for transport of the horses whose sword-hacked skeletons were included with the Nydam I find (Brøndsted 1960, 251–3; Engelhardt/Ørsnes 1970a, xv–xvii). The known Nydam boats are unlikely to have carried a particularly large army particularly far.

Although one may judge that Ilkjær and Lønstrup's arguments in this regard need to be treated with a degree of caution with reference, particularly, to Vimose, Illerup 2 and Nydam I, there is nothing especially extraordinary about their conclusions which need occasion our scepticism. There may indeed be an element of significant consistency in these findings in that the major deposits of Torsbjerg, Illerup 2 and Vimose, all datable around the beginning of the 3rd century, may present the best evidence in the bog finds for relatively long-distance military hostilities involving Schleswig, Jutland and Fyn, from the south, around or beyond the Elbe, in the case of Torsbjerg, and from the north or east in Scandinavia in the cases of the other two deposits. Whether these represent invasion of the areas or raiding out of them is another matter. By the 4th century, however, sufficiently distinctive spear- and shield boss-types appear in graves west of the Elbe and not in the bog-finds to render it most unlikely that this is the provenance of the material deposited (Figs. 3.20–23). Within Scandinavia, regional differentiation in the weapon-types of weapon graves remains quite limited, but comparing the contents of the major bog-finds of Jutland and Fyn with the contents of graves from Gotland and Norway one may at least attest that at this distance certain tendencies appear, such as the long barbed spears of Norway and the stockier shield bosses of both areas, that render it less likely that these are the sources of the weapons in contemporary bog-deposits rather than closer to hand (Figs. 3.24–29). It would certainly appear that there are only exceptional items in the later bog deposits which, on the evidence of grave distribution, could not have come from the immediate vicinity of their final deposition (cf. Ilkjær & Lønstrup 1983, 100–5).

A note may be added on the subject of the runic inscriptions, of which a number accompany the weapon deposits. It is sufficient for our purposes to note that the early history of runes is insufficiently clear for these to determine the attribution of a provenance to most of the material in the bog-finds, and that for the most part the bog-finds are of too early a period for the identification of significantly distinctive regional or tribal dialects in the language of the inscriptions. Finds from Illerup 2 and Torsbjerg indicate, according to Ilkjær and Lønstrup's attribution of provenance, the use of runes both around or south-west of the Elbe and somewhere in southern Scandinavia around the year 200, both of which possibilities are intrinsically acceptable (cf. Barnes 1986). A long inscription on a spearshaft from Kragehul begins with the words **ek erilaz**, containing what is subsequently a distinctively North Germanic variant of the nominative case of the singular first personal pronoun, *ek/ik* (> Norwegian/Danish 'jeg'/English 'I', German 'ich'), and a puzzling word *erilaz* familiar from Scandinavian runic inscriptions. This inscription is therefore unlikely to have been made much to the south of Fyn. Krause has also speculatively identified North and East Germanic elements in the vocabulary and morphology of inscriptions on three items from Vimose (Krause & Jankuhn 1966, 50–69). The geographical bounds of East Germanic *circa* 200 A.D. are however entirely obscure.

For this particular topic to be taken any further, consideration is required of the question of what sort of area could turn out an army of the proportions of that at Ejsbøl-North, bringing us face-to-face with the problems of military organisation as an aspect of social organisation. It has already been noted that there is some evidence to support the view that the major deposit sites stand in their own geographical zones, even within their own archaeological culture provinces, but that this evidence fails to support the exclusive association of any one site with any known, named national group. If these bog sites can represent areas then it is at least possible for either of the armies to represent particular areas rather than being rootless bands, formed around successful captains or 'lords'. It

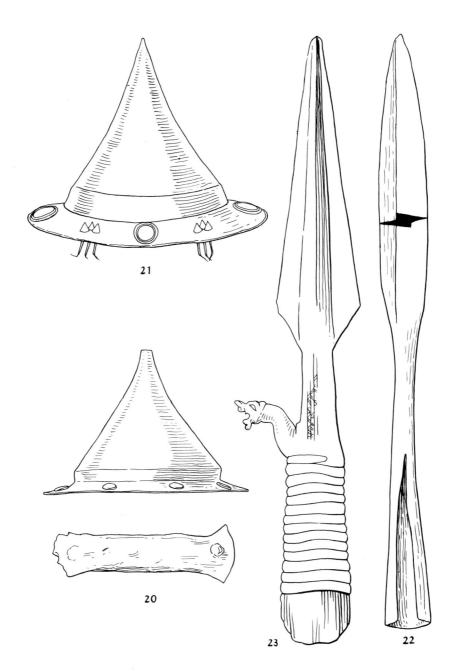

Figs. 3.20–23:   20, Shield boss, Rhenen, Netherlands, grave 833; 21, Shield boss, Vermand III, France, grave B; 22, Spearhead, Rhenen, Netherlands, grave 819; 23, Spearhead, Vermand III, France, grave B.

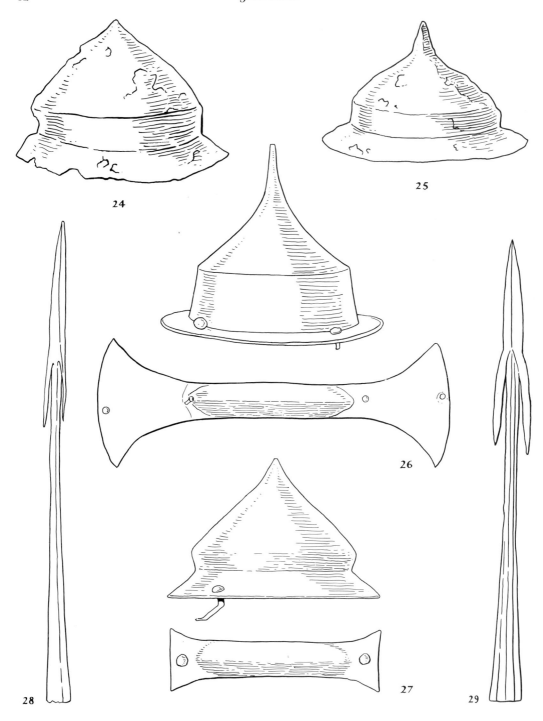

Figs. 3.24–29: *24, Shield boss, Hordaland, Norway; 25, Shield boss, Hordaland, Norway; 26, Shield boss, Kornettskogen, Gotland; 27, Shield boss, Kälder, Gotland; 28, Spearhead, Buskerud, Norway; 29, Spearhead, Sogn og Fjordane, Norway.*

would, however, be possible for there to be rival bands or lords within an area, and also for a local area militia to meet and defeat a rootless band. As is well known, the existence, organisation and structure of lordships amongst these folk at this time is a deeply obscure issue, but it is noteworthy that some presumably central authority amongst the Angles was apparently able to organise the construction, maintenance and development of the *Olgerdige* barrier at the same time as the major Torsbjerg deposit was made. The other 'Anglian' bog deposits are largely later in date.

At this point the distribution of weapon graves becomes relevant. In southern Scandinavia in particular it is noticeable that only relatively small numbers of weapon graves are ever recorded from any one cemetery site. Of late Roman Iron-age cemeteries on Fyn, Nybølle produced four graves containing just shields out of more than 62 burials, at Møllegårdsmark seven weapon graves out of nearly 1,400, apparently concentrated towards the earlier part of this period, and Øregård two weapon graves out of 34. There were clearly at least half-a-dozen weapon graves at Ringe to judge by unstratified weapons found, but just one weapon grave out of the 52 properly recorded. Some 17 other sites had just one weapon grave each, and there are on Fyn cemeteries of up to 80 recorded burials with no weapons at all. Altogether weapon graves constitute only 1–2% of the recorded late Roman Iron-age graves on Fyn published by Albrectsen. Jutland has few large cemeteries, but nevertheless there are only four examples of two weapon graves from a single site, at Vogn, Lærkenfeld, Næsbjerg and Hjortbro. At Hjemsted, South Jutland, a 4th- and 5th-century inhumation cemetery of 88 graves produced no military material (Ethelberg 1986). There are very few weapon graves at all from the remaining Danish islands (excepting Bornholm). The situation begins to change as we move south and west through Anglian and Saxon regions. The large cemeteries at Hammoor, Krummensee/Pötterberg, Sahlenberg, Sörup I and Westerwanna have produced between seven and sixteen weapon graves each, although not particularly richly furnished burials except perhaps for seven at Westerwanna containing sword-fittings and one, possibly two, at Sörup I with mailcoats represented, and generally still representing a very small percentage of the total graves found: 8% of the graves recorded at Hammoor is a high score. The large Anglian cremation cemeteries of Husby, Bordesholm and Borgstedt have produced respectively three, four and five weapon graves of the late Roman Iron Age or early Migration Period. At Bordesholm Borgstedt, Hammoor and Krummensee/Pötterberg the proportion of recorded graves furnished with sword, spear or shield lies consistently between 2 and 4%, but the proportion of weapon graves amongst the total of burials in Schleswig-Holstein is not significantly different from the figure recorded for Fyn. Within these thinly spread weapon graves in the area from the Weser to the Danish islands there appears no consistent and significant difference between the cremation and inhumation rites. The situation is rather different in early Anglo-Saxon England. Weapons are very much more frequent in inhumation cemeteries, regularly occurring in between 10 and 30% of the graves, and are found in 18% of the graves of a large sample of some 50 or so cemeteries reported by Härke (this volume). Weapons might appear to be very scarce in cremations here (Hills 1977, 23–4) but the new evidence of the carefully excavated, processed and published cremation cemetery at Spong Hill, with two cremations with sword-pommels, four with possible scabbard mounts and three or four with arrowheads out of *circa* 2,300 burials of this type shows a situation not particularly dissimilar in general to that in the homelands between Saxony and Fyn (Hills 1977; Hills *et al.* 1987 and forthcoming; information kindly supplied by Dr. Catherine Hills).

Obviously one need not suppose that weapon graves represent the complete distribution of soldiery within a given region at a given time. Not all warriors must have been buried with weapons, nor need all weapon graves be those of warriors. These graves are not the resting places of the bodies or weapons of those defeated on campaign like the Ejsbøl army. Nevertheless the thinly spread distribution of weapon graves, particularly in southern Scandinavia but also right across northern Germany west of the Elbe provides a tempting invitation to postulate a thinly spread military élite, an élite within which even the non-sword bearers could be counted. Warfare would seem to have been the business of this élite and few others: the lowest-class fighters represented at Ejsbøl seem to be the archers, and these would seem to have made up a pitiable supplementary minority rather than a massed peasant host supporting their better armed masters. Such a concept of the élite may fit with Tacitus's account of the 'Hundred' units of young men selected from individual areas, although of course one must acknowledge the distance in time and probably in area between 4th-century Anglia and Jutland and the area(s) from which Tacitus drew his account (cf. Wallace-Hadrill 1975). How additionally an élite may have been constituted – whether one man might be drawn from each extended household at a farmstead or per village; whether there were a system whereby communities could compound to support a professional; whether military duty were an hereditary duty; whether the swordsmen might have constituted an established élite, with a broader body of spearmen turned out and armed at need; whether the expense of weapons limited the size of the élite – such questions may for now be enumerated but left unpursued.

If the proportions of weapon graves amongst Anglian and southern Scandinavian burials of the 4th and 5th centuries give us any sort of reliable figure to work with – and if they do not we have no other figure to use – then the élite theory would imply that an army of the size of the one represented at Ejsbøl-North could have been drawn from a population of several thousand people, and that even the small numbers represented at other bog sites would plausibly have been drawn from populations of several hundred if not a thousand or more. A crucial question is whether or not at the same time they formally represented that population in the sense of acting, somehow, on their behalf. Given the evidence for central organisation amongst the Angles in the 3rd century there is no overwhelming reason why they should not, but given too the case for the relatively local character of warfare in the Schleswig-Jutland-Fyn area towards the end of the Roman Iron Age and in the early Migration Period, we must also recognise that such armies are unlikely to represent particularly large neighbouring groups and territories and may therefore represent rival factions within national groups. There is no impossible contradiction here. The point is worth focussing on particularly because it may represent a significant point of contrast between political developments in this area and those to the east and the south-west. In the 3rd and 4th centuries the Saxons and the Franks appear to emerge as previously unknown confederacies of separate groups. It is conceivable that they united under the leadership of some elected war-king, although the process of the formation of these confederacies remains sadly unexplored (cf. Wallace-Hadrill 1962, 148–63; James, forthcoming). There is no reason why the Saxons and Franks thus constituted should not have been capable of coordinating some activities, although to repeat the point, they are not presented by Ammianus as being part of a *barbarica conspiratio*. Such confederation, evidently, would not seem to be the case with the Angles and Jutes, but may quite plausibly have been the case with an emerging power-block to their east, centred on Sjælland, the channel for trade between Scandinavia and the Romanized or Roman south, an area with few military bog deposits, particularly ones containing weapons, and very few weapon graves, perhaps thriving on and maintaining a divided war zone in the west. This looks to be a convincing origin for the Danes, a group recorded as expelling the *Heruli* from somewhere in southern Scandinavia early in the 3rd century but otherwise very little known before the 6th and 7th centuries (cf. Hedeager 1978 and 1980). It is at least reasonable to postulate an association between this process and the proposed easterly source of material in the major deposits of Illerup 2 and Vimose of about the beginning of the 3rd century.

How, finally, may these tentative and gross politico-military possibilities affect our model of the *adventus Saxonum*? Primarily the model of an élite does provide ready-formed bodies of men capable of transplantation into the Roman defensive system as regular *numeri* or *laeti*, although not necessarily appearing in the authentic guise of national armies. It is of little relevance to the model of the less-controlled *foederati*, but in general terms it does not match with any image of anarchic hordes of barbarians, all men armed to the teeth, divulging upon a civilized Britain from over the North Sea. Unless, that is, there were some rapid and radical military and social adaptation on the part of the Germanic folk to the opportunities open to massed military forces in 5th-century Britain. Some change would certainly appear to have taken place along with or shortly after the migration to Britain, with the substantially higher frequency of weapon graves occurring in the early Anglo-Saxon inhumation cemeteries and the simpler range of weapons and weapon-sets occurring within them. A recent conference on early Anglo-Saxon kingdoms very clearly underlined the Anglo-Saxonist's view of Migration-period England as a primeval political chaos out of which a number of kingdoms eventually emerged (publication forthcoming: see James, forthcoming, for bibliographical details). This has best to be reconciled with the recurrent evidence for powerful and extensive polities in Roman Iron-age northern Germany by accepting that these polities, such as the powers of the Angles or the Sjælland-based Danes, had unstable foundations and were capable both of burgeoning rapidly and being swiftly overtaken. Migration and colonization provides almost a classic situation for social and political divergence between branches of a dividing group: a well-documented example is provided by the different developments in Viking-age and early medieval Norway and Iceland. Despite the evidence of social stratification amongst earlier Germanic folk, there is some justification for regarding the culture of Migration-period England, certainly for several decades after *circa* 475, as being fundamentally egalitarian in the sense that positions of power were open to any with the strength to seize and hold them, not restricted by non-utilitarian qualifications such as birth. It may be the case that any recasting there was of an inherited hierarchical system, any broadening and simplification of the military élite mirrored by such material remains as cemeteries with more weapon graves and simpler and more practicable weapon sets, is best dated not to the earliest stage of migration, nor to the first generation of Germanic settlement in Britain, relating to which the numbers of sites and gravefinds are few, but to the period of virtually unrestrained expansion and consolidation of Germanic settlement falling in a conventionally-datable way between *circa* 475 and 525. Whatever the date, if the (relatively) egalitarian character of Migration-period England is true – and as yet it stands as a convenient but unproven and problematic hypothesis – in itself it must be understood not as an original void, but as the result of a process and the product of circumstances, a process and circumstances worthy of our serious investigation.

Postscript

Since this paper was prepared and read, in January 1987, considerable additions have been made to the published literature on the bog finds. Full catalogues of most of the categories of material at Torsbjerg have been made by Klaus Raddatz: (1) *Der Thorsberger Moorfund. Katalog. Teile von Waffen und Pferdegeschirr, sonstige Fundstücke aus Metall und Glas, Ton- und Holzgefässe, Steingeräte*, Offa-Bücher Neue Folge 65 (1987), and (2) 'Der Thorsberger Moorfund. Gürtelteile und Körperschmuck. Katalog', *Offa* 44 (1987), 117–152. The first volume of a comprehensive publication and discussion of the Ejsbøl excavations and finds, Mogens Ørsnes, *Ejsbøl I – Waffenopferfunde des 4.–5. Jahrh. n.Chr.*, Nordiske Fortidminder Ser.B, Bd.11 (1988), has recently appeared. Nydam III has been published, with a discussion of the topic of *pars pro toto* offerings, by Peter Vang Pedersen, 'Nydam III – et våbenoffer fra ældre germansk jernalder', *Aarbøger for nordisk Oldkyndighed og Historie* 1987, 105–137. Discussion of various finds and issues in the foregoing paper would undoubtedly have been modified if these publications were taken into account, but I do not believe that any essential changes to the argument or (such as they are) conclusions would have resulted.

John Hines, January 1989

References

Albrectsen, E. 1968: *Fynske Jernaldergrave 3*, Yngre Romersk Jernalder.

Albrectsen, E. 1971: *Fynske Jernaldergrave 4*, Gravpladsen på Møllegårdsmarken ved Broholm.

Alcock, L. 1971: *Arthur's Britain*.

Almgren, B. and Nerman, B. 1923: *Die ältere Eisenzeit Gotlands*.

Andersen, H. 1951: Det femte store Mosefund, *Kuml* 1951, 9–22.

Andersen, H. 1956: Afsked med ådalen, *Kuml* 1956, 7–22.

Andreae, B. 1973: *The Art of Rome* (translated by R.E. Wolf).

Barnes, M. 1986: The new runic finds from Illerup and the question of the twenty-second rune, *Saga och Sed* 1984, 59–76.

Becker, C.J. 1971: Mosepotter fra Danmarks Jernalder, *Aarbøger for nordisk Oldkyndighed og Historie* 1971, 5–60.

Böhme, H.W. 1974: *Germanische Grabfunde des 4. bis 5. Jahrhunderts zwischen unterer Elbe und Loire*.

Brøndsted, J. 1960: *Danmarks Oldtid III – Jernalderen*.

Caesar *dBG*: de Bello Gallico. T. Rice Holmes (ed.) *Caii Iulii Caesaris Commentarii Rerum in Gallia Gestarum VII* (1914).

Englehardt, C. 1863 [Englehardt/Ørsnes 1969]: *Thorsbjerg Mosefund*. Reprinted as *Sønderjyske og Fynske Mosefund* Bd.I, with foreword by M. Ørsnes, 1969.

Englehardt, C. 1865 [Englehardt/Ørsnes 1970a]: *Nydam Mosefund*. Reprinted as *Sønderjyske og Fynske Mosefund Bd.II*, with foreword by M. Ørsnes, 1970.

Englehardt, C. 1867 [Englehardt/Ørsnes 1970b]: *Kragehul Mosefund*. See also Engelhardt 1869 (below).

Engelhardt, C. 1869 [Engelhardt/Ørsnes 1970b]: *Vimose Fundet*. Reprinted with Engelhardt 1867 (above) as *Sønderjyske og Fynske Mosefund* Bd.III, with foreword by M. Ørsnes, 1970.

Ethelberg, P. 1986: *Hjemsted – en gravplads fra 4. & 5. årh. e.Kr.*

Fett, P. 1938–40: Arms in Norway 400–600, *Bergens Museums Årbok*, 1938 (Historisk-antikvarisk rekke 2) and 1939 (Historisk-antikvarisk rekke 1).

Gebühr, M. 1980: Kampfspuren an Waffen des Nydam-Fundes, *Beiträge zur Archæologie Nordwestdeutschlands und Mitteleuropas*, Materialhefte zur Ur- und Frühgeschichte Niedersachsens 16, 69–84.

Genrich, A. 1954: *Formenkreise und Stammesgruppen in Schleswig-Holstein.*

Gildas, *de Excidio: de Excidio Britonum.* In M. Winterbottom (ed. & trans.) *Gildas. The Ruin of Britain and other works* (1978).

Hedeager, L. 1978: Processes towards State Formation in Early Iron Age Denmark, *New Directions in Scandinavian Archaeology*, 217–22.

Hedeager, L. 1980: Besiedlung, soziale Struktur und politische Organisation in der älteren und jüngeren römischen Kaiserzeit Ostdänemarks, *Prähistorische Zeitschrift* 55, 38–109.

Hills, C. 1977: The Anglo-Saxon Cemetery at Spong Hill, North Elmham, Part I, *East Anglian Archaeology* 6.

Hills *et al.*, 1987: The Anglo-Saxon Cemetery at Spong Hill, North Elmham, Part IV, *East Anglian Archaeology* 34.

Hills *et al.*, forthcoming: The Anglo-Saxon Cemetery at Spong Hill, North Elmham, Part V, *East Anglian Archaeology.*

Ilkjær, J. 1975: Et bundt våben fra Vimose, *Kuml* 1975, 117–62.

Ilkjær, J. and Lønstrup, J. 1975: Nye udgravninger i Illerup ådal, *Kuml* 1975, 99–115.

Ilkjær, J. and Lønstrup, J. 1977: Illerup ådal. Udgravningen 1976, *Kuml* 1977, 105–17.

Ilkjær, J. and Lønstrup, J. 1981: Runefundene fra Illerup ådal, *Kuml* 1981, 49–65.

Ilkjær, J. and Lønstrup, J. 1982: Interpretation of the Great Votive Deposits of Iron Age Weapons, *JDA* 1, 95–103.

Ilkjær, J. and Lønstrup, J. 1983: Der Moorfund im Tal der Illerup-Å bei Skanderborg in Ostjütland (Dänemark), *Germania* 61, 95–116.

James, E. forthcoming: The origins of the barbarian kingdoms: continental evidence, in S.R. Bassett (ed.), *The Origins of Anglo-Saxon Kingdoms*, forthcoming.

Jankuhn, H. 1966: [contributions to] O. Brandt, *Geschichte Schleswig-Holsteins.*

Jankuhn, H. 1977: Archäologische Beobachtungen zur Religion der festländischen Angeln, *Studien zur Sachsenforschung* 1, 215–34.

JDA : Journal of Danish Archaeology.

Jordanes, *dOAG: De origine actibusque Getarum* ed. A. Holder (1882).

Keen, M. 1984: *Chivalry.*

Krause, W. & Jankuhn, H. 1966: *Die Runeninschriften im älteren Futhark.*

Livy, *aUC: ab Urbe Condita*, vol. XIV ed. & trans. A.C. Schlesinger, Loeb Classical Library (1959).

Lund Hansen, U. 1976: Das Gräberfeld bei Harpelev, Seeland, *Acta Archaeologica* 47, 91–158.

Mackeprang, M.B. 1943: *Kulturbeziehungen im nordischen Raum des 3.–5. Jahrhunderts.*

Mackeprang, M.B. 1952: *De Nordiske Guldbrakteater*

Neumann, H. 1982: *Olgerdiget.*

Orosius, *HaP: Historiae adversum paganos. Libra VII*, ed. C. Zangemeister (1889).

Ørsnes, M. 1964: The weapon find in Ejsbøl Mose at Haderslev, *Acta Archaeologica* 34, 232–47.

Ørsnes, M. 1970: Die Moorfund von Ejsbøl bei Hadersleben, in H. Jankuhn (ed.), *Vorgeschichtliche Heiligtümer und Opferplätze in Mittel- und Nordeuropa*, 172–87.

Raddatz, K. 1957: *Der Thorsberger Moorfund. Gürtelteile und Körperschmuck.*

Raddatz, K. 1963: Pfeilspitzen aus dem Moorfund von Nydam, *Offa* 20, 49–56.

Raddatz, K. 1981: *Sörup I.*

Rech, M. 1979: *Studien zu Depotfunden der Trichtbecher- und Einzelgrabkultur des Nordens.*

Salway, P. 1981: *Roman Britain.*

Särlvik, I. 1982: *Paths towards a Stratified Society.*

Skedemose I–III: U.-E. Hagberg et al., *The Archaeology of Skedemose*, 3 vols., 1967–68.

Stjernquist, B. 1955: *Simris I.*

Strabo, *Geography* ed. & trans. H.L. Jones, Loeb Classical Library, 8 vols., 1917–50.

Tacitus *The Annals of Tacitus*, ed. H.Furneaux, (1894)

Tacitus *Germania*: in H. Furneaux (ed.) *C. Taciti Opera Minora*, (1900).

Vale, M. 1981: *War and Chivalry.*

Wallace-Hadrill, J.M. 1962: *The Long-Haired Kings.*

Wallace-Hadrill, J.M. 1975: War and Peace in the earlier Middle Ages, *Transactions of the Royal Historical Society* 5th series no. 25, 157–74.
Zimmer-Linnfeld, K. 1960: *Westerwanna I*.

Figs. 3.2–18 from Engelhardt 1865–1869; Fig. 19 drawn by Eva Koch-Nielsen, reproduced by permission of the editor of the *Journal of Danish Archaeology*; Figs. 21–24 from Böhme 1974, reproduced by permission; Figs. 26–27 from Almgren and Nerman 1923. All redrawn to a consistent style and scale by Marion Cox, Oxford.

Chapter 4

Early Saxon Weapon Burials:
frequencies, distributions and weapon combinations

Heinrich Härke

The aim of this paper is to discuss some general aspects of the Anglo-Saxon weapon burial rite. It will concentrate on the absolute and relative frequencies of weapon burials, and on the types of weapon combinations occurring in Early Saxon inhumation graves. Other aspects, such as typology, technology, the deposition of weapons in the graves, or the archaeological and anthropological correlates of the weapon burial rite, cannot be dealt with here, nor can the question of weapons in cremation burials.

The following discussion is based on a sample of 54 inhumation, or mixed, cemeteries, 47 of which were analysed in detail (Appendix). The geographical coverage is somewhat uneven due to a number of reasons: regional differences in burial rite and in the state of cemetery excavations, and some problems concerning access to finds and data. The regions best covered are Wessex and Kent; regions with a sample of problematic size are Sussex and the north. In terms of chronology, the sample spans the entire Early (Pagan) Saxon Period, from the earlier fifth to the end of the seventh centuries.

Weapon Burial Frequencies

In the cemeteries analysed, 18% of all inhumations were found to have weapons, i.e. about one out of five Pagan Saxon inhumations contained weapons. Limiting the analysis to the identifiable male adult burials in the sample, we find that 47% of them had been furnished with weapons. Almost half of all male adults of this period were, therefore, buried with arms.

But there are marked variations at regional, and particularly at local, level. Differences between cemeteries, even neighbouring ones, are sometimes striking. Weapon burials represented between 1% and 36% of all inhumations, or between 11% and 90% of male adults, in any one cemetery. Such marked local variations are typical of all aspects of the Anglo-Saxon weapon burial rite.

It is only at regional level that interpretable patterns emerge. In most regions, between 15% and 22% of inhumations had been equipped with weapons. If we exclude the 'late' cemeteries of seventh/eighth century date which are unevenly distributed in the sample, regional proportions of weapon burials still vary from 17% to 22%, except for the north with only 8%. These regional differences show up more clearly when we look at the

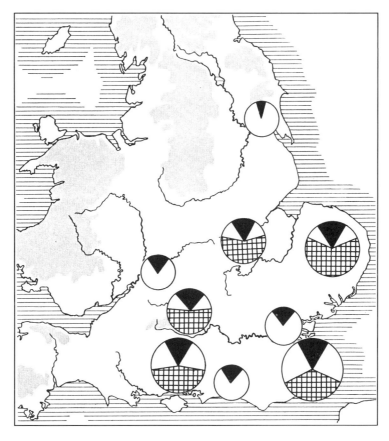

black – per cent of all inhumations   hatched – per cent of male adults

Fig. 4.1 Relative proportions of weapon burials by regions.

proportions of male adult burials furnished with weapons: the percentages vary from 36% to 62%. If we exclude, again, the late cemeteries, two regional groupings may be identified (Fig. 4.1):

- Saxon and Anglian areas (except for the north where the sample is rather small for this analysis): 50–65% of male adults had weapons;

- Kent (and the north?): less than 40% of male adults had weapons.

This is an intriguing pattern because it is the 'rich' areas that appear to have a smaller proportion of weapon burials than the 'poorer' regions. In this sample, Kent and the north stand out by having the highest average number of finds per male burial and the highest proportion of male burials with precious metals (excluding unfurnished burials from the analysis). They also have the highest average number of weapons per weapon burial: in Kent and the north, there are (relatively speaking) more weapons in fewer weapon burials.

It would therefore seem that the regional differences in weapon burial frequencies are not directly related to differences in regional wealth (*pace* Arnold 1980, 86). Differences between the regions in their respective social structures may be presumed, and these may well have played a role in determining the geographical pattern of weapon burial frequencies.

But apart from wealth and social structure, there is a third factor that has to be taken into account: the burial rite, or more precisely, the regional proportions of cremations. In most Anglian areas, the high percentage of weapon burials among inhumations coincides with a high overall proportion of cremations, whereas in Kent and the north, the virtual absence of cremations coincides with a low percentage of weapon burials among inhumations. In both respects, the Saxon areas are in between these two extremes. The most likely explanation of this correlation is that some of the social groups not practising weapon burial would have tended towards cremation wherever the latter was an accepted burial rite.

The chronological analysis of weapon burial frequencies presents several problems, the first of which is the system of absolute dates as used in Anglo-Saxon archaeology. This kind of dating does not facilitate chronological comparisons. In order to trace changes over time, the weapon burials were grouped in four different ways:

- by centuries (V–VII)
- by half centuries (Va–VIIb)
- in overlapping chronological groups (1–6)
- by absolute median dates.

Analysis by centuries and half centuries shows up a peak of weapon burial numbers in the first half of the sixth century. But these two methods can evaluate only 30% to 40% of the sample because too many weapon burials straddle the dividing lines between the horizons and cannot be fitted into the rigid systems. For this reason, a system of six overlapping 'burial date groups' has been devised; each spans about a century or slightly more. In this way, three quarters (77%) of all weapon burials in the sample can be assigned to a group. Thus, the system of burial date groups makes the best use of the available data, and provides the most reliable results (Fig. 4.2). It places the maximum of weapon burial numbers in group 3 (which has a median point around AD 535/540).

The analysis by absolute median dates does not require a grouping by date spans, but operates with individual cases. These median dates are derived by converting approximate date spans into absolute figures: e.g. first half of sixth century into 500–550, median date 525. Depending on the selection of date spans deemed acceptable for this kind of analysis, the peak of the weapon burial distribution falls between *c.* AD 535 and 555. Although not too much weight should be given to such 'exact' dates, the overall agreement of the results from all four approaches is remarkable.

This describes the changes over time in *absolute* numbers, which need not reflect variations in the *relative* proportions of weapon burials. But the chronological analysis of the latter presents a second problem: in contrast to weapon burials which usually can be dated closely enough, most other male burials lack closely datable finds. The only way to overcome this problem is to group entire cemeteries according to their date spans, and work out the relative proportions of weapon burials for each of the 'cemetery date groups'. Burial sites with a very wide date span (typically mid/late fifth to late seventh centuries) had to be omitted from the analysis in order to obtain meaningful results.

The resulting curve of weapon burial proportions (Fig. 4.3) closely resembles the curve of absolute numbers of weapon burials: a steep rise to a peak in the sixth century (with 20% of all inhumations, and 61% of male adults being equipped with weapons), and a subsequent, slow decrease in the later sixth and seventh centuries. The end of the weapon burial rite can be dated to around AD 700 or very shortly afterwards, in contrast to the Continent where weapons continued to be placed in status burials well into the eighth century (Stein 1967). It should be noted, however, that the decline of this rite in England is a decrease in numbers of individuals buried with weapons – it is *not* a decrease in the average number of weapons deposited in each weapon grave: that number (1.6 weapons) remained surprisingly stable throughout the entire Pagan Saxon Period.

It is obvious that in the final phase of the Anglo-Saxon weapon burial rite, few of those who actually fought as warriors were buried with arms. Conversely, the maximum of the absolute weapon burial frequencies, late in the first half of the sixth century, falls into Myres' phase IV, the post-Badon phase of "reaction and British recovery" (Myres 1969, 64) for which far fewer battles are recorded than for the phases before and after (cf. Arnold 1980, 85 fig. 4.2). It was with the renewed Anglo-Saxon expansion in the second half of the sixth century that the decline in absolute and relative numbers of weapon burials began. The weapon burial rite, therefore, was not directly related to the level of military activity; if there was any correlation at all, it was a negative one.

Weapon Types and Combinations

The frequencies of weapon types in Pagan Saxon inhumations show very marked variations (Table 4.1). Spears occur in most weapon burials, shields in slightly less than half of them, swords in only one out of ten. Seax, axe and arrow are all well below 10% each. These figures contrast with the frequencies of weapon types in Frankish and Alamannic graves (Table 4.2) where swords accompanied between a quarter and half of all weapon burials (Steuer 1968). More significantly, they also differ from the frequencies of weapon types in contemporary Saxon inhumations in Northern Germany (Table 4.2) where seaxes and arrows were found with about half of all burials, but shields with only one fifth of them (pers. comm. T. Taitl-Kröger, Hamburg).

The frequencies of Anglo-Saxon weapon sets ('combinations') reflect these preferences (Table 4.3). The most frequent set is a single spear on its own, found in almost half of all weapon burials. The second most popular set is the combination of 'shield + spear' which occurs in a quarter of all inhumations with weapons. Other combinations represent less than 10% each, most of them much less than that. Thus, Anglo-Saxon weapon burials contained mostly single weapons or very simple, basic sets of weapons.

Some patterns of recurring combinations can be identified. Half of all spears in the sample occurred on their own, without further weapons. Most shields were associated with a spear, most swords with a shield and/or a spear. Seaxes were deposited together with a spear or on their own, but only rarely with a shield. Most axes and arrowheads were found without other weapons; arrows were hardly ever part of a set, and were only combined with spears.

For the discussion of geographical and chronological patterns, it is necessary to form groups of related combinations (Table 4.3). The subdivisions are not based on functional

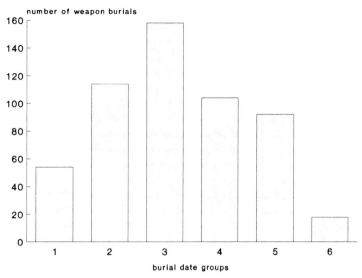

Burial date groups:
1   early V–early VI cent.;   4   mid VI–early VII cent.;
2   mid V–mid VI cent.;   5   late VI–late VII cent.;
3   late V–late VI cent.;   6   mid VII–mid VIII cent.

Fig. 4.2   Numbers of weapon burials in the sample over time.

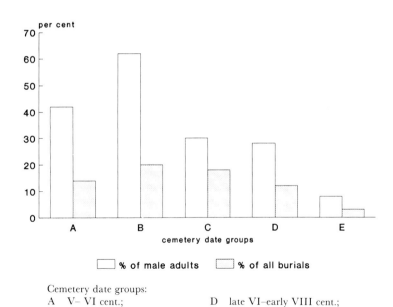

Cemetery date groups:
A   V– VI cent.;   D   late VI–early VIII cent.;
B   (late) V–early VII cent.;   E   VII–VIII cent.
C   VI–VII cent.;

Fig. 4.3   Changes in the proportions of weapon burials over time

Table 4.1   Frequencies of weapon types in Early Saxon inhumation burials

	Number of burials with this type of weapon	as % of undisturbed weapon burials
spear	460	86.1
shield	238	44.5
sword	62	11.6
seax	23	4.3
axe	14	2.6
arrow	6	1.1
Total of undisturbed weapon burials	534	

Table 4.2   Comparison of frequencies of weapon types in England and on the Continent

| | ENGLAND | | | | CONTINENT | | | |
| | Anglo-Saxons VI–VII cent. | | Saxons V–VII cent. | | Franks VI–VII cent. | | Alamanni VI–VII cent. | |
Weapon Type	no. of burials	%	no. of burials	%	no. of burials	%	no. of burials	%
spear	589	83.9	32	56.1	73	45.6	55	45.6
shield	317	45.2	10	17.5	25	15.6	49	23.8
sword	76	10.8	10	17.5	17	10.6	76	36.9
seax	30	4.3	34	59.6	77	48.1	148	71.8
axe	14	2.0	7	12.2	38	23.8	–	–
arrow	7	1.0	23	40.4	43	26.9	66	32.0
helmet	–	–	–	–	–	–	1	0.5
horse bit, spurs	1	0.1	–	–	2	1.3	20	9.7
Total of weapon burials evaluated	702		57		160		206	

Note:

no. of burials – number of inhumations with the respective type of weapon

% – as a percentage of total weapon burials evaluated for the region

The above figures include all burials (undisturbed and disturbed) as information on the absence or presence of post-depositional disturbance was not available in all cases.

considerations (which would require an *a priori* decision by the archaeologist), but on the premise that a weapon type was usually the more valuable (in whatever sense) the less often it was used to furnish a burial. In creating the actual groups of weapon combinations, the sword has been given precedence over the less frequent axe and seax because its use in burials spans virtually the entire Pagan Period, whereas axe and seax are limited to the earlier and later phases, respectively.

The frequencies of the various weapon combinations differ considerably from cemetery to cemetery, and as with the weapon burial frequencies, the regional variations and patterns are more easily interpretable (Fig. 4.3). A common feature of all regions is the proportion of spear combinations, between 40% and just over 50%. The major difference between them is the way the remaining 50% to 60% are divided up into the other types of combinations.

The most intriguing observation is that the proportions of sword combinations and shield combinations appear to be closely linked. Where sword combinations are frequent, the proportion of shield combinations is low; where sword combinations are rare or absent, the proportion of shield combinations is correspondingly higher. 'Rich' areas such as Kent have a high proportion of sword combinations whereas in 'poorer' areas, particularly in the Anglian regions, shield combinations replace some, or all, of the sword combinations. The seeming absence of sword combinations north of the Wash is a consequence of the small sample for this region; swords have been found there, e.g. in Bernicia (Alcock 1981; Miket 1980). The seax, axe, and arrow combinations are rare, and occur mainly in the south.

The chronological analysis reveals only gradual changes in the proportions of weapon combinations over time (Table 4.4). The oscillations of the proportions of spear combinations and shield combinations in chronological groups 2, 3 and 4 are probably more apparent than real: they seem to be a consequence of typological dating. The clearest trends are the steady increase of seax combinations (from group 3), the disappearance of axe combinations (from group 4), the decrease of shield combinations (from group 5), and the disappearance of sword combinations (in group 6). Datable arrow combinations are too few for a meaningful chronological analysis.

The overall process, then, was one of simplification and standardisation: types of weapon combinations became fewer, and less varied, as time went on. In the later phases of the Pagan Period, the seax, and possibly also the shield, took over some of the roles of the axe and the sword in the burial rite. That does not imply, of course, that the seax was the functional replacement of the axe, and later of the sword, in the actual fighting equipment. For practical reasons alone, this is rather unlikely. After all, the sword remained one of the principal Anglo-Saxon weapons throughout the Middle and Late Saxon Periods, as far as we can tell from historical sources.

This problem highlights the likelihood that there was a discrepancy between weapons used in the burial rite, and weapons used in real life. The discussion of Anglo-Saxon weapon burials cannot, therefore, be concluded without a look at functional and practical aspects. It is all too often assumed that the weapon combinations found in Early Medieval graves in England and on the Continent are functional sets of weapons and may, thus, be used to reconstruct fighting practices and the armouries of individual warriors (e.g. Arnold 1980, 84–90; Steuer 1968, 19; id. 1970, 354; Werner 1968, 100). But is this assumption correct?

Some Pagan Saxon weapon combinations (Table 4.3) look practical enough: e.g. 'shield

Table 4.3   Frequencies of weapon combinations in Early Saxon inhumation burials

Group	Weapon combination	Number of burials	%
SPEAR COMBINATIONS	SP	237	44.4
	SP + SP	6	1.1
	SP + SP + SP	2	0.4
SHIELD COMBINATIONS	SH	36	6.7
	SH + SP	139	26.0
	SH + SP + SP	14	2.6
SWORD COMBINATIONS	SW	9	1.7
	SW + SP	10	1.9
	SW + SH	11	2.1
	SW + SH + SP	24	4.5
	SW + SH + SP + SP	4	0.7
	SW + AX + SP	1	0.2
	SW + AX + SH + SP	1	0.2
	SW + SX + SH + SP	1	0.2
	SW + SX + AX + SH + SP + SP	1	0.2
SEAX COMBINATIONS	SX	6	1.1
	SX + SP	9	1.7
	SX + SH	–	–
	SX + SH + SP	4	0.7
	SX + SH + SP + SP	2	0.4
AXE COMBINATIONS	AX	8	1.5
	AX + SP	2	0.4
	AX + SH + SP	1	0.2
ARROW COMBINATIONS	AR	4	0.7
	AR + SP	2	0.4
Total of undisturbed weapon burials		534	100

Abbreviations: AR – arrow; AX – axe; SH – shield; SP – spear; SW – sword; SX – seax.

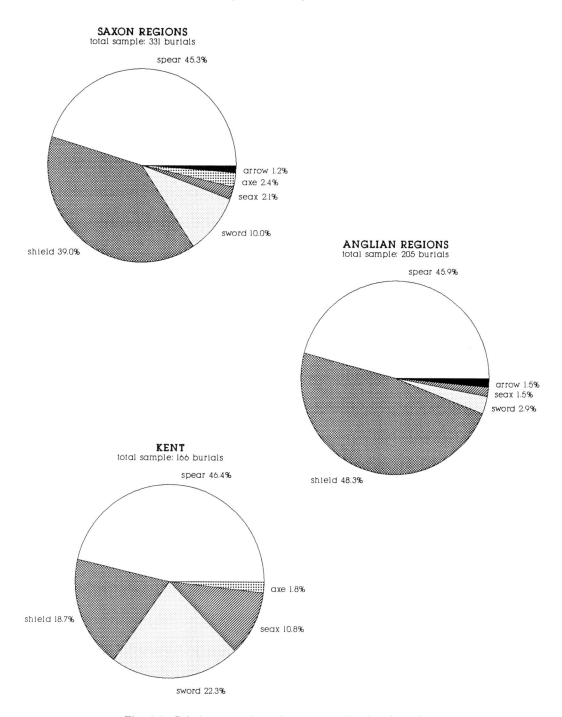

Fig. 4.4 Relative proportions of weapon combinations by regions
(for groups of weapon combinations, cf. Table 4.3).

Table 4.4   Changes in the proportions of weapon combinations over time

Weapon combinations	Burial date groups					
	1	2	3	4	5	6
spear combinations	31%	42%	46%	26%	51%	47%
shield combinations	46%	47%	37%	62%	24% H	18%
sword combinations	16%	7%	11%	9%	13%	–
seax combinations	–	–	2%	3%	12%	35%
axe combinations	7%	1%	4%	–	–	–
arrow combinations	–	3%	–	–	–	–
Total sample of datable burials	55 (100%)	113 (100%)	158 (100%)	105 (100%)	92 (100%)	17 (100%)

Burial date groups:
1   early V – early VI cent.   4   mid VI – early VII cent.
2   mid V – mid VI cent.   5   late VI – late VII cent.
3   late V – late VI cent.   6   mid VII – mid VIII cent.

+ spear' or 'sword + shield + spear'. But many others are decidedly less practical, and sometimes not really functional at all. By far the most popular set is the single spear which, of course, can be sufficient armament depending on the type of spear and the style of fighting. However, one third of all single spears in the analysed sample have small points (types C1, D1, E1, F1 and H1 after Swanton 1973; id. 1974) which would seem to indicate throwing spears – and a single throwing spear on its own does not make sense as a functional set.

Combinations of several spears (with or without a shield, sword, or seax) do not give the impression of having been selected on practical grounds, either. There are no recurring sets of spearhead types or sizes in the sample. No combination of spear types occurs more often than twice (out of a total of 37 cases of multiple spear sets). The combination of a long and a short spearhead, indicative of a set of pike and throwing spear, occurs only twice.

If it seems difficult to find a functional interpretation for many single spears, it is even more difficult in most cases where the weapon set consists of a single seax or axe. In the analysed sample, no less than five of the six single seaxes without additional weapons are of the narrow variety: small and light blades that may be useful as supplementary equipment, but not as main arms. Likewise, six of the eight single axes are franciscas: this is the only axe type which can be used as a throwing axe and, therefore, requires additional weapons to make up a functional set. By way of contrast, other axe types which could be used as main weapons are usually found in combinations with other weapons.

Finally, there can be no doubt about the total lack of functionality in the case of single shields without supplementing weapons – and they are the third most popular weapon set. Only some of these cases are the result of post-depositional disturbance (already excluded from Table 4.3). The remaining 36 cases in this sample cannot be explained by the total decay of supplementing weapons made entirely from organic materials (such as clubs or spears without iron points). A considerable number of unassociated shield-bosses were unearthed in the course of modern, careful excavations (e.g. Mucking, with five single shields) where the remains or shadows of such 'organic' weapons would have been detected if they had existed.

It should also be noted that the provision of a single shield or a single seax in a grave is not an Anglo-Saxon peculiarity. Iron bosses without accompanying weapons have been observed in Roman Iron Age burials of Northern Germany and Southern Scandinavia (Schirnig 1965; and cf. the contribution by John Hines in this volume), while single shields and single seaxes are also found in Early Medieval burials on the Continent (Steuer 1968, 24, 61, 63).

Conclusions

Thus, all weapon sets found in Anglo-Saxon burials cannot have been the result of functional considerations, and their interpretation in terms of fighting practices and complete warrior equipment may, in many cases, be misleading. The analysis suggests that weapons were a largely symbolic burial deposit. Regional variations may have been the result of differences in social structure and wealth, and these factors must be presumed to have played an important role at the local and individual levels, too.

The background of the weapon burial rite as such is much more difficult to identify. James (1979, 72), elaborating ideas put forward mainly by Werner and Böhme, has suggested that this custom originated in the mid-fourth century in Western Europe out of a need to emphasize the status of the Germanic military aristocracy. Steuer (1982, 522, 528) has recently speculated that the Germanic weapon burial custom was the consequence of the comitatus system ('Gefolgschaftswesen') and is, thus, indirect evidence of the military service of free warriors. On the basis of the Anglo-Saxon archaeological evidence, however, it seems clear enough that the frequency of the weapon burial rite was not related to the level of historically attested military activity. It was influenced by regional differences in burial rites and by the decline, over time, of the grave-goods custom. Further analysis suggests social factors (mainly wealth, age, family relationships, and possibly ethnicity) to have determined and shaped the Pagan Saxon weapon burial rite.

Appendix

Burial sites analysed (by Regions)

Region	Cemetery	Inhumations with weapons	Publication
KENT	Sarre	70	X
	Finglesham	28	+
	Dover B	(27)	(X)
	Broadstairs I	24	
	*Polhill	17	X
	Orpington	13	X
	Lyminge II	6	+
	*Holborough	4	X
	Bekesbourne II	4	
ESSEX	Mucking II	58	
	Mucking I	15	
SUSSEX	Alfriston	35	X
	Highdown	(11)	X
WESSEX	Pewsey	19	
	Worthy Park	19	
	Petersfinger	14	X
	Andover	12	X
	*Bargates	11	X
	Droxford	9	X
	Harnham Hill	7	X
	Charlton Plantation	6	(X)
	*Snell's Corner	5	X
	Collingbourne Ducis	4	X
	Winterbourne Gunner	3	X
	*Portsdown I	2	X
	Ford	2	X
	*Winnall II	–	X
UPPER THAMES	Long Wittenham I	51	X
	Berinsfield	25	
	Abingdon I	23	X
	Brighthampton	11	X
WEST MIDLANDS	Bidford-on-Avon	32	+
	Stretton-on-Fosse II	17	
	Broadway Hill	1	X
EAST MIDLANDS	Empingham II	34	
	Wakerley I	16	
	Nassington	11	X
	*Dunstable	3	X
	Leighton Buzzard II	2	X
	*Leighton Buzzard III	2	X
	Ruskington	(1)	
EAST ANGLIA	Morning Thorpe	(66)	(X)
	Holywell Row	21	X
	Westgarth Gardens	21	(X)

Region	Cemetery	Inhumations with Weapons	Publication
	Bergh Apton	14	X
	Spong Hill	12	X
	Swaffham	6	X
	Little Eriswell	3	X
	*Burwell	(1)	X
THE NORTH	Welbeck Hill	(6)	
	Sewerby	5	X
	West Heslerton	(4)	
	Fonaby	3	X
	Worlaby	2	

key:
*   late cemetery (VII/VIII cent.)
X   all evaluated evidence published
(X)   published after completion of analysis
+   part of evaluated evidence published
( )   only limited evaluation

References

Alcock, L. 1981: Quantity or quality: the Anglian graves of Bernicia, in: V.I. Evison (ed.). *Angles, Saxons, and Jutes. Essays presented to J.N.L. Myres* (Oxford: O.U.P), 168–183.

Arnold, C. 1980: Wealth and social structure: a matter of life and death, in: Rahtz *et al.* 1980, 81–142.

James, E. 1979: Cemeteries and the problem of Frankish settlement in Gaul, in: P.H. Sawyer (ed.). *Names, Words and Graves: Early Medieval Settlement* (Leeds), 55–89.

Miket, R. 1980: A restatement of evidence from Bernician Anglo-Saxon burials, in: Rahtz *et al.* 1980, 289–305.

Myres, J.N.L. 1969: *Anglo-Saxon Pottery and the Settlement of England* (Oxford: Clarendon).

Rahtz, P., Dickinson T. and Watts L. (eds.) 1980: *Anglo-Saxon Cemeteries 1979. The Fourth Anglo-Saxon Symposium at Oxford* (Oxford. British Archaeological Reports 82).

Schirnig, H. 1965: Waffenkombinationen in germanischen Gräbern der Spätlatène- und älteren Kaiserzeit, *Nachrichten aus Niedersachsens Urgeschichte* 34, 19–33.

Stein, F. 1967: *Adelsgräber des achten Jahrhunderts in Deutschland* (Berlin. Germanische Denkmäler der Völkerwanderungszeit A IX).

Steuer, H. 1968: Zur Bewaffnung und Sozialstruktur der Merowingerzeit. Ein Beitrag zur Forschungsmethode, *Nachrichten aus Niedersachsens Urgeschichte* 37, 18–87.

Steuer, H. 1970: Historische Phasen der Bewaffnung nach Aussagen der archäologischen Quellen Mittel- und Nordeuropas im 1. Jahrtausend n.Chr., *Frühmittelalterliche Studien* 4, 348–383.

Steuer, H. 1982: *Frühgeschichtliche Sozialstrukturen in Mitteleuropa* (Göttingen. Abhandlungen der Akademie der Wissenschaften in Göttingen, Philologisch-Historische Klasse, 3. Folge, Nr. 128).

Swanton, M.J. 1973: *The Spearheads of the Anglo-Saxon Settlements* (London: Royal Archaeological Institute).

Swanton, M.J. 1974: *A Corpus of Pagan Anglo-Saxon Spear-Types* (Oxford. British Archaeological Reports 7).

Werner, J. 1968: Bewaffnung und Waffenbeigabe in der Merowingerzeit, in: *Settimane di studio del centro italiano di studi sull'alto medioevo* XV (Spoleto), 95–108, 199–205.

Chapter 5

The Development of Anglo-Saxon Swords from the Fifth to the Eleventh Century

Peter Bone

Introduction

The double-edged swords used by the Germanic peoples of the Early Medieval period developed from Romano-Celtic and Sarmatian cavalry swords over the period 100–400 AD. These swords generally have relatively narrow, acutely pointed blades, often of a diamond-shaped cross-section, suited to a cut-and-thrust type of fighting.

Germanic sword blades typically have broad, flat blades, frequently with one or more fullers (grooves) which are best suited to cutting blows. Blades change relatively little over the period under consideration, and surviving blades are often in poor condition, and so Early Medieval swords are usually classified according to the form of the hilt, which tends to vary according to date and geographical origin. The form at the hilt thus gives an indication of the age and 'ethnic origin' of a good sword: the fact that sword hilts are often richly decorated allows dating and origin to be cross-checked with other decorative metalwork. One point to be borne in mind however is that swords were regarded as precious heirlooms in Germanic society, and could remain in use for a considerable period, during which the hilt might be redecorated or even replaced. Blade and hilt were not necessarily made by the same smith: there is evidence of a thriving export trade in both blades and finished swords from the Frankish Rhineland, though there is growing evidence for sword-blade production in England, especially Kent, during the sixth and seventh centuries (Lang & Ager, this book, 100–113).

The Anglo-Saxons certainly developed their own distinct forms of sword hilt from those used in their continental homeland in southern Scandinavia and north-western Germany following the settlement of Britain. By the ninth century, English hilts had evolved a clearly different form from those used by the other German peoples.

Parts of the Sword

The schematic diagram below (Fig. 5.1) shows the terminology used in this article to describe the parts of the sword.

The general dimensions of swords vary little during the period: overall length at 81–97 cm (32–38″), blade length of 68–81 cm (27– 32″), and blade width at the lower guard of

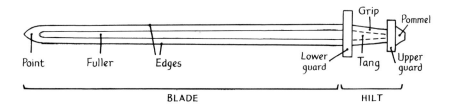

Fig. 5.1 The parts of the sword.

4.5–6.5 cm (1.77–2.56″). The grip itself is usually from 8–10 cm (3.15–3.94″) long, confirming that these swords were designed to be used one-handed.

The Hilt – The Fifth Century

There is little evidence for the earliest Anglo-Saxon swords, but what there is shows that the swords in use were similar to those found in the bog deposits of Angeln. These early forms had lower and upper guards and grip of wood, bone or horn rather than metal, and no real pommel – merely a large 'washer' over which the tang was rivetted. Three variants of such hilts were in use in southern Scandinavia during the late third to early sixth centuries, two of which appear to have usually been coated in silver foil, although I am not aware of any such being found in Britain. Indeed, I am only aware of two examples of the early forms of hilt, from Cumberland and Feltwell in Norfolk. The Cumberland sword hilt is decorated with goldwork possibly of 7th century style, but is quite probably an older sword that was re-embellished late in its career. It is possible that the other forms found in the bog deposits were used in Britain, but have yet to be discovered or published. The Feltwell sword, found hidden in a disused Roman bath house is the nearest known example but the find circumstances are obscure.

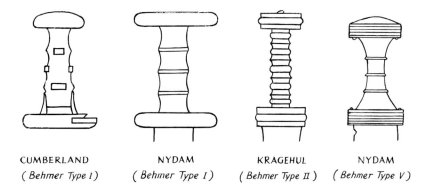

Fig. 5.2 South-Scandinavian hilts, fourth–fifth centuries (after Behmer).

The Sixth and Seventh Centuries

For this period, there is abundant evidence from grave-finds for a sword form which seems to have been adopted by all the Germanic peoples – it is found in Britain, Scandinavia, Germany, France, Italy, and Hungary. Swords of this type are the first to feature a large metal pommel, rather than an oversized washer. The upper and lower guards seem sometimes to have been of wood, bone or horn, or often of a sandwich construction of two layers of metal rivetted to a central layer of organic material (Fig. 5.3). Some do have all-metal guards, but where this is the case they usually mimic the sandwich construction, complete with rivets. These swords are often very rich, with gilded (or even solid gold) metal parts.

This form of hilt includes the 'ring-swords'. These have an upper guard embellished with a ring-and-staple. In the earliest examples the ring is free-running through the staple, whilst on later forms it is replaced by a single solid casting of the ring-and-staple. The significance of these rings is not really known, but since literary sources indicate that both rings and sword-hilts were considered worthy of having oaths sworn upon them, this may have been their function. Some swords show signs of having had such rings removed, and so it is possible that they were personal to a particular owner and were removed if the sword passed on to someone else. In a few cases, 'rings' have been found attached to items other than swords (eg the shield at Sutton Hoo, and a drinking horn at Valsgärde). The early free-running rings are found in England and southern Scandinavia, whilst the later solid rings are more widespread. It would thus seem likely that this custom originated amongst the Anglo-Saxons in Britain or their continental homeland, and then spread to the other Germanic peoples – solid rings have been found on sword hilts in Lombard cemeteries in Italy.

One of the most remarkable things about swords of this type is their uniformity throughout Europe, which contrasts strongly with the regional variations which are apparent before and after this period. This may perhaps reflect a considerable degree of contact and exchange between the Germanic peoples, and a 'pan-Germanic' cultural similarity such as is also expressed in the Anglo-Saxon poem 'Widsith', which purports to describe the travels of a poet amongst the Germanic tribes and their neighbours of the fourth to sixth centuries.

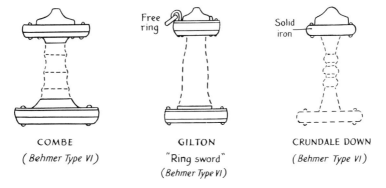

COMBE
(*Behmer Type VI*)

GILTON
"Ring sword"
(*Behmer Type VI*)

CRUNDALE DOWN
(*Behmer Type VI*)

Fig. 5.3 Kentish hilts, sixth–seventh centuries (after Behmer).

The Eighth Century

With the abandonment of weapon-burials, we enter another period of sparse evidence – I only know of two English sword hilts dated to the eighth century, neither of which is complete. These are a pommel from Windsor, and the upper half of a hilt from Fetter Lane (Fig. 5.4). There is little to go on, but it would appear that these continue the evolutionary trend from the swords of the seventh century. Whereas earlier pommels were roughly triangular, both of the eighth century examples have a pronounced central lobe, flanked by rather lower triangular 'wings'. There was a similar development in both North and South Germany in the first half of the eighth century, cf. Stein's sword types Mannheim and Haldenegg, so perhaps there were connexions. In both cases the upper guard is, or would have been, straight, and the lower guard was probably also straight and a little longer, as on the Continental examples. The guards were probably of solid metal, although some may still have been of sandwich construction. Interestingly the surviving half of the decorated grip from Fetter Lane is of a similar shape to the Danish examples of Behmer's type V. Some Scandinavian examples of the sixth/seventh centuries (Behmer's type VI and type VII) also have grips of this shape, and others have the 'finger-grooved' shape of Behmer's type I. From this it would seem that both forms of grip had been imported from Europe by the Anglo-Saxon migrants.

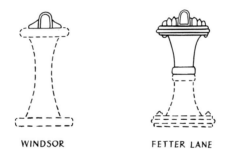

WINDSOR   FETTER LANE

Fig. 5.4   English hilts of the eighth century (after Dunning & Evison).

The Ninth, Tenth, and Eleventh Centuries

Following the dearth of evidence for the preceding century, the late Saxon period again has a wide range of evidence, largely from river-finds. The frequency of river-finds of weapons has lead to speculation that, since grave-goods were no longer in vogue, weapons may have been deposited in rivers on the owner's death.

   The ninth century sees the appearance of probably the most distinctively English sword-hilt of all, included in Petersen's survey of Viking age swords as type L. Although very distinct from seventh and eighth century hilts, the pommel forms part of the same evolutionary trend, with a pronounced central lobe. Even more striking is an entirely new development – the upper and lower guards are curved away from the grip, rather than straight. This seems to have been a particularly English development that later spread to Scandinavia. Pommels and guards are of iron, richly embellished with silver. By this time,

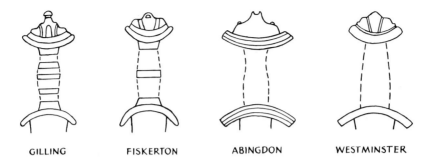

Fig. 5.5 English hilts of the ninth century (after Evison 1967 and Wilson 1965).

guards are always of solid metal. This hilt form is found from the ninth to the eleventh century. Early examples have a very pronounced central lobe on the pommel and relatively narrow, strongly curved guards, whereas later ones have a more subdued, rounded pommel and thicker, less curved guards which tend to widen slightly towards the ends. No grips survive, but the silver bands that decorated them show that either a gently curved or perhaps finger grooved shape was in use. Swords of this kind have also been found in Scandinavia (hence their inclusion in Petersen's classification), but their distinctive Trewhiddle style decoration confirms their English origin.

In the tenth century another new form also appears – the so-called 'teacosy' or 'mushroom' pommel. This is probably the result of Danish influence, as other early examples of this hilt point towards an origin in Scandinavia. English examples appear to show an evolutionary trend developing from the trilobate type L form, in which the contours of the pommel become more rounded and the guards become straighter. Ultimately, the upper guard and pommel are no longer made as separate pieces, but as a single piece of metalwork. I am not aware of any evidence for the grip shape used on such later swords, but it would seem likely that the earlier variants noted above remained in use in some form.

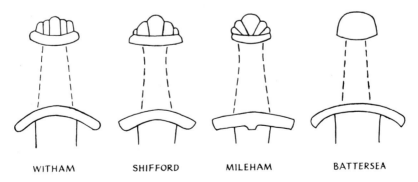

Fig. 5.6 English hilts of the tenth century (after Evison 1967 and Wilson 1965).

The Blade

As noted in the introduction, the blade of the Germanic sword changes relatively little over the period under study. In many cases, blades survive in poor condition, if at all, and may have deteriorated too far for any detailed study to be made. For these reasons, the blade can rarely be used as a basis for dating the sword.

Throughout the early medieval period, the sword blades used by the Anglo-Saxons and other Germanic peoples are relatively long, and broad, tapering slightly towards the point, which is typically rather rounded. The blade often has a fuller (shallow, rounded groove) in either face – the purpose of these was to render the sword lighter, without losing strength. Not all swords had fullers – they seem to be relatively uncommon on swords of Behmer's type VI and VII of the seventh century, and also on Petersen's type L of the ninth century: it would seem likely that this was also the case in the eighth century, but in the absence of evidence this is merely supposition. On both later Anglo-Saxon swords and the early examples of Behmer's types I, II, and V, fullers are common, although Danish examples of the earlier types frequently have between two and five narrow fullers down the face of the blade. Some of these early blades also have angular points, rather than the smooth curve that is more usual.

The Anglo-Saxons appear to have made sword blades by the pattern-welding process, which has been written about extensively elsewhere (this volume, Lang and Ager, 85–122). This was a complicated process whereby twisted iron rods were forge-welded together, probably with the intention of creating a blade combining strength and flexibility. Radiographic examination of sword blades shows that they usually consisted of two or three layers of pattern-welded iron, perhaps indicating that Dark Age swordsmiths could not produce sufficient material to produce a sword blade in a single piece. If so, this makes the late ninth century discovery by the Frankish smiths of the Rhineland, of a method of producing sword-blades without pattern-welding, even more remarkable. Some blades bear maker's marks, but are otherwise undecorated apart from the various patterns produced by the manufacturing process. Although blades were plain, however, hilts were often richly decorated with brass, copper, silver and gold inlay or plating in contemporary style, aiding considerably in dating.

Scabbards, Belts and Baldrics

No scabbards survive intact in England, but from those that have done in Europe and in the remaining fragment it is possible to reconstruct their form. The scabbard comprised two thin slats of wood that formed a 'sandwich' around the blade. Some may have been of wood only, but a covering of leather or cloth seems to have been more usual. A lining of cloth, thin leather, or fur inside the scabbard also seems to have been usual, probably to protect the blade from rust – grease or oil would be retained by these materials.

Either end of the scabbard could be protected by metal binding – a chape at the bottom end, and a locket at the mouth. These are quite common in the sixth and seventh centuries, but later finds are rare. It is probable that not all sword scabbards had chape or locket, and these items may have been subject to the whims of fashion.

Pictorial sources show that swords, although sometimes worn on waist belts, were normally carried slung from the right shoulder on a baldric. These same sources normally show the sword hilt riding quite high, above the hip, and the scabbard is usually shown hanging at an angle, rather than straight down. Practical experimentation shows that is the most efficient way to carry a sword. A baldric distributes the weight better, and is more comfortable than a waist belt, which tends to drag down because of the weight. Wearing the sword high and/or at an angle, helps to prevent the scabbard becoming tangled with the legs when moving fast. In some cases, (eg Sutton Hoo) strap distributors have been found in association with swords, and it seems likely that these were used with a Y-shaped baldric strap to hold the scabbard at an angle. In a few cases such an arrangement can even be seen in manuscript illustrations. Practical experimentation also shows that where the sword hangs relatively low on the baldric, wearing a waist belt clasped over the baldric helps considerably in avoiding the problems of tripping over the scabbard as it bounces around whilst running, although so far as I am aware no manuscript shows this use of a waist belt and baldric together.

The Sword in Society

Some of the surviving Anglo-Saxon swords are richly decorated with gold or silver, and surviving wills attest that swords could be worth considerable sums of money – King Alfred left one sword worth 3600 silver pennies. Swords were prestige items, one of the attributes of thegnly status, and were considered worthy gifts between men of high rank. Charlemagne, for example, presented Offa of Mercia with a sword captured from the Avars. Both heroic poetry and wills testify to the passage of swords from generation to generation as treasured heirlooms. In poetry the weapon of the hero is primarily the sword, although the spear would have been the most common weapon on the battlefield. The relative scarcity of swords in pagan burials, although it does not necessarily indicate their frequency in life, probably does illustrate their relative scarcity. Unlike spear or bow, which could also be used in hunting, the sword's only use was in warfare. As such it would have been a potent symbol of the aristocratic warrior class, marking its bearer as both wealthy and a warrior.

The Sword in Use

Wielding reconstructions of Anglo-Saxon swords confirms the view that they are primarily slashing weapons. They can be used for a thrust, but the balance of the blade makes such movements tiring. That same balance, however, means that a potentially devastating cut can be delivered, ensuring that even a relatively weak blow will cause the maximum damage. Surviving archaeological evidence confirms that powerful sword cuts, backed by the flow of adrenalin in combat, could shear through skulls and cut through iron mail. The poetic descriptions of severed limbs and heads are probably not greatly exaggerated, if at all.

Using a sword is tiring, but to an extent the momentum of each blow can be used to start the next, enabling a flurry of blows to be delivered in quick succession. Facing an opponent with a shield, the most natural blows would be directed at the opponent's head and knee, over and under the protection of the shield. In either case there would be a good chance of killing or disabling the opponent if the blow landed. A harder, but tempting, stroke would be an attempt to disable the opponent's weapon hand with a sword cut, reducing the threat to oneself. It is quite possible also that a powerful cut would be capable of lopping off an enemy's spearhead.

References

Behmer, E.H. 1939: *Das Zweischneidige Schwert des Germanischen Völkerwanderungszeit* (Stockholm).

Davidson, H.E. 1962: *The Sword in Anglo-Saxon England* (Oxford).

Dunning, G.C. and Evison, V.I. 1961: The Palace of Westminster Sword, *Archaeologia* 98, 123-58.

Evison, V.I. 1967: A Sword from the Thames at Wallingford Bridge, *Archaeological Journal* 124, 160-88.

Hawkes, S. Chadwick 1986: The Sword from the Feltwell Villa, in David Gurney, *Settlement, Religion & Industry on the Roman Fen-Edge, Norfolk* (East Anglian Archaeology 31), 32-37.

Menghin, W. 1983: *Das Schwert im frühen Mittelalter* (Nürnberg).

Oakeshott, R. Ewart 1960: *The Archaeology of Weapons*, (London).

Oakeshott, R. Ewart 1964: *The Sword in the Age of Chivalry*.

Oakeshott, R. Ewart 1974: *Dark Age Warrior*.

Petersen, J. 1919: *De Norske Vikingesvaerd. En Typologisk – Kronologisk Studie over Vikingetidens Vaaben* (Oslo).

Stein, F. 1967: *Adelsgräber des achten Jahrhunderts in Deutschland* (Germanische Denkmäler der Völkerwanderungszeit, A, IX, Berlin).

Wheeler, R.E.M. 1935: *London and the Saxons* (London).

Wilson, D.M. 1965: Some Neglected Late Anglo-Saxon Swords, *Medieval Archaeology* 9, 32–54.

Chapter 6

The Seax

David A. Gale

The seax is a heavy single-edged knife or short sword that was used on the Continent from the end of the Roman period but which found favour in England only after an interval of more than two centuries.

The origins of the seax are unclear. It can be observed that some late Gallo-Roman and early Merovingian knives display features that possibly influenced the development of the seax (Fig. 6.1).

However Böhner (1958, 130–45) and others have stressed the importance of the large single-edged knife of the Nordic Roman Iron Age and of the Hunnic sabre, adaptations of which have been found in rich fifth-century graves in both Alamannia and Frankia, as influencing the eventual forms of the seax which became such a regular feature of male equipment in the Merovingian world.

The seaxes used so extensively by the Franks and Alammanni were categorized by Wheeler (1935, 177) as his type I amongst seaxes used in England and are characterized by the back and edge both curving inward to make the point. They were further classified by Böhner, in his influential study of cemeteries in the region of Trier, and his division of the corpus of seaxes into three major types still stands. Thus we have the small (narrow) seax (class A), the broad seax (class B) and the long seax (class C) representing the developments of the seax on the Continent during the fifth/sixth, seventh and eighth centuries respectively (Fig. 6.2).

Down to the end of the seventh century, when weapon-burial fails us, seaxes appear much less commonly in England than in the Frankish dominions, and such as they are seem mostly not to be imports but insular adaptations of the form. The blades tend to be less substantial and a few display what seem definitely insular characteristics such as a two-handed grip and tiny curved upper guards (Evison 1961) (Fig. 6.3).

A major change in the shape of the seax-blade in England occurs with the development of the angled (broken) back. There are difficulties in dating this change as there are very few datable associated objects found with seaxes. Most late seax finds are from rivers. However, it should be noted that small knives with angled backs feature in seventh- and eighth-century graves both on the Continent and England (Böhner 1958, 215, type C, table 60, 5 & 6; Hawkes 1973, 199, figs. 57–58). It may be that the later English seax was a development from or in parallel with these knives (Fig. 6.4). The beginnings of the angled-back form occur before the end of the so-called 'pagan' period in graves of the late seventh century, with such seaxes as that from Shudy Camps (Figs. 6.3.2).

The Scramasax

The all embracing term for knife is the seax. However, Gregory of Tours in his *History of the Franks*, iv, 51, writes of a murder committed by young men with a weapon he names as a 'scramasax'. It is tempting to associate this weapon with the seax as discussed here but, as Professor Evison (1961) has pointed out, we should not assume that they are one and the same. I shall therefore use the word seax when referring to the weapon in question, although, as I shall point out, to assume that the seax was only a weapon has its drawbacks.

Later Seaxes in England

The Seax and the Long Seax

If we use blade length and, by virtue of this, probable usage as criteria for placing seaxes into groups, two basic forms can be identified; the long seax (Wheeler's type III, corresponding to Böhner's type C) and the shorter type of seax. As finds of this shorter type are more numerous than that of the long seax, I shall use 'common seax' as a term of convenience for the shorter type when discussing the late English seaxes.

The long seax is found with blade lengths ranging from 54 cm up to 76 cm, while the blades of the common seax range from a mere 8 cm up to 36 cm, with a predominance of blades around 24 cm. These measurements give us a clear distinction between the long seax and the common seax, as there is a complete absence of blade lengths in the 45 cm region, although it should be noted that the projected length of the broken long seax from Keen Edge Ferry (Evison 1964) is around 50 cm.

Types of Seax

This is not an attempt to classify seaxes by shape or decoration but merely to point out blade shapes that occur and only broadly group them by common factors; also to look at some forms of decoration.

All later common seaxes and most of the long seaxes show the same basic characteristics of a plain tang, angled back and a blade wedge-shaped in cross section.

Blade shapes

Three broad groups of common seax can be identified although some examples will inevitably fall between them (Fig. 6.5).

(i)   The first group has a broad blade with the angle on the back occurring approximately halfway along its back. The blade edge is usually markedly curved.

(ii) The second group has a narrow blade with a straight edge. The angle on the back occurs approximately two-thirds of the way along the blade towards the point.

(iii) The third group has a broad blade with a straight or slightly curving edge with the back angled at a point slightly more than halfway towards the point. It can be argued that this type is, perhaps, later than the other two.

A dozen or so examples of the long seax have been found in England and these display a variety of blade shapes (Fig. 6.6). Several of these are Frankish in style and dates and place

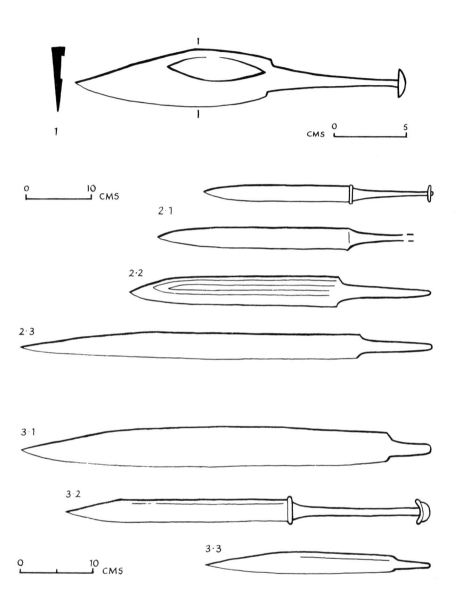

Figs. 6.1–6.3 Fig. 6.1 Late Gallo-Roman knife (Abbeville). Fig. 6.2 Frankish seax-types: 2.1. Narrow seaxes, class A (Rittersdorf gr. 65 & Kelsen); 2.2. Broad seax, class B (Oberlenken); Long seax, class C, (Hillesheim). Fig. 6.3 English seax-types, all adaptations rather than imports: 3.1. Large broad seax or broad long seax (Colchester Mus.), 7–8th centuries; 3.2. Two-handed narrow/broad seax with tiny pommel and guard (Shudy Camps, Cambs.), 7th century; 3.3. An early seax, Wheeler's 'Frankish' style (Thames, Brentford).

of manufacture are very difficult to secure. Long seaxes with angled back seem to be exclusively English (including an example from Norway, Gjessing 1934, pl. 26, which Evison regards as an import) and a badly corroded example from Hurbuck, Co. Durham, was found with associated objects that included a sword with a pommel datable to about the late ninth century.

Blade Decoration

Not all blades are decorated and also there is, perhaps, a tendency for the practice to be abandoned on very late seaxes. Types of decoration found include incised lines, grooves and a variety of metal inlays or combinations of these. When decoration does occur it is not restricted to any particular shape or form of seax. This is well exemplified by the practice of setting plaited wire into the blade (creating a herringbone pattern when laid in two or more rows side by side). This can be seen on seaxes of all lengths and occurs with other types of decoration. However, for notable examples of plait alone we have a tiny seax with one line from St. Augustine's Abbey, Canterbury (Graham-Campbell 1978, fig. 11), also a similar tiny seax with three lines of plaited inlay from Cheddar (Rahtz 1979, fig. 90); the Honey Lane, London, seax (Fig. 6.7), with a blade length of 23 cm, which has three lines of inlay joined by a plaited triangle (Wilson 1964, no. 43); a similar damaged seax from the Thames at Hampton (Museum of London A27086) and finally the long seax from Hurbuck with a single strand of plait. An early example of herringbone patterned inlay can be seen on a Frankish seax from Iversheim, West Germany (Enskirken 1972, table 33, gr. 155,1).

The practice of inlaying names and inscriptions, although rare indeed, also occurs on blades of all lengths, along with a variety of other decoration. This can be seen on the tiny 'Osmund' seax (Clark 1980, pl. 66; Fig. 6.8), the highly ornamented seax from Sittingbourne, Kent (Backhouse, Turner and Webster 1984, 102), with a blade length of around 25 cm, and a long seax from the Thames at Battersea (*Ibid.* 101), thus encompassing all blade lengths. The Battersea long seax also displays, uniquely, an inlaid Runic *futhorc*.

Grooves or shallow incised lines are a common form of decoration. They usually occur singly or in groups of twos or threes and are found in a variety of depths, widths and cross-sections even within the same blade (Fig. 6.9).

The long seaxes from Battersea and Keen Edge Ferry have both grooves and inlay (consisting of plaited wire and inset triangles of coloured metal) and this combination of inlay, but without the grooves, appears on a very small seax from Wicken Bonhunt, Essex (Musty *et al.* 1973, 287: Fig. 6.10). There is a very similar seax-shaped knife in the British Museum, from Utrecht. An early example of both inlay and grooves appearing on the same blade can be seen on the late seventh-century seax from Northolt (Evison 1961, fig. 58,4).

A further form of inlay appears on several seaxes found in the east of England. This type can be seen at Moyses Hall Museum, Bury St Edmunds and the Cambridge Museum of Archaeology and Anthropology (from the River Ouse) and presumably these seaxes were made in a workshop local to that region. The inlay consists of tiny chips of yellow metal set in two rows along the back of the blade (Fig. 6.11), which are linked beneath the angle of the back by a similarly constructed triangle. Curious little pendent crescents hang beneath the rows and the triangle.

As far as I am aware this form of decoration occurs only on seaxes of blade shape (i). However, other forms of decoration can be seen on shape (i) seaxes, for example three rows of plaited inlay on a damaged blade in the British Museum (Wilson 1964, no. 50).

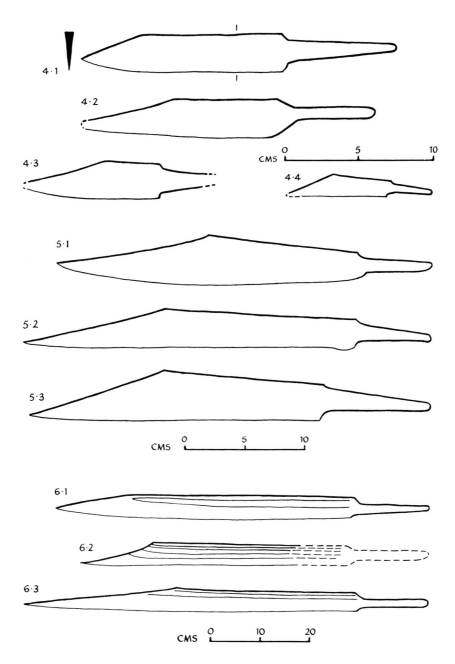

Figs. 6.4–6.6 Fig. 6.4 Knives with angled (broken) backs, 7th century: 4.1. Holborough, Kent; 4.2. Abingdon, Oxon; 4.3, 4.4. Mindelheim & Strasskirchen, W. Germany. Fig. 6.5 English common seaxes: 5.1. Blade-shape (i) (Thames, Brentford); 5.2. Blade-shape (ii) (Princes St., London); 5.3. Blade-shape (iii) (Thames, ?London). Fig. 6.6 Long seaxes: 6.1. Baexam, Holland; 6.2. Thames, Keen Edge Ferry, Berks. 6.3. Little Bealings, Suffolk.

I have not so far come across a seax of blade shape (ii) with inlay, grooves and lines being favoured, whereas seaxes of blade shape (iii) encompass a wide range of decoration.

Pattern-Welding

Most seaxes are constructed by a method usually known as pattern-welding (see also Lang, this volume). The arrangement of the welded bars within the seax varies widely (Tylecote and Gilmour 1986, 126–44). The two seaxes illustrated (Fig. 6.12) were studied at the Museum of London (by courtesy of John Clark who made the reserve collection of seaxes available for inspection). There seems to be no obvious connection between any particular shape of seax blade and any of the various arrangements of the pattern-welded bars that are found.

Handles and Sheaths (Scabbard)

No late seax handles have survived, although imprints of wood grain or horn are known on the tangs of early seaxes. Suggestions concerning fittings, materials used and shape will be conjectural. A few knives of the Viking period have surviving horn, bone and wooden handles (TVIE 1981, 109, YD44, YD 45a, 114 YAB 27; Waterman 1959, 73, fig. 7, nos. 8–12; Arbman 1940–3, table 6; Saunders 1978, 133–5). Seax tangs are flat, wide, plain and invariably taper to some extent. As notches and rivet holes are never found it is not easy to arrive at a satisfactory solution to the problem of fixing a handle. It should be noted, however, that a long seax from the Thames with a Frankish-style blade (presently in Reading Museum) was found with iron fittings about the tang which may have had a decorative function or been a device for securing the handle.

If the handle were of wood the practice of repeatedly heating the tang and ramming it into a central hole in the handle till a good fit is achieved seems feasible. I am indebted to Carole Morris for this suggestion. However, the tang of a seax is not ideally suited to either this process or this type of fitting as it rarely comes to anything approaching a point at its tip. Moreover, the substantial nature of the seax tang, along with the shape and section of its blade, suggests that this was a hacking implement. That being so, fitting the handle as above would be inadequate to prevent it splitting in use unless the grip were fairly large and/or additionally reinforced with a binding, for example of leather. The problems of hafting a seax have been put to realistic experimentation and I have received comments about this from Sam Finton Shelbourne. The chief problem is that the handle works loose and slips off the tang, but apparently this can be prevented by the insertion of tiny softwood wedges.

Sheaths (scabbards)

Unlike the handles a few sheaths have survived; from London (Museum of London); Northumberland (Wilson 1960, fig. 25); and from York (*V.C.H. Yorks* ii, 91; TVIE 1981, 119, YL10 with fig., YL11). They are of folded leather, usually with tooled decoration reflecting the shape of the seax within (*London Museum Catalogue* 1954, 186; Fig. 6.13). A sheath from York shows a coiled animal roundel at the junction of the blade and handle, which may be a regional or even Viking variation in the design. Sheaths are fixed along one edge with iron rivets or stitching. Early seax sheaths in England appear to be of similar construction but, coming as they do from graves, sometimes have additional fittings

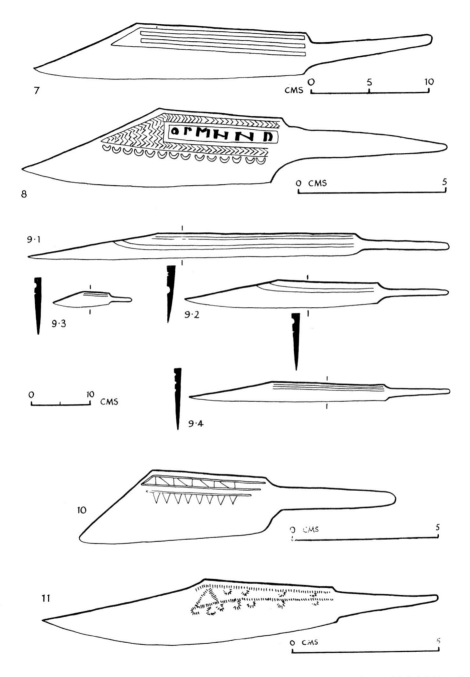

Figs. 6.7–6.11 Fig. 6.7 Seax with inlaid lines, Honey Lane, London. Fig. 6.8 Seax with inlaid inscription, Thames, London. Fig. 6.9 Seaxes with grooved decoration from London: 9.1. Thames, Battersea; 9.2. Thames, Wandsworth; 9.3. Mus. of London, C 727. Figs. 6.10, 6.11 Tiny seaxes with complex inlay, Wicken Bonhunt, Essex, and River Ouse, Cambridge.

preserved such as buckles, chapes and strips around the mouthpiece (Swanton 1973, 162, fig. 62h). Wooden scabbards for early seaxes are known from the Continent and England.

The method of slinging the various forms of seax is open to dispute, but there are some helpful figural depictions. A Frankish tombstone of about AD 650 from Niederdollendorf in the Rhineland (Fig. 6.15.1) shows a man wearing a seax, apparently of Böhner's type B, diagonally across his stomach with handle towards his right hand: it was worn with the cutting edge upwards as the simulated row of rivets indicate (Wilson 1980, 54 with fig.). This mode of wearing the seax is confirmed by grave finds both here and on the Continent (Biddle & Kjølby-Biddle 1985, 269–70). On a cross fragment from Repton, Derbyshire, there is the figure of a rider with a seax similarly placed (Biddle & Kjølby-Biddle 1985, fig. 3, pl. vi: Fig. 3.2). This is not a Merovingian broad seax, however, but a depiction of the English variant with angled back and developed pommel such as one knows from late 'pagan' graves, for example Shudy Camps (Fig. 6.3.2) or Ford, Laverstock, Wiltshire (Musty & Evison 1969, 114–6, fig. 5). According to shape of the blade and the suggestion of rivets, this Repton seax was also hung blade upwards at the belt. The date of this carving is plausibly placed towards the middle of the eighth century, which would suit the form of the seax depicted. Two carved stones in Middleton church, Yorkshire, show warriors, possibly tenth-century Norsemen, with their seaxes slung horizontally from the belt at the front (Bailey 1978, pl. 9.2, 9.4 and fig. 9.3; Kerr & Kerr 1982, 40–1, with fig.). As befits the period these resemble common seaxes with blade shape (iii): again they are worn blade upwards with pommel to the right (Fig. 6.15.3).

Saxon figures in manuscript illustrations are invariably viewed from the front and are not shown with seaxes. One could imply from this that seaxes might be worn at the back except that a study of these figures reveals that they rarely show belts or other fittings: warriors fighting with swords, for example, are often shown without scabbards.

No evidence exists for the method employed for slinging the long seax. It is too long to be hung from the belt across the waist and as there are no pommels or guards to counteract the weight of the blade it is unlikely that it was slung in the manner of late Saxon and Viking swords, balanced at an angle at the hip from a belt or from a baldric.

Difficulties are also encountered with a group of early seaxes with very long tangs (Swanton 1973, 166, fig. 64a; Werner 1953, 102–3, also table 36; Werner 1955, table 28, A2; table 32,C1). These appear to have been used double handed. The arms of combat in England and elsewhere at that period would normally be the shield and spear. If these seaxes were indeed used in the above manner, then to face a fully armed warrior, who had all the advantages of reach and defence, with just a double-handed seax, and hence no shield, would surely result in a quick death.

The Norse and the Seax

Two types of long seax are known from Scandinavia in the eighth and ninth centuries; the single-edged sword (Wheeler's type II seax: Wheeler 1935, 177–8, fig. 42; Grieg 1922, figs. 1, 2, 48, 49, 50, 62. Fig. 6.14) and the long seax proper (similar to Böhner's class C). The origins of the single-edged sword seem to be in Scandinavia itself, where smaller versions of this weapon are known from the fourth century. The class C long seaxes were probably imports into Scandinavia, as was an English long seax, with an angled back, found in Norway. At the onset of their westward expansions, however, the Norse do not seem to have

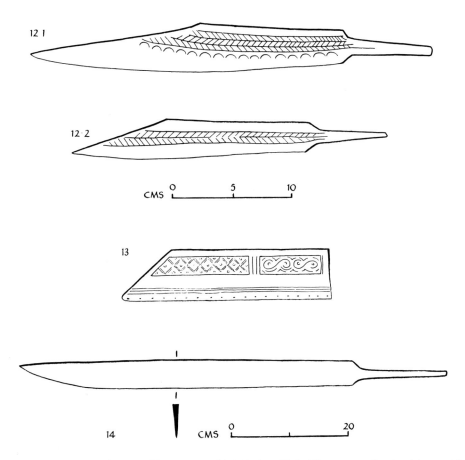

Figs. 6.12–6.14 *Fig. 12 Seaxes with pattern-welded blades: 12.1. Three rows of twisted bars with dog-toothing beneath (Mus. of London, 1655a); 12.2. Two rows of twisted bars (Mus. of London, 1655b). Fig. 6.13 Decorated seax-sheath (Mus. of London). Fig. 6.14 Single-edged sword, Haldasnosi, Loedal, Sogn og Fjordane, Norway.*

had an object of similar shape or size to the common seax. As finds from York verify, it was adopted as a result of contact with the English.

The Roles of the Common Seax and Long Seax

Writings contemporary with the seax give it the status of a weapon (as opposed to a tool). Dorothy Whitelock (1974, 106) states that smiths worked 'daggers' for battles, daggers being presumably some sort of seax. Two wills state that *handseaxe* (and we have no way of knowing precisely what is meant by that term) formed parts of heriots (Brookes 1978), that is payments upon death of war gear to one's lord. Of sixteen wills surveyed, two, those of an Ealderman and of a King's Thegn, mention 'handseaxes' forming parts of heriots. The heriot of the King's Thegn mentions two swords, four horses, etc. and one seax, whereas the

Ealderman's heriot contains six swords, six horses, six spears, etc., and one seax. These Wills put the seax in distinguished company without rating it as an important weapon in its own right. Indeed, as we have seen, by the very nature of warfare in this period the seax must have played a very secondary role as a weapon. Some of the tiny seaxes are obviously far too small to have had any effective military use at all. And yet the sculptured representations agree with the testimony of the wills in showing that the seax was worn by men of the highest rank. The Repton rider is wearing body armour and brandishing sword as well as shield; he wears a fillet around his forehead and he is thought possibly to represent a king. The warrior on the sculpture known as Middleton B is depicted not just with the seax but surrounded with his weapons, either as symbols of his rank or as actual grave goods: the weapon set includes a sword, an axe, a spear and shield, and the man appears to be wearing a helmet (Fig. 6.15.3). These are the accoutrements of a nobleman. Contexts such as these stress the importance of the seax.

Granted that it was not a major weapon, what other uses could the common seax have had?

In everyday life on the farm and in the ordinary household, the ubiquitous domestic knife was used for eating, skinning, whittling, etc., and the axe was a very versatile tool for a whole range of heavier duties from felling timber, through the whole range of activities involved in house construction and decoration, to chopping firewood (personal comment, Alan Baxter, West Stow Country Park). Skilled use of these domestic tools leaves no clear role for the seax. Furthermore, one would not expect to find elaborate (and expensive) decoration on ordinary domestic implements. Neither warrior nor farmer can have had any fundamental use for the common seax, which was both too small and too highly ornamented for everyday functional usage. The long seaxes have obvious uses as swords, but the highly decorated examples would obviously be grievously damaged after the first blow if used for that purpose.

The Anglo-Saxon with any wealth and social standing displayed these openly in his life-style and dress. Seaxes have a wide range of blade decoration and clearly this was meant to be seen. It follows that seaxes were functional and frequently used, as indeed their portrayal in sculpture tends to affirm. A possible area of use we might look at is hunting. A short heavy bladed knife, designed for hacking rather than thrusting, would be useful for finishing a quarry such as a deer,[1] certainly for the ritual of the 'gralloch' or disembowelling after the kill. Most hunting men could easily carry one in the chase, whether riding or on foot: the horizontal slinging facilitates this. Great play might be made of the seax's use in the final kill. To take the argument a stage further, the seax may eventually have acquired a symbolic role; the badge of the hunting man, perhaps even the mark of a freeman. Seaxes, as we have seen, are plain and also decorated to various degrees and these could cover the range of social status from ceorl to ealdorman and even king. The Norse may have quickly adopted the seax not just to acquire a useful tool but also to emulate the social structures and their symbols as displayed amongst the contemporary English.

Acknowledgements

I should like to thank the curators of the various museums in which I was enabled to study and draw seaxes. Mrs Sonia Chadwick Hawkes helped me finalise this paper for publication, herself arranging and paying for the drawings in Fig. 6.15.

Fig. 6.15 Contemporary sculptures showing the wearing of the seax: 15.1. Niederdollendorf, Rhineland, 7th century; 15.2. Repton, Derbyshire, 8th century; 15.3. Middleton, Yorkshire, 9th–10th century.

Notes

1. A Frankish pictorial calendar, *The Labours of the Months* (Osterreichische Nationalbibliothek, Vienna, Cod. 387, fol. 90v.), shows two men (hunters) killing a boar. The first man (November) is shown thrusting a spear into the boar. The other man (December), who is brandishing a long seax, is performing a more secondary role (he has the boar by the hind leg). It is a possibility that his function is that of actually slaughtering and perhaps cutting up the boar. D. Bullough, *The Age of Charlemagne* (London, 1980), fig. 98.

References

Arbman, H. 1940–43: *Birka II* (Stockholm).

Backhouse, J., Turner, D.H., Webster, L. 1984: *The Golden Age of Anglo-Saxon Art* (British Museum Publ., London).

Bailey, R.N., 1978: The chronology of Viking Age scupture in Northumbria, *Anglo-Saxon and Viking Age Sculpture*, ed. James Lang (BAR British Ser. 49, Oxford), 173–203.

Biddle, M. & Kjølby-Biddle, B. 1985: The Repton Stone, *Anglo-Saxon England* 14, 233–92.

Böhner, K. 1958: *Die Fränkischen Altertümer des Trierer Landes* (Germanische Denkmäler der Völkerwanderungszeit, Ser. B, I, Berlin).

Brookes, N.P. 1978: Arms, status and warfare in late Anglo-Saxon England, *Ethelred the Unready*, ed. D. Hill (BAR British Ser. 59, Oxford), 81–103.

Clark, J. 1980: A Saxon knife and a shield mount from the Thames foreshore, *Antiquaries Journal* 60, 348–9.

Enskirken, K. 1972: *Das Fränkischen Gräberfeld von Iversheim.*

Evison, V. 1961: The kitchen area of Northolt Manor, Middlesex: The Saxon objects, *Medieval Archaeology* 5, 226–30.

Evison, V. 1964: A decorated seax from the Thames at Keen Edge, *Archaeological Journal* 61, 28–36.

Gjessing, G. 1934: *Studier in Norsk Merovingertid.*

Graham-Campbell, J. 1978: An Anglo-Scandinavian ornamented knife from Canterbury, Kent, *Medieval Archaeology* 22, 133–5.

Greig, S. 1922: *Merovingisk og Norsk enegge Sverd fra VII og VIII Aarhundrede.*

Hawkes, S. Chadwick, 1973: The dating and social significance of the burials in the Polhill cemetery, *Excavations in West Kent 1960–1970*, ed. Brian Philp, 180–201.

Kerr, N. & M., 1982: *A Guide to Anglo-Saxon Sites.*

Musty, J. 1969, The excavation of two barrows, one of Saxon date, at Ford, Laverstock, near Salisbury, Wiltshire (with a contribution by Vera Evison on 'the seax'), *Antiquaries Journal* 49, 98–117.

Musty, J., Wade, K., Rogerson, A., 1973: A Viking pin and an inlaid knife from Wicken Bonhunt, Essex, *Antiquaries Journal* 53, 287.

Pirling, R. 1974: *Das Römisch-Frankische Gräberfeld von Krefeld-Gellep 1960–1963* (Germanische Denkmäler der Völkerwanderungszeit, Ser. B. 8, Berlin).

Rahtz, P., 1979: *The Saxon and Medieval Palaces at Cheddar, Excavations 1960–2* (BAR British Ser. 65, Oxford).

Saunders, A.D., 1978: Excavations in the church of St. Augustine's Abbey, Canterbury, *Medieval Archaeology* 22, 25–63.

Swanton, M.J., 1973: *The Spearheads of the Anglo-Saxon Settlements* (Royal Archaeological Institute, London).

Tylecote, R.F. & Gilmour, B.J.J. 1986: *The Metallography of Early Ferrous Edge Tools and Edge Weapons* (BAR British Ser. 155).

TVIE 1981: *The Vikings in England. Anglo-Danish Viking Project*, ed. E. Roesdahl, J. Graham-Campbell, P. Connor, K. Pearson.

Waterman, D.M. 1959: Late Saxon, Viking and early Medieval finds from York, *Archaeologia* 97, 59–106.

Werner, J. 1953: *Das Alamannische Gräberfeld von Bülach* (Monogr. zur Ur- und Frühgeschichte der Schweiz 9).

Werner, J. 1955: *Das Alamannische Gräberfeld von Mindelheim* (Materialhefte zur Bayerische Vorgeschichte 6).

Wheeler, R. M. 1935: *London and the Saxons* (London Museum).

Wilson, D. M. 1960: *The Anglo-Saxons* (London).

Wilson, D. M. 1964: *Catalogue of Anglo-Saxon Ornamental Metalwork 700–1100 in the British Museum* (London).

Wilson, D.M. ed. 1980: *The Northern World: the History and Heritage of Northern Europe* (London).

Chapter 7

Swords of the Anglo-Saxon and Viking Periods in the British Museum: A Radiographic Study

Janet Lang and Barry Ager

1. Introduction

A radiographic study of swords of the Anglo-Saxon and Viking periods in the British Museum was undertaken at the request of the Department of Medieval and Later Antiquities in order to facilitate their study. The corroded state of the swords often makes it impossible to determine without radiography whether or not the blades are pattern-welded or have inlaid pattern-welded inscriptions. Both are well recognised forms of decoration for the swords of the period, inscriptions being introduced at about 800 AD. In all, 142 swords were radiographed in the British Museum Research Laboratory. A few swords were in such a fragile condition that they could not be handled safely, and these were omitted from the study. This paper presents the results obtained and is not intended to be an extensive scholarly study of the swords. It is hoped that the information made available here will contribute to further research and comparative studies.

2. Definition and Origins of Pattern-welding and Damascening

The term pattern-welding is used to describe a process of welding together twisted rods to build up patterned blanks from which swords, daggers and spear heads were made. It is characterised by the presence of patterns on the blade which were originally visible to the eye, although in corroded specimens a radiograph may be needed to reveal them. The process of damascening with which pattern-welding is often confused, produces decorative gradations by varying the carbon content throughout so that a pattern appears at the surface. The best known examples of the latter technique are found on oriental blades. Tylecote (1976, p. 66) has commented that it is possible that there is no real difference in principle between pattern-welding and damascening, but at the same time, he also said that pattern-welding differs from damascening in that the starting material is low carbon iron and the strips are more elaborately twisted, agreeing with the earlier work of Maryon (1960), who distinguished clearly between the two. In Maryon's definition of pattern-welding, the patterns were produced by welding together twisted strips or rods of low carbon steel or even wrought iron, often with very similar compositions; in damascening, fine patterns are produced in steel by variations in composition which respond differently to etching and wear. The carbon content is often very high, thus increasing the hardness of the

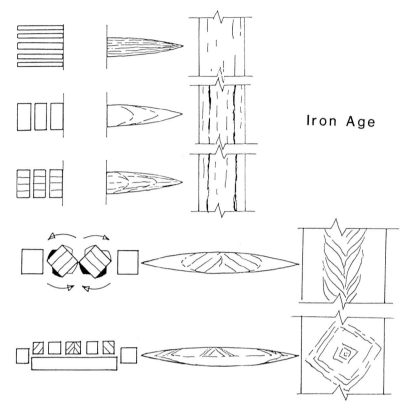

Iron Age

Fig. 7.1   Development of Pattern Welding

blade. These variations on damascened pieces may be (i) in the original piece of metal, for example wootz steel, which was produced in the East by a crucible process or (ii) introduced by welding together smaller carburised pieces or (iii) introduced by deliberately carburising at each stage as in the Japanese processes (Smith 1957) where a blade is made up by reworking and reforging the same piece of metal many times. Damascening has been discussed in detail by Belaiew (1918), Smith (1957, 1960), Wadsworth and Sherby (1979) and Yater (1983–84) amongst others.

The technique of pattern-welding, with which the present paper is mainly concerned, is known to have been used from the third century AD and appears to have evolved from the piled structures made by the Celts and Romans (Lang 1984). These piled structures were constructed by forge-welding together a number of sheets or strips of iron laid on top of each other. The composite structure was then forged to the required shape. The components were frequently arranged with layers of carbon-rich iron alternating with layers of low carbon iron. A late British Iron Age sword from Waltham Abbey, for example, was forge-welded from at least 24 separate layers with different carbon contents (Lang 1984). The metal almost invariably contained slag, which had a strengthening effect if the inclusions were small and well dispersed throughout the structure; however if the slag inclusions were large, they had an embrittling effect. The use of a number of relatively small strips of metal for the blade probably helped to reduce the risk of large lumps of slag remaining. In the middle of the La Tène period another method of constructing composite blades was developed. In this, several long rods or strips of iron or carburised iron were placed side by side and welded together, so that the joins ran parallel to the edge of the blade, perpendicular to the flat surfaces, instead of in layers with the joins parallel to the flat surfaces, (from cutting edge to cutting edge) as they had in the earlier period (see Fig. 7.1). Then, during the late La Tène period, i.e. the first century BC to the first century AD, the smiths began to twist the strips before welding them together. A sword from Llyn Cerrig Bach, Anglesey (no later than the first century AD) showed evidence of twisting (McGrath 1973) and is believed to be one of the earliest examples of the use of deliberate twisting.

Later, sometime in the third century AD, the twisting became more complicated and true pattern-welding could be said to have started. In this process a complex structure was built up by plaiting or twisting iron strips (which were sometimes themselves made up from a number of strips) and then welding them together (Anstee & Biek 1961). The patterned piece was used to make the central sections of a sword blade, or part of a knife or spear head. Some of the earliest pattern-welded swords, from the third and fourth centuries AD, were found at Nydam in Schleswig Holstein (Schürmann 1959), the Rhine, South Shields (Rosenquist 1967) and at Canterbury (Webster 1982).

The first scientific study was made of the Nydam swords in 1927, by Neumann, and then the next was Maryon's examination of a Nydam-type sword from Ely in 1948 and this was followed by many papers, particularly on material from Eastern Europe, notable contributors being Pleiner (1969), Anteins (1966, 1968) Piaskowski (1961). Studies have also been made by France-Lanord (1949, 1952), Liestøl (1951), Salin (1957), Panseri (1963), Emmerling (1972, 1978, 1979), Menghin (1974, 1983), Ypey (1960, 1973, 1982, 1983), and Müller-Wille (1970, 1977, 1982), as well as Maryon (1948, 1950, 1960), Anstee and biek (1961) and Gilmour (in Tylecote 1986). Experimental pattern-welding by Anstee and Biek (1961) showed that patterns can be obtained even with strips of the same virtually carbon free iron. They also observed that the convolute patterns produced by sectioning a screw thread longitudinally near the axis were replaced by a curving herringbone structure when more of the surface was ground away. This feature makes grouping the swords by their patterns difficult. Neumann (1927) distinguished three types of pattern, streifendamast, winkeldamast, and rosendamast, which could be translated as "straight", "chevron" or "herringbone" and "curving", a system followed by Schürmann (1959). Emmerling (1972) also suggested three categories of patterns: V-forming, N-forming and M- or W-forming. Although these categories provide useful visual descriptions, in the present study it was decided that a simple but slightly more fundamental distinction could be made on the basis of the number of strips or strip composites making up the patterns. Some of the rods were twisted for their whole length while others had straight sections interspersed with twisted sections and these characteristics provided sub-divisions of the main categories. Anstee (1961) also recorded the number of strips used in each blade in his paper, describing the patterns as standard (continuously twisting) and alternating (alternating twisting and straight sections). Koch (1977) also used the number of strips as a type indicator. There are drawbacks to this method of categorising the patterns, which are inherent in the radiographic method. It is difficult to see if two layers of pattern are present, if they are superimposed, many patterns cannot be fully understood from radiographs and the number of strips making up each

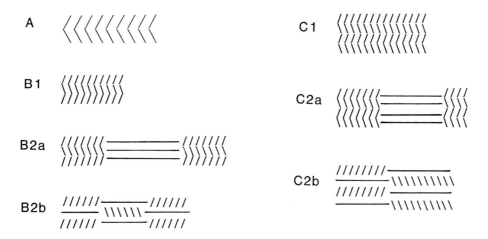

Fig. 7.2 Diagram of pattern types on welded swords.

band or element cannot be distinguished. Radiographs have other disadvantages: they do not show the presence of complex edges, which Gilmour (Tylecote 1986) found to be quite common, or cores, which also may consist of more than one layer. Schürmann (1959), for example, has described the metallographic examination of three of the Nydam swords. One of these was constructed from eleven pieces, all with different carbon contents. The edges and pattern-welded surfaces were welded onto a core which itself was made as a sandwich, with a medium carbon steel sheet between thin soft iron plates. The carbon content of the pattern-welded strips varied between 0.1 and 0.6%. After examining a number of Scandinavian swords metallographically, Liestøl (1951) suggested that slices cut from welded twisted composite bars were welded together with their sliced faces uppermost, to form surface sheets sandwiching a core of plain metal.

It was not possible in the present study to make metallographic cross sections which would have shown the number of layers immediately and also incidentally allow some assessment of the quality of the sword as a weapon, such as the hardness (and therefore sharpness) of the edges, for example. However, it has been found in this study that stereo radiography helps to identify swords which have two layers of pattern, a number of which have been found in the survey. (See 4, ii below)

3. Experimental

Radiography was carried out using a Raymax machine (nominal maximum 150 KV), with either Kodak Industrex 'C' or 'A' strip film. The film to source distance was 1 metre and the current 10 mA. The voltage in almost all exposures was 70 KV, while the exposure time varied between 2 and 20 minutes, depending on the film and the thickness of sound metal. A number of swords were so badly corroded that not enough of the pattern could be distinguished to determine the pattern types. These are recorded in the column (P) in Table 7.1 at the end of the chapter. This category also includes some swords with unusual patterns which do not fall into the categories. Inscriptions were found on both sides of the blade so that the images of both were superimposed on a radiograph, making it very difficult to distinguish them. Stereoradiographs were therefore made of these swords, which showed the layers or inscriptions much more clearly. For this, two separate exposures were made (left and right), the x-ray source being moved about 100 mm across the width of the sword which remained in exactly the same position. The films were examined with a stereo viewer, being laid side by side (left and right as marked). This made it possible to see which inlaid shapes were on the top and bottom surfaces, or to see if two pattern layers were present. The same technique was used to distinguish different pattern layers, notably on the Sutton Hoo sword. A visual survey was also made of the corroded swords, many of which were splitting, as is shown in Fig. 7.3a, and the number of layers were recorded (Table 7.1). Xeroradiographs were made at the Royal Marsden Hospital by Dr R. Davis, providing an excellent image for a selected number of swords.

4. Results

In the present survey 142 Anglo-Saxon and Viking period swords found in the British Isles were examined. Nearly all the swords are in the collection of the Department of Medieval and Later Antiquities of the British Museum. It was found that more than half were pattern-welded, a small proportion had pattern-welded inscriptions on both faces and the remainder were without pattern-welded decoration of any kind. It is interesting to note that the blades of the inscribed swords from England were not pattern-welded, although the inserted letters themselves were patterned-welded. This seems to be true of most similar swords described in other studies and perhaps is further evidence for the decorative rather than functional purpose of pattern-welding. The results are recorded in Table 7.1, the swords being listed in registration order, and are summarised in Table 7.2. In Table 7.2 the swords are recorded according to their dates and constructional types. These types are discussed in detail in the next section.

i) The Construction Types

The swords were divided into groups according to the number of bands or main elements which could be seen on the radiographs. These groups were further subdivided on the basis of the arrangement of the straight and twisted sections. (See Fig. 7.2) The other groups included the swords with inscriptions and the seaxes. The British Museum's collection of seaxes was also examined and grouped as patterned and inlayed or non-decorated. It should be noted that almost all the patterned swords had non-patterned edges which were welded on, and the decorated seaxes had non-patterned back and cutting edges, which were also welded on.

Some swords are listed in Tables 7.1 and 7.2 as patterned (P): these either have patterns which cannot be distinguished clearly enough to fit them into one of the categories, usually because of their corroded state, but also because the pattern or structure of the sword is unusual and does not fit into the constructional types described below. For example, the

Janet Lang and Barry Ager

Fig. 7.3a Registration number 1936 5–11 54. Late fifth–Early sixth century Anglo-Saxon sword from Howletts, Kent, grave 16. This shows how the sword has split into three layers (two are patterned).

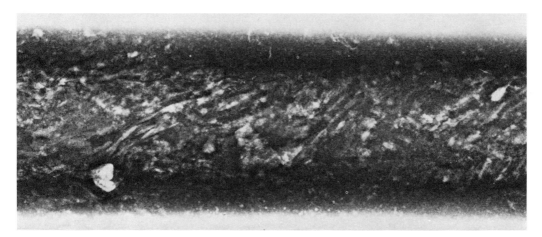

Fig. 7.3b Registration number 1869 3–15 1. Fifth–sixth century Anglo-Saxon sword from Waterbeach, Cambs. showing a broad diffuse surface band. Xeroradiograph by courtesy of the Royal Marsden Hospital.

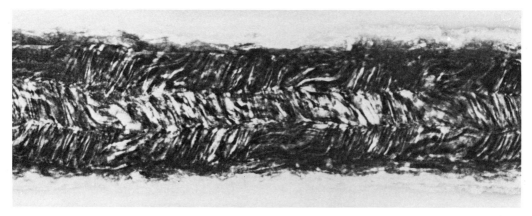

Fig. 7.3c Registration number 1912 7–23 1. Late ninth century Anglo-Saxon sword from Hurbuck, Durham, showing an unusual pattern with two layers of three continuously twisting rods, with a change in the pitch of twisting every 30–40 mm. A similar Anglo-Saxon patterned sword was found at Borgstedt in Schleswig-Holstein. Xeroradiograph by courtesy of the Royal Marsden Hospital.

Table 7.2 Frequencies of welding patterns according to date of swords.

Date	A	B1	B2a	B2b	C1	C2a	C2b	T	2 layer	P	O	total P	total	no. type	undec.	dec.	cent. A.D.
400–500	2	2	4	2	–	1	–	–	2	4	19	15	34	9	–	–	5–6
400–700	1	1	2	1	–	–	–	–	2	1	3	9	5	6	–	–	5–7
500–600	1	7	6	5	–	2	1	–	8	3	7	24	31	9	1	–	6
500–700	1	1	4	–	–	–	–	–	–	1	1	7	8	4	4	–	6–7
600–700	4	3	2	3	–	1	1	–	6	1	–	15	15	7	–	1	7
800–1000	2	2	–	1	1	1	–	8	3	3	4	10	22	7	7	8	9–10
Totals	11	17	18	12	1	6	2	8	21	13	34	76	119	–	12	6	

fifth–sixth century sword from Waterbeach, Cambs. (1869.3–15.1) (Fig. 7.3b) is the single example in the British Museum's collection of a broad diffuse band which spiralled around the blade; it resembles the blade made by Anstee and Biek (1961) by twisting a bar with a rod on either side, and could have been made by this method. A similar type of pattern was found on a sword from Waal-bij-Nijmegen (Ypey 1973). Two swords (1936.5–11.76, Howletts early sixth century and 1929.2–6.1 from Windsor, Viking tenth–eleventh) exhibited an interlace pattern on the radiographs; this might have been achieved by less frequent twists along the bar than was usual. The central element of the sword from Windsor was made by using two wires or strips together, arranged as a series of flattened loops (see Figs. 7.4a, 7.5a). Another example of individual variation is shown by a sword from Hurbuck (1912.7–23.1, Fig. 7.3c) which has a triple continuously twisting pattern, but at intervals of about 25 mm along each strip composite, the twist is much wider making a variation in the pattern. In contrast, the simplest variation was found: for example, three fifth–sixth century swords (two from Mucking 618, and one from Kempston 1891.6–24.79) were made from three strips, welded together side by side but were otherwise unpatterned. The central sections appeared to be strongly striated on the radiographs and could have presented a visual contrast with the smoother surfaced edges; this effect was often employed by late Iron Age smiths.

The preferred number of strips or strip composites used for the sword blades seems to have been three.

no. of elements	2	3	4	6
% of total number of pattern-welded swords	16	68	13	1

The reasons for this preference may be aesthetic or practical. It may be that it was found to be easiest to produce a sound blade with three strips or strip composites. Of course it is easier to twist a strip or rod with a thin cross section than a thicker one but once this has been done the strips still have to be welded together side by side, and this must have been an operation requiring some skill. The degree of difficulty increases with number and thinness of the strips, as there is an increasing danger of inclusion of oxides and incomplete welding.

It would be very difficult to ensure metallic contact as the twisted elements lay side by side ready for welding. (Anstee and Biek 1961, Maryon 1948, 1950). Gilmour's metallographic studies have shown that incomplete welding often did occur (Tylecote 1986).

The radiographs indicate that a number of strips or rods was used to make the strip composites, but it was extremely difficult to see how many were used in each bundle, so that it seemed better not to attempt to determine the numbers in most cases. For example the sword from Dover, grave C (1963.11–8.751) (see Fig. 7.5b) has straight sections made from three rod composites, lying side by side, each of which appears to consist of three thinner strips or rods, however it is possible that more strips are present in the bundle, but masked on the radiograph. Metallographic cross sections might provide answers to this question. Some of the corroded swords were examined visually and were found to be splitting into two or three layers. The results of this visual examination are given below.

Results

| Patterned swords | 3 layers 28 | 2 layers 5 | 1 layer 4 |
| Non-patterned swords | 3 layers 7 | | 1 layer 6 |

It should be noted that this list is not exhaustive and represents a self selecting sample, ie. fairly severely corroded blades.

ii) Swords with two Pattern Layers

A number of swords with two layers of pattern were found by stereo radiography. These are noted below. As it is not easy always to detect two layers it is possible that some of the swords with very indistinct patterns may also be of this type. Of the 21 two layered swords found, 16 had similar patterns in both layers while five had different patterns. Two were from Faversham (nos 956–70, 957–70) with B2a and B2b patterns (see below for explanation), Lyminge (1890.9–2.1) with B2b and B1, Ardvonrig, Barra (1895.6–13. 22) with opposed B1 patterns in each layer, Howletts (1936.5–11.166) with B1 and a layer with strips running across the blade with B2a.

Note. The Sutton Hoo sword (1939.10–10.95,19–29) was the subject of a recent paper by Ypey (1983). He suggested that its arrangement of rods viewed in cross section could be described schematically either as

layer 1   SCSASCSAS or SSSSSSSS
layer 2   SSSSSSSS or SCSASCSAS

depending on the distance of the section along the blade (S = straight, C = clockwise twist, A = anticlockwise twist). A close examination of recent stereo radiographs, however, shows an arrangement which can be represented schematically thus, as

layer 1		layer 2
SCSC	or	ASAS
ASAS	or	SCSC

Fig. 7.4a   Registration number 1929 2–6 1. Tenth–eleventh century Viking sword from the Thames at Windsor. This shows a straight part of the central loop with twists on either side and twisted cutting edges.

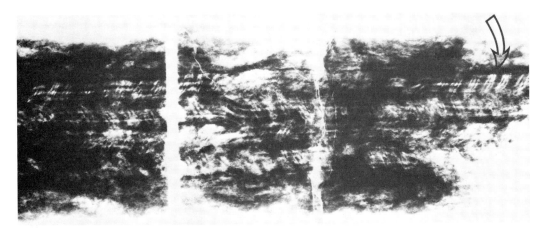

Fig. 7.4b   Registration number 1939 10–10 95, 19–29. Seventh century sword from Sutton Hoo, Suffolk. This shows the two layered pattern. The area where the twist layers overlap slightly is arrowed.

Fig. 7.5a   Registration number 1929 2–6 1. Tenth–eleventh century Viking sword from the Thames at Windsor with superimposed loop pattern.

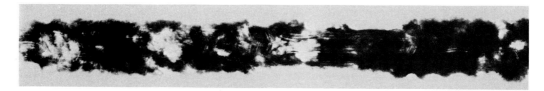

Fig. 7.5b   Registration number 1963 11–8 751. 525–600 AD Anglo-Saxon sword from Dover, Kent, grave C, showing three bands clearly made from several strips in a coincident straight and twist pattern, with two layers, apparently not coincident.

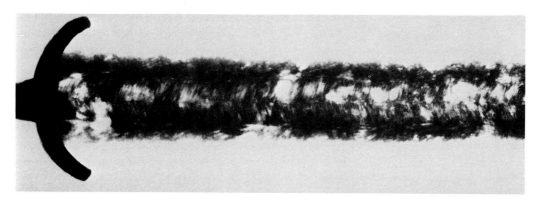

Fig. 7.5c   Registration number 1856 7–1 1405, Anglo-Saxon ninth–early tenth. This sword has a typical two band continuous twist pattern.

Fig. 7.5d   Registration number 1912 7–23 2. Late ninth century Anglo-Saxon seax from Hurbuck, Durham, this was found with the sword (1912 7–23 1); it shows an unpatterned separate edge, a central section with whorls merging into an interlace region adjoining the back edge which has an inlaid plait.

depending on the distance of the section along the blade (Fig. 7.4b). Reproduction of the radiograph (Bruce-Mitford 1978, fig. 211) is poor and could be considered misleading.

Lists of the swords in each constructional group are given below. A double layered construction is indicated by: +

Type A Two Bands
The bands are twisted in opposite directions for the whole length:

1839.10–29.144a Chartham Down, Kent AS 7
1856.7–1.1405 London AS 9–E10 (Fig. 7.5c)
1891.6–24.80 Kempston, Beds AS 5–7
+ 1895.6–13.22 Ardvonrig, Barra AS 9
1902.7–22.171 Droxford, Hants AS 5–6
1936.5–11.164 Howletts, Kent AS 5–6
1963.11–8.416 Dover (gr 71) Kent AS earlier 7
1963.11–8.483 Dover (gr 93) Kent AS 6
1963.11–8.502 Dover (gr 96a) Kent AS earlier 7
1963.11–8.509 Dover (gr 96b) Kent AS earlier 7
1963.11–8.782 Dover (unassoc.), Kent AS 6–7

Type B Three bands
B1 Each band is twisted for its whole length usually in opposite directions:

+ 953–70 Faversham, Kent AS 6
955–70 Faversham, Kent AS 5–6
+ 1839.10–29.144b Chartham Down, Kent AS 7
*1853.4–12.89 Barham Down, Kent AS 6–7
*1853.4–12.90 Barham Down, Kent AS 6–7
1869.10–11.13 Chessell Down, IOW AS 6
1869.10–11.17 Chessell Down, IOW AS L5–6
1880.5–21.1 Longbridge, Warwicks AS 6
+ 1890.9–2.1 Lyminge, Kent AS 6(?)
1891.6–24.78 Kempston, Beds AS 6
1902.12–16.2 Windmill Hill, Bucks AS L5–6
+ 1912.7–23.1 Hurbuck, Durham AS L9–E10
+ 1912.12–20.2 Twickenham (?), Surrey AS 7
+ 1936.5–11.166 Howletts, Kent AS 5–6
+ 1963.11–8.174 Dover, Kent AS 7
1964.7–2.381 Gt Chesterford, Essex AS 6

* These are parts of one sword.

Type B2a Three bands with coincident twist and straight sections across the width.

+ 954–70 Faversham, Kent AS 6
+ 956–70 Faversham, Kent AS L5–7
+ 957–70 Faversham, Kent AS 6
1848.7–27.1 Battle Edge, Burford, Oxon AS L5–E6
1867.7–29.150 Chessell Down, IOW AS c500
+ 1873.6–2.104 Tissington, Derbyshire AS 7
+ 1875.3–10.40 Long Wittenham, Oxon AS 6
1883.12–13.612 Sittingbourne, Kent AS 6
+ 1888.7–19.57 unprovenanced AS 5–7
1894.11–3.1 Crundale Down, Kent AS 7

+ 1894.12–16.4 Broomfield, Essex AS 6–7
+ 1936.5–11.99 Howletts, Kent AS 6
1963.11–8.124 Dover, Kent AS 5–6
1963.11–8.281 Dover, (grave 41), Kent AS 6–7
1963.11–8.340 Dover, Kent AS 6–7
1963.11–8.493 Dover (grave 94b) Kent AS 6–E7
+ 1963.11–8.751 Dover (gr C) Kent AS 6
1963.11–8.783 Dover, Kent AS 6–7

Type B2b   Three bands, with alternating straight and twisted sections along the length and across the width.

952–70 Faversham, Kent AS 6
+ 956–70 Faversham, Kent AS 5–7
+ 957–70 Faversham, Kent AS 6
1869.10–11.16 Chessell Down, IOW AS L5–6
+ 1873.6–2.104 Tissington, Derbyshire AS 7
1883.12–13.621 Sittingbourne, Kent AS E7
1887.2–9.1 London V 10–E11
+ 1890.9–2.1 Lyminge, Kent AS 6
1915.5–3.2 Herringswell, Suffolk AS 5–6
1915.12–8.353 Astwick, Beds AS 5–6
1963.11–8.128 Dover (gr 27) Kent AS E7
1963.11–8.469 Dover (grave 91) Kent
1963.11–8.603 Dover (grave 131) Kent A E7

Type C   Four bands
C1   Four bands of continuous twist (Emmerling's M or W forming type)
1854.11–7.12 Norwich AS L 9–E10

C2a   Four bands of coincident twist and straight sections across the width

OA 6610 Barnet, Herts AS 5–7
+ 1875.3–10.40 Long Wittenham, Oxon AS 6
+ 1883.12–13.646 Faversham, Kent AS 6
+ 1883.12–14.4 Taplow, Bucks AS E7
1894.8–3.87 Strood? Kent AS 5–6 (Fig. 7.6a)
+ 1965.7–3.1 Wensley, Yorks. AS 9

C2b   Four bands of alternating twist and straight sections across the width and along the length
1936.5–1.75 Howletts, Kent AS 6

+ 1939.10–10.95, 19–29 Sutton Hoo, Suffolk AS E7

Type F2b   Five bands
1913.7–17.1 Barlaston, Staffs AS 7
1963.11–8.511 Dover, Kent AS 6–E7

Type P
a) Pattern present but not identified
1891.6–24.79 Kempston, Beds AS 5
1902.7–22.175 Droxford, Hants AS 5–6
1906.6–12.1 Farnden, Notts 9–10
1936.5–11.99 Howletts, Kent AS 5–6
1936.5–11.165 Howletts, Kent AS 5–6

Fig. 7.6a   Registration number 1894 8–3 87, Later fifth–sixth century Anglo-Saxon sword from Strood, Kent, showing four coincident bands of straight and twist. Xeroradiograph by courtesy of the Royal Marsden Hospital.

Fig. 7.6b   Registration number AL116/775. Ninth century Viking sword from the Thames at Windsor. This shows two layers with three twisted bands in each, the central band having an elongated twist at intervals.

Fig. 7.6c   Registration number 1856 7–1 1408. Anglo-Saxon seax (ninth–tenth century).

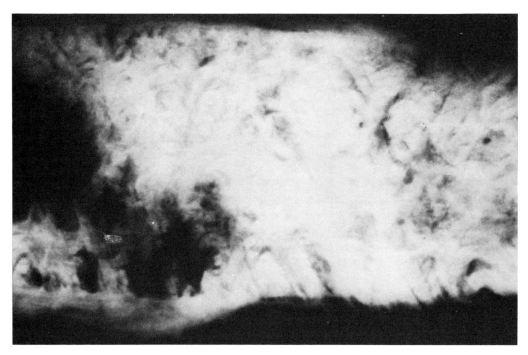

Fig. 7.7a   Registration number 1894 11–3 1. Mid seventh century Anglo-Saxon sword from Crundale Down showing curving elements in the pattern near the tip of the blade.

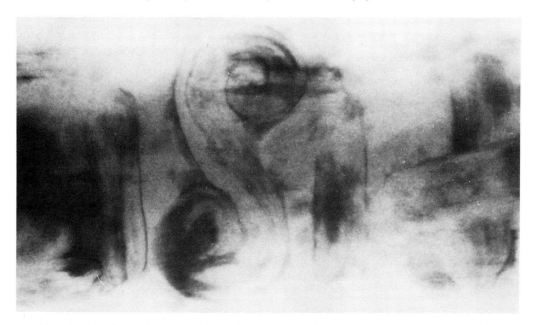

Fig. 7.7b   Registration number 1848 10–21 1. Late ninth or early tenth century Anglo-Saxon sword from the R. Witham at Lincoln. This shows part of the inscription, with the S-scroll on the reverse clearly visible.

b) Unusual patterns

Acklam sword (Yorkshire Museum)
This sword has six bands of alternating twist and straight, probably in two layers.

AL 116/775 Thames, Windsor V 9 (Fig. 7.6b)
(British Museum sword, on loan to the Royal Armouries, Tower of London) This has a two layer structure, with three bands of twist in each layer. The middle band in each layer has an elongated twist at about 3 cm intervals. The two layers are not entirely coincident.

1839.10–29.144b Chartham Down, Kent AS 5–6
This has a two layered structure with three bands of continuous twist in each layer. One layer also contains some short straight sections.

1854.11–7.12 Norwich AS 9–E10
This sword has four elements, giving a herringbone pattern of continuous twists. Visual inspection of the sword itself suggests that there may be two layers.

1869.3–15.1 Waterbeach, Cambs AS 5–6 (Fig. 7.3b)
This sword has an unusual diffuse pattern and was discussed above.

1869.10–11.13 Chessell Down, grave 26 IOW AS 6
This sword has a patterned strip down the middle, consisting of three continuously twisting bands, with two straight strips on each side.

1894.11–3.1 Crundale Down, Kent AS 7 (Fig. 7.7a)
This sword has two layers of non-superimposed twist and straight, of type B2a. The twists become very tight near the tip and take a cruciform pattern, which suggests that that area has been ground.

1895.6–13.22 Ardvonrig, Barra AS 9
This sword has a two layered pattern with two continuously twisting bands in each. The two layers, unusually, appear to be in opposition, thus;
   1st layer C A
   2nd layer A C

1912.7–23.1 Hurbuck, Durham AS L9 (Fig. 7.3c)
This sword has two layers consisting of three continuously twisting bands, not completely superimposed. The bands have a longer twist at intervals, and have been arranged to coincide across the width.

1913.7–17.1 Barlaston AS 7
Fragmentary sword which appears to have 5 bands of twist, possibly with some straights alternating across the width, probably two layers of pattern.

1929.2–6.1 Windsor V 10 (Fig. 7.4a, 7.5a)
The whole blade appears to be patterned including the cutting edges. It has been constructed from two narrow twisted sections forming the cutting edges, next to them are two broader twisted sections, and in the centre a band made from a continuously looped strip of metal. The plate shows that each band is made up of a number of thin strips.

1936.5–11.76 grave 20, Howletts, Kent AS E6
This sword apparently does not have separate edges but has a long continuously twisting pattern, in which it is difficult to distinguish the number of elements.

1936.5–11.166 Howletts, Kent AS 5–6 (Fig. 7.8)
This sword is fragmentary, but the remains showed two layers, one consisting of three bands of continuous twist (B1), while the other showed partly B2a structure, but with cross bands (cutting edge to cutting edge) for part of the length.

Type 1 Inscriptions
Lyle collection cat.no 236 (not available at British Museum)

Westminster, Thames AS 10–E11

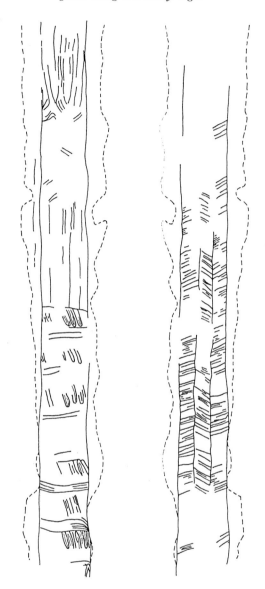

Fig. 7.8 Drawing from the radiographs of reg. no. 1936 5–11 166 from Howletts, Kent.

Tr 169 No provenance AS L10–11*
Tr 174 Nottingham V E10*
1848.10–21.1 Lincoln AS 10
1856.7–1.1404 Temple, Thames V 10–11
1864.1–27.3 Lough Gur, Grange, Co. Limerick, Ireland V 10
1875.4–3.169 Burneston, Yorks AS 9
1891.9–5.3 Kew, Thames V 10
1915.5–4.1 Edmonton, Middx V 10

* on loan from the Royal Armouries

iii) Inscriptions

As the lists given in the preceding sections show, in England true pattern-welded blades continued to be forged by Anglo-Saxon swordsmiths into the late ninth and early tenth centuries, i.e. swords of Petersen's type L (Petersen 1919, 112–6; his typology is based on the form of the hilt, not on the pattern-welding of the blade). Meanwhile, on the Continent, a new type of blade of plain steel, not pattern-welded, but often carrying ferrous inlaid pattern-welded inscriptions of various forms (see below), had already come into production as early as c. 800 AD. This type had largely replaced the pattern-welded blade during the course of the ninth century (Müller-Wille 1970, 82; 1982, 135–7, 145–9) During the ninth century the new form of blade appears in England. It seems, from the limited number of examples surviving, to have taken over by the end of the century and some may even have been made here (Evison 1967, 181). These inscribed blades can be seen as an end refinement of the technique of pattern-welded veneering (Fournierdamast) described by Menghin (1983, 17–18). In this process, thin pattern-welded sheet was inlaid on blades of otherwise homogeneous steel. It was adopted on the continent towards the end of the Merovingian period, apparently purely for decorative effect, but does not seem to have been much favoured in England.

On the continental blades, the inscriptions usually took the form of a name in large Roman capitals in the fuller of one side (towards the hilt end) and of a pattern-welded design or motif on the side immediately opposite; or, less often, of motifs alone on both sides. By far the commonest of these inscriptions are renderings of the names "Ulfberht" (Müller-Wille op.cit., and 1977; East and Brown, forthcoming), and "Ingelrii" (for both see also Lorange 1889, 12–20; Wegeli 1902–5; Petersen 1919; Davidson 1962, 42–50; Kirpichnikov 1966 and 1969; Evison 1967, 177–83). From the numerous repetitions of the same name, they seem originally to have been makers' (not owners') names from the middle Rhineland. In another area this is explicitly stated on an eleventh century late Russian sword from Foshchevatya which bears, in pattern-welded Cyrillic letters, a name on one side and the slavonic word for "smith" on the other (Kirpichnikov 1966 41, figs. 14–15; 1969, 176–7, figs. 6–7). Furthermore there are also the well-known non-ferrous inlaid inscriptions with both makers' and owners' names (e.g. the Sittingbourne seax, Wilson 1964, 172–3). Typological studies based on the hilts show that the names Ulfberht and Ingelrii were in use over several generations, into the eleventh and (in the latter case) even twelfth centuries. Each was probably first used in just one workshop, but once they became recognised as marks of good quality blades they were probably imitated at other centres. Indeed, one sword from the Old Nene near Peterborough appears to carry both the name "Ingelrii" on one side and, less certainly, "Ulfberht" on the other (Ypey 1960–1, afb, 30; Davidson 1962, 47; Müller-Wille 1970, no. 11 on p. 84). The motifs seem to have served as a kind of trade mark, either alone or on the reverse of the name blades. The distribution of inscribed sword-blades, largely in grave and river finds right across northern and central Europe from Iceland and Ireland to the Dnieper and middle Volga results from the combined effects of both trade and warfare.

The inscriptions appear to have been made by hammering short lengths of plain or twisted wires into a chased channel in the surface of the blade while it was white-hot. The characters were secured in place by further hammering after reheating (Davidson 1962, 45). There is some evidence to show that a form of punch was also used to drive the inlays into position (East, 1985). Finally the surface was ground smooth and polished so that the patterned metal of the inlay contrasted with the plain steel of the blade. Modin (unpublished report) found that the pattern-welded letters on an Ulfberht blade (from Claud, Hulterstad, Sweden) were pattern-welded from ferritic iron which might have contained phosphorus. This would have remained bright and shiny while the blade dulled.

Often the inscriptions are still visible, or if obscured by corrosion can be revealed by cleaning and treatment (Maryon 1950, pls. 21–2; Oakeshott 1951, pl. 14; Kirpichnikov 1969, 170). Where this is not possible, examination by x-radiography (Fig. 7.7b) can prove invaluable and the present study has added a further five inscriptions to the corpus which were not otherwise visible to the naked eye (nos. 2, 3 and 7 below). All the pattern-welded inscriptions are discussed in more detail below.

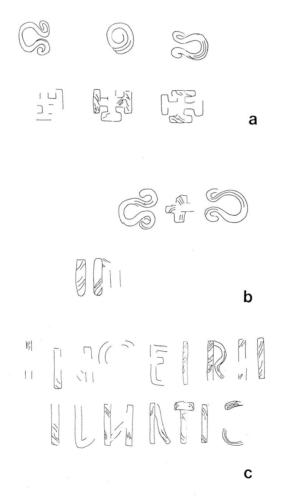

Fig. 7.9 Pattern-welded inscriptions drawn from radiographs: a) Lyle collection no. 236 (R. Thames near Westminster); b) Reg. no. 1915 5–4 1 (R Lea at Edmonton, Mddx); c) Reg. no. 1891 9–5 3 (R Thames at Kew, Surrey).

1   *Sir Gavin Lyle's Collection, Cat. no. 236 (River Thames near Westminster)*
(Fig. 7.9a. Sir Gavin Lyle's Collection, Cat. no. 236); Wilson 1965, 42, no. 10 and fig. 13.
Evison's Wallingford Bridge type; 10th–earlier 11th cent. (Evison 1967, 186). Stereo
radiographs show that the published figure of the inlaid marks can be improved on and
that the 'inscription' is in fact double-sided. It consists of an eyelet loop either side of a spiral
scroll on one side and three crosses potent on the other. This arrangement is one of several
ninth–eleventh century variations using similar loops and crosses in groups of three.
Another sword of Wallingford Bridge type from Lempäälä, Finland, carries a cross potent
between eyelets on one side and a spiral scroll between two similar crosses on the other
(Leppäaho 1964, Taf. 10, 2). Related marks can also be seen on a sword of Petersen's type
Z from Neuzvestno and on another of Petersen's type E from Ust'-Ruibezhna, Russia
(Kirpichnikov 1966, fig. 18, 3 & 8; for dating see Stalsberg 1981). The different
arrangements of symbols may indicate different workshops, or it could be that they are
simply variant marks of one centre. The same symbols, but with wholly different patterns
on the reverse, are used on swords of Petersen's type E from Gnezdovo, Russia
(Kirpichnikov 1966 fig. 18, 7) and of type R or S from Lempäälä, Finland (Leppäaho 1964,
Taf. 9, 4) while a circle and cross potent on a type Z sword from Kangasala, Finland are
perhaps all that remain of a similar inscription (ibid., Taf. 9, 2). A plain equal-armed cross
between the eyelets can be seen on an early tenth cent. sword from Edmonton (inscription
no. 9, below; Fig. 106). Penannular and scrolled loops of rather different forms appear on
swords of the ninth cent. from Maarhuizen and Wijk-bij-Duurstede, Holland and one of
tenth cent. from Brekendorf, Germany (Ypey 1960–1, afb. 12–13, 16–17; Müller-Wille
1977, Abb. 13, 5). There appears to be a relationship, perhaps of imitation, between
inscriptions combining crosses and eyelets, but without names, on the one hand, and the
pattern of horse-shoe loops on either side of a cross crosslet on an ULFBERHT sword from
Rapola, Finland on the other (Leppäaho 1964, Taf. 16c; Müller-Wille 1970, 87, no 78).

2   *Tr 169 On loan from the Royal Armouries, Tower of London (No provenance)*
(Fig. 7.10a. B.M., on loan from the Royal Armouries, no. Tr. 169). This is a sword of
Petersen's type Z of the later tenth–eleventh cent. (Evison 1967, 171). The inscription is
possibly only single-sided: a circle or C-scroll between groups of transverse bars, cf. a sword
(of Petersen's type O?) from Myklebost, Norway (Lorange 1889, Tab. 3, 6).

3   *Tr 174 On loan from the Royal Armouries, Tower of London (Nottingham, Notts.)*
(Fig. 7.10c. Anon 1851, p. 425 central figure). This is a Viking sword of c. 900–950
belonging to Petersen's type X with a short guard. A C-shaped loop is all that remains of
the inscription on this sword, which may originally have been a C between two reversed Ns,
as on a tenth to eleventh cent. sword of the Wallingford Bridge type from the Thames
(Evison 1967 pl. 9 and figs. 1f and 5a), or it may be part of the 'G' in 'INGELRII',
although this is perhaps less likely because there is no trace of other letters.

4   *Reg. no. 1848 10–21 1 (R. Witham at Lincoln)*
(Fig. 7.11a. Maryon 1950, pls. 21–2 Wilson 1964, cat. no. 32, with full bibliography).This
is a sword of Evison's Wallingford Bridge type, perhaps of an early stage and is dated late
ninth or early tenth cent. by Wilson (1965, 44) although the absence of Trewhiddle style
silver plates usual on later ninth–early tenth cent. Anglo-Saxon swords noted by Evison

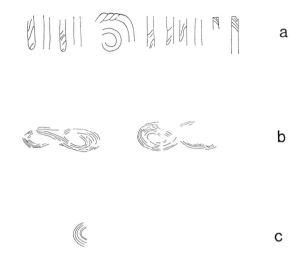

Fig. 7.10   Pattern-welded inscriptions on sword blades drawn from the radiographs: a) Tr 169 (unprovenanced); b) Reg. no. 1875 4–3 169 (Camphill, Burneston); c) Tr 174 (Nottingham).

(1967, 163) would seem to place it within the tenth century. The inscription is double sided; side (a) +LEUTLRIT (with an inverted final T); side (b): reversed S-scroll. The name is Continental Germanic and is probably to be read Leuterit/Leutirit or Leutfrid, or perhaps Liudrid (Page 1964, 90). Evison (1967, 180–1) notes two other blades with this inscription from Estonia and Russia and a possible Anglo-Saxon copy from the Thames at Battersea. A reversed S-scroll, (although with the addition of tendril terminals), is seen on another sword from Al'myet'yevo, Russia, with an indistinct symbol on the reverse (Kirpichnikov 1966, fig. 21).

5   *Reg. no. 1856 7–1 1404 (R. Thames opposite the Temple, London)*
(Fig. 7.11b. Oakeshott 1951, fig. 1 and pl. 14; Davidson 1962, fig. 28, 30; Evison 1967, pl. 12a). This is a sword of Evison's Wallingford Bridge type of tenth or earlier eleventh cent. and has a double-sided inscription; side (a): INGELRII; side (b): a cross potent flanked by groups of triple bars. References to other 'Ingelrii' swords are given above.

6   *Reg. no. 1864 1–27 3 (Lough Gur, Grange, Co. Limerick, Ireland*
(Fig. 7.11c. Bruce-Mitford 1953, 321; Davidson 1962, fig. 27). This is a sword of Petersen's tenth cent. type Q, and has a double-sided inscription; side (a): a cross potent between horseshoe-shaped loops with rings at the terminals and flanked by groups of triple bars either side; side (b) a circle between crosses potent and groups of triple bars either side. Evison (1967, 179 no.75) compares this inscription with an almost identical one on a ninth–tenth cent. sword from Loppi, Finland.

7   *Reg. no. 1875 4–3 169 (Camphill, Burneston, North Yorkshire)*
(Fig. 7.10b). This is an Anglo-Saxon sword of the later ninth century belonging to

Petersen's L type and has a single figure of eight loop inlaid lengthwise on either side of the blade towards the hilt end. The loops are of similiar size but are not directly opposite to each other and one begins about 8 mm further down the blade, so that they overlap on the x-ray. As it stands the pattern appears to be unique, but it can be compared with the figure of eight loops set transversely between groups of triple bars on two Ulfberht swords from Vad and Visnes, Norway: the former is of Petersen's tenth century type R and the latter is of his ninth to mid tenth century type H (Müller-Wille 1970, Abb. 6, 25 and 7, 30). The pattern may also be related to the simple lengthwise knot between bars on another Ulfberht sword from Sassinsaari, Finland (ibid. Abb. 8, 76) and, less closely, to the pair of-apex-to-apex triangles between triple bars on a type H sword from Shestovitsy, USSR (Kirpchnikov 1966, fig. 17, 6) and to the similar pattern on an Ingelrii sword from the Thames at Wandsworth (Evison 1967, fig. 4a). The loops of the Camphill sword possibly

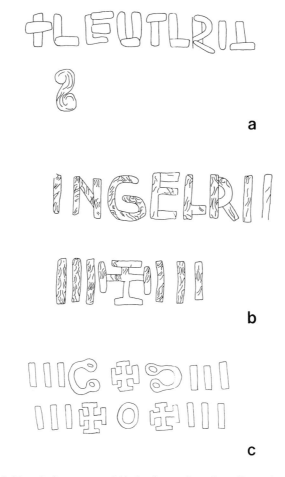

Fig. 7.11 Pattern welded inscriptions on sword blades drawn from the radiographs: a) Reg. no 1848 10–21 1 (R. Witham at Lincoln); b) Reg. no 1856 7–1 1404 (R. Thames at The Temple, London); c) Reg. no 1864 1–27 3 (Lough Gur, Co. Limerick, Ireland).

then represent an Anglo Saxon attempt to imitate the Continental marks incorporating similar motifs.

8 *Reg. no. 1891 9–5 3 (R. Thames at Kew)*
(Fig. 7.9c. Unpublished). The pommel is missing, but the brass-inlaid guards are close in form to those of Petersen's type Q of the tenth cent. and lasting into the later Viking period. A double-sided inscription is obscured by scabbard remains and accretions. Superimposition of letters on the x-ray plates makes it extremely difficult to read and the following interpretation is purely tentative: side (a) INGELRII; side (b) SITAN(B)I if (a) is read correctly, or possibly I(B)NATIS if not. The name INGELRII occurs frequently in blade inscriptions (see above), but the reading of side (b) is so uncertain that it seems pointless to speculate further than to say that it may be the name of the owner. Although the maker/owner formula appears to be unknown on the Continental sword blades of the period under discussion it can be paralleled on the ninth–tenth cent. Anglo-Saxon seax from Sittingbourne, Kent, except that in the latter, the inscriptions are incised on inlaid plates on one side and inlaid in silver on the other (Wilson 1964, cat. no. 80, pl. 30). In his account of a sword of Petersen's type X of the tenth or beginning of the eleventh century from Den Hool, "Oosterhesselen", Holland, which has a different inscription on either side of the blade (viz. INGERIH FECIT and SIGBRHANI), Ypey (1984) makes the alternative suggestion that the use of the two different names could have been to deceive the purchaser into thinking that these blades were of especially high quality. In support of this suggestion he comments on the number of imitations of maker's names that were prevalent.

9 *Reg. no. 1915 5–4 1 (Old bed of R. Lea at Edmonton, Middx)*
(Fig. 7.9b; Read 1915; Shetelig 1940, fig. 25; Davidson 1962, fig. 69). This is a Viking imported sword of Petersen's tenth cent. type U; its metal inlays date it early in this period (Wilson 1966, 44). Double-sided inscriptions: side (a), a pair of eyelet loops with scrolled ends flanking a plain equal-armed cross; side (b), two transverse bars only, but nothing more of the pattern can be seen. The closest parallels, though both with crosses potent instead of the plain form, are on the swords from Lempäälä, Finland and Ust'-Ruibezhna, Russia mentioned under no. 1 (Leppäaho 1964, Taf. 9. 4 and 10, 2; Kirpichnikov 1966, fig. 18, 8).

iv) Seaxes
Twenty seaxes were examined fourteen of which were dated to the ninth or tenth centuries. Nine of the blades had pattern-welding or inlays which were non ferrous. The blades consisted of three sections, the back edge, the patterned middle section of the blade, and the hammered cutting edge, although the simplest forms appeared to have been made from only one or two pieces of metal, rather than three.
    The forms of the decoration were:-

(a) Pattern-welded strip inlays (1857.6–23.1) and Oliver's Battery Hampshire, on loan from Hampshire County Council.
(b) Welding (1856.7–1.1408 (Fig. 7.6c), 1912.7–23.2 (Fig. 7.5d), possibly 1883.12–12.1).

(c) Non ferrous inlay (copper and brass) as a braid (1912.7–23.2, 1856.7–1.1413, 1859.1–22.12, 1881.6–23.1, 1857.6–23.1) the seax from Sittingbourne (1881.6–23.1) also has an inscription.

Four of the remaining blades were made from a blade section and a back-edge section, the latter having one or more grooves, running parallel to the edge of the blade. The radiographs showed that the blade consisted of two sections, the back edge was strongly striated, with the grain running parallel to the edge while the blade section showed a less directional, more uneven appearance, with rounded areas of less radiographic density, which is typical of hammered metal. This suggests that after the two segments of the seax had been welded together, the blade was forged out to the required shape. Two seaxes appeared to have been made from a single piece of metal, but had grooves, while three were also from a single piece of metal, but were completely undecorated. The construction of the remaining two could not be determined.

5. Discussion

The discussion section is in two parts. The first is concerned with comments or observations arising directly from the radiography results, while in the second part there is a more general discussion on the purpose of pattern-welding, the origins of the swords and the social or economic changes which might be inferred from the results.

(A) Comments on the results

1. 64% of the Anglo-Saxon and Viking period swords examined are pattern-welded.

2. The proportion of swords with pattern-welded blades rose dramatically after about 500 AD. and fell again during ninth–tenth centuries.

Table 7.3 Pattern-welded swords, percentages according to date.

Centuries AD	5–6 AD	5–7	6	6–7	7	9–10
% all swords coming from all sites	44	55	77	88	100	45 pw

From the table it can also be seen that:-

(a) The proportion of patterned to non-patterned swords rose to a peak during the seventh century.
(b) No sword-blades which could be firmly dated to the eighth century have been found.
(c) Making swords with pattern-welded inscriptions was restricted to the period after 800 AD.

3. In the British Museum sample, the use of the two patterned layered structure seems to have been mainly in the sixth and seventh centuries. Anstee (1961) listed 21 Anglo-Saxon

swords, all but one of which had double layers. Gilmour (Tylecote 1986) has also sectioned 18 swords from fifth–seventh centuries, all of which were found to have two patterned layers. However in the British Museum sample only 58% of patterned swords were identified as having two layers. This difference may be the result of the difficulties of identification when radiographs alone are used.

4. A total of 141 provenanced swords were found and 43 of these came from Kent. The cemeteries in East Kent represented here by Dover, Faversham, Crundale Down, Sittingbourne, Howletts, Lyminge, Chartham Down and Barham Downs are noted for their rich furnishings, not least the swords. The Dover site was remarkable, not only because it produced 17 swords, but also, because all of them were patterned. On the other hand Mucking (Essex) yielded 5 swords none of which was patterned. Similarly only two of the 6 Droxford (Hants) swords had a pattern (1902.7–22.171 and 175). Of the swords found in Kent, 89% were patterned while only 31% of the swords found in other locations were decorated.

Table 7.4   Percentages of pattern-welded swords from Kent.

Centuries AD	5–6	5–7	6	6–7	7	9–10
% All swords coming from Kent	20	44	83	75	47	–
% All decorated swords from Kent	40	20	66	75	47	–
% Kent sword decorated	86	50	80	100	100	–
% Other swords decorated	35	55	72	50	100	37 pw
inscript.						36

The reason for the Kentish sites being rich in pattern-welded swords may reflect the preferences and economic status of its inhabitants (or transients) and also its proximity to the Continent, in particular the Rhineland and Northern Germany, Denmark and Northern France, whose inhabitants made extensive use of pattern-welding. Kent already had a long tradition of iron working and it has been argued by Cleere (1983) that there was a Roman Imperial Estate in the Weald, with direct state working in the eastern part, though whether or not there was any direct continuity into the Anglo-Saxon period is not known as yet.

5. The results were also examined to see if there was any change in the number of pattern types being used which could be related either to the location of the finds or their chronology. A and B types were found throughout the period in most areas. The rich site at Dover (Evison 1987) yielded a total of 5 A type swords, 3 each of type B2a and B2b, and two F types, but none of the B1, C or D types. This suggests either some degree of aesthetic selection or that they came from the same workshop or group of workshops. Looking at the number of different patterns being used throughout the Anglo-Saxon period there was little change in the variety of the patterns on the swords. Seven different pattern types were recorded during this period. Comparison with material from other sites kindly made available by Sonia Hawkes, suggests that other more complex patterns, some with curving

elements, were being used in the fifth, sixth and seventh centuries. This material is being reviewed and it is hoped will soon be published.

6. The seax first appeared in the sixth century as an undecorated blade, but apparently did not come into common use until the ninth–tenth centuries.

Table 7.5 Percentages of decorated seaxes.

Date	Total no. of seaxes	Decorated welded or inlayed seaxes
6	1	0
6–7	4	0
7	1	1
9–10	15	8

Ten seaxes were found in London, and eight elsewhere. It is interesting to note that the decorated seaxes were later ones. Perhaps a weapon which was less costly to produce when it was introduced was adopted by wealthier clients who preferred patterned blades. Swords with inscriptions constituted 4% of the total number of swords during the whole period and 32% of those dating from the 9–11th century; four were found in the London area, and one each in Ireland, in Lincoln, in Yorkshire and in Nottingham.

(B) General discussion of pattern-welded blades

Three questions arise in connection with the pattern-welded blades. These are:

(1) was pattern-welding decorational or structural in intention;
(2) were the blades made in England or imported from the continent;
(3) what social and technological changes taking place can be inferred from the swords themselves and their deposition.

The Purpose of Pattern-Welding

Pattern-welding has been considered to have been be employed mainly for strengthening the blade, but some recent papers suggest rather that it was used mainly for decoration and a consensus of opinion seems to be gradually emerging to this effect. Tylecote (1962 p. 250) remarked that the pattern was a by-product of the method of manufacture and not an intended effect. It was used, he suggested, to introduce carbon into the blade to a greater depth and thus to increase its hardness. At the same time the embrittling effect concomitant with increasing hardness would be mitigated by the softer tougher strips also incorporated in the pattern-welded structure, and gross slag inclusions would be also eliminated. Later, however, Tylecote (1976, p. 57) has commented that it is not clear that artifacts made in this way were appreciably stronger than most of the weapons made by simple piling, but if well polished, they would look beautiful. Most recently (1986), Tylecote said that the pattern-welded sword appears to have been designed in its earliest phase as an ornamental or prestige weapon and its military usefulness seems to have taken second place to its appearance. He adds "If it were not for the fact that we know that such swords were used for fighting (Beowulf etc) we would have supposed that its purpose was like the ceremonial sword of today."

Some early work supported the idea that the swords had superior properties; certainly Salin (1957) and France-Lanord (1947) found that the pattern-welded swords which they examined were extremely hard and apparently could cut like razors. France-Lanord (1947) also tested the blades he was examining and found that pattern-welded blades were three times more flexible than ordinary blades (Salin 1957, p. 65).

It is clear from Old Norse and Irish literature that the springiness of the blades was much valued in a good sword: the Svarfdaela Saga (Davidson 1962) describes how, ideally, the tip of a good blade could be bent back to touch the hilt and spring back undamaged. During conservation in the British Museum Conservation workshop a seventh-century pattern-welded sword in good condition from Acklam still exhibited considerable springiness when being straightened in spite of lying in the ground for fourteen centuries. Menghin (1983) also stressed the importance of pattern-welding and the resilience of the blade.

Although the resilience of the blade is important, pattern-welding is not necessarily the best way of achieving it. Ypey (1984), as a result of his own experimental work, has suggested that the purpose of pattern-welding was almost entirely decorative, at least in the later Carolingian and Viking periods. This must be the case with pattern-welded spearheads which are of rigid construction. Menghin (1983) has reported thin surface layers of pattern-welded material on sword blades which must be also entirely decorative, although it should not be forgotten that these developments are relatively late. So many swords have been identified as having three layers, a relatively plain layer (Schürmann 1959) between two pattern-welded ones, that it is difficult to believe that their presence is entirely functional. Cutting edges and cores were constructed from more than one strip (Schürmann 1959, Tylecote 1986) but often with a layered structure, and this was probably intended for stengthening. Gilmour (Tylecote 1986) sectioned a number of patterned-welded swords and found that the blades were variable both in relation to soundness and their hardness although there seemed to be a technical improvement from the eighth century onwards. The majority were made from wrought iron, both phosphorus rich and phosphorus free, while some contained some iron richer in carbon. Gilmour discussed the use of phosphorus iron, which he concluded was employed to improve the pattern, rather than for its structural properties. Phosphorus iron was frequently used during the Iron Age (Schultz 1965) and a Roman blowing iron was constructed from low and high phosphorus irons. In this case it was concluded (following Rollason 1978, 170) that these irons were used to facilitate welding (Lang 1976). If this were the case, it might have been a factor in its use in pattern-welding. Goodway (1987) also points out that phosphorus has a considerably hardening effect and in the absence of carbon can be worked and used satisfactorily. On balance it seems most likely that pattern-welding was largely decorative. It is quite possible that pattern-welding was thought to improve the properties of the swords, and it might be remembered that a smith with the skill to produce fine pattern-welding might be likely to produce a good quality sword anyway.

English or Continental origins
The next question to be considered is whether the sword blades were made in England or on the continent. According to tenth-century Arabian authors there were two Teutonic peoples producing pattern-welded swords: the Franks (Farang) and the East Scandinavians (Rus) (Liestøl 1951) while references to swords in Anglo-Saxon and

Scandinavian literature describe patterned blades and are discussed by Cramp (1957, 63–67), Liestøl (1951) Davidson (1962, 121–152) and Brady (1979, 90–110). Unfortunately the Anglo-Saxon and Scandinavian poets give us no direct information about where these swords were made. Cramp (p. 65) suggests that the reference in Beowulf to the manufacture of a sword by giants 'no doubt arose because the best pattern-welded swords were imports – the products of imported trade secrets'. This may have been the case, though as Brady observes (p. 121), supernatural smiths were part and parcel of Germanic legend and mythology both here and abroad, so we cannot be certain of the significance of the giant myth. Davidson (p. 34) sees no convincing reason why pattern-welded swords should not have been made in England, if only in a few workshops.

The question of origin is a difficult one to resolve since stylistically diagnostic features appear mainly on the hilt and other mounts which could and often were fitted in different centres from those where the blades were made (Davidson 1962). For example the sword from Lincoln, (1848, 10–21, 1) has a Continental blade and an Anglo-Saxon hilt. However in order to make some comparison with the patterns on the continental sword blades a brief survey of the technical literature was carried out. The quality of the illustrations varied, some only showed a small part of the blade and clearly the sample of surviving swords would not be representative (the same being true of the British Museum's collection). The survey therefore had its limitations, but the results are interesting, especially those from the cemetery at Schretzheim (Koch 1977). The 105 swords found there have been thoroughly investigated and are included in the table separately.

Table 7.6 Distribution of welded patterns on swords compared.

Types present	A	AS	B1	B2a	B2b	C1	C2(a+b)	Two pattern layers
Continent	12	1	2	1	1	3	1	8
British Museum	12	1	17	18	12	1	8	21
England (Gilmour)	3	2	7	4	1	1	2	
Schretzheim	17	2	12	5	–	3	4	8

(AS is a coincident straight and twist with two rods) Gilmour's results are published in Tylecote (1986).
Many of these continental patterns showed curving elements, which were the result of the surface being removed by grinding (Anstee 1961). The suffix X indicates this form

Many of these continental patterns showed curving elements, which were the result of the surface being removed by grinding (Anstee 1961). The suffix X indicates this form

Table 7.7 Distribution of curving patterns on swords.

	AX	B1X	B2bX	B2aX	C1X	C2X
England (Not British Museum*)	7	3	2	–	3	
Continent	10	17	3	5	2	2

* Only Crundale Down sword (1894.11–3.1). None were found by Gilmour.

The use of surface removal to vary the patterns is the most obvious difference in technique or pattern, the only example found in the British Museum was the lower end of the sword from Crundale Down (1894, 11–3, 1, mid seventh century). Several blades in the British Museum have close counterparts on the Continent, for example, Waterbeach with one side of the blades from Waal-bij-Nijmegen and Inversheim (Ypey 1982). Most inscribed swords appear to have been Frankish in origin, but some Anglo-Saxon copies may also have been made locally. The radiographic evidence suggests that the technique of grinding away the surface or slicing, as Liestøl suggested, were not much used in England, whereas they were frequently employed on the Continent to produce the curving patterns. Fullers (the so-called 'blood channel', a depression running down the blade on both sides) were thought to have been ground in and it may be inferred that they were made in this way on the Continent. However, in England, even where fullers are present, (predominantly on later blades), the absence of curving patterns shows that they were not ground but probably hammered. The results of Gilmour's metallographic studies of swords found in England were in agreement with this suggestion, showing hammered not ground fullers. This is strongly indicative that there was some kind of sword-making industry in England.

If Anglo-Saxon swords were made in England, what was the source of the iron, and where were they fabricated? In the area of Kent and Sussex there are two documentary pieces of evidence for iron working in the Anglo-Saxon period. A charter of AD 689 mentions an iron mine near Lyminge, Kent, while the Domesday book lists iron working near East Grinstead, Sussex. Crossley (1981) and Hill (1981) have used maps to show the distribution of Domesday and archaeological evidence of iron working. This is sparse, but an increasing number of sites are being discovered and no doubt other sites are yet to be discovered. Iron production debris can be difficult to date if other archaeological evidence is lacking. If forging took place at some distance from the smelting site (or imported iron had been used) it would not be easy to trace the forging site. Identification of such a site might have to rely on the discovery of traces such as the small spherical particles of slag which spray out around the anvil during forging; these have been found on an Iron Age site (Crew 1984). The only smelting or smithing remains from the early Saxon period at present appear to be slag bottoms of a north German type from Aylsham, Norfolk and Mucking, Essex and tap slag from Witton, Norfolk (Wilson and Hurst 1969, 1965), Shakenoak, Oxfordshire (Brodribb 1972), while Middle Saxon remains have been found in Northamptonshire (Williams, 1979; Addyman 1964); Ashdown forest (Tebbutt 1982) Southampton (Holdsworth 1980) and Wharram Percy (MacDonnell, personal communication). It is surprising that there is not more evidence for manufacture in the period from fifth to seventh centuries, as so many swords were being interred, many probably being made locally. Work at a royal smithying site at Ramsbsury, Wiltshire (Haslam 1980) has suggested that at least during the eighth and ninth centuries changes in technology occurred which point to the rediscovery of processes lost in England since the Roman Age. Site continuity would seem to have been extremely rare in this country.

On the Continent the picture is different. Although, according to Crossley (1981), it can be supposed that the same level of iron production was maintained on the Continent as during the Roman period, it seems likely that the departure of the Roman army reduced the demand somewhat in some areas. Unfortunately the evidence for post-Roman iron working, as in Britain, is sparse, except for Scandinavia, where there was a continuous increase in iron production which continued uninterrupted from the Iron Age to Medieval times (Martens 1983). Many extraction and working sites have been found, some with very large slag deposits. Large hoards of iron bars have also been found; for example 650 bars were found at Skedstand and bundles of iron bars from the migration period were found at Eketorp in Öland (Calissendorff 1979). Interestingly there is linguistic evidence for iron being sold in "garba" from the twelfth century onwards in England (Rogers 1865). This is a Latin trading term for a bundle or sheaf. Long thin round-sectioned bars forged together to make double tweezer-shaped bars were excavated at Helgö (Haglund 1978, 38). Could these have been intended for pattern-welding, perhaps even for export? Anstee (1961) tack-welded his rods together for ease of handling in his experiments. The Frisians traded in iron as is shown by finds from the port of Hedeby in Schleswig (Crossley 1981). These finds are from the Carolingian period (corresponding to the start of the Later Anglo-Saxon period in England) when there were edicts by the Holy Roman Emperors forbidding the export of weapons from the Carolingian Empire. In view of the large scale Scandinavian iron production (e.g. Martens 1983) it is conceivable that iron was imported thence into England, through north Germany or the Low Countries, but there is no evidence for this at present. No currency bars dating from the Anglo-Saxon period have been found in England.

On the present evidence, it must be concluded that while some swords were imported or else brought by their migrating owners, others were probably made in this country, from local iron or from iron transported over fairly short distances, rather than from imported bars and blooms. It is, however, not impossible that new archaeological evidence may be found for iron imports. Perhaps further excavations on urban sites may also reveal more iron production sites (like Southampton), or provide evidence for imports.

Socio-economic implications

The final question to be considered concerns whether changes in socio-economic patterns can be inferred from the swords and their deposition. To some extent, this topic awaits a detailed study of the swords and their fittings in relation to their find sites, but in the absence of such a study at present it is possible to draw some inferences from the data given above.

The results show that some changes occurred after the sixth century. All the swords datable to the seventh century were pattern-welded, but it would be a mistake to conclude that only pattern-welded swords were being made. A trend is detectable at this time towards isolated aristocratic graves and an increasing poverty can be seen in the other graves. Evidence from swords dated to the eighth century is sparse, as a result of changing burial practices, and none were examined in this project. In the ninth and tenth centuries the seax became a much more popular weapon than before among the Anglo-Saxons. In a recent paper Hodges (1985) suggested that, in the late first millenium, smiths were no longer few in number and attached to royal smithies like Ramsbury, Wiltshire (Haslam 1980), but increasingly were found in expanding towns, where there was a growing demand for domestic iron. Hodges argues that the weapons and tools of the smiths of this period which have been found indicate that cost consciousness was increasing a tendency towards standardisation. Hodges suggests that smiths could no longer afford to become engaged in making swords which took a month to produce. This may well have been true in England, although not necessarily true elsewhere; in Scandinavia for example, some smiths' graves are rich in the variety of metal working equipment. Probably the Rhineland

'Ulfberht' swords and most of the Anglo-Saxon seaxes required less time to construct as they were more simply made. The seaxes have only one cutting edge, are usually shorter in length, require less metal and probably had a handle which was simpler than the more complex sword hilt. Sometimes they were made from one piece of metal, but even when they were made from pattern-welded elements, the back edge and the blade were plain, and the whole would have been easier to weld together because it was shorter. Strengthening was given by the heavy back edge. As long as this was sound the weapon could be used. Perhaps the smiths felt more confident of producing a sound thicker sectioned blade than before. Evidence of the increasing popularity of the seax during the ninth to tenth centuries, tends to support Hodges' economic analysis of Anglo-Saxon iron production. The sudden increase in the number of swords surviving from towards the middle decades of the ninth century until the end of Late Saxon period can probably be attributed to two main factors. The first was the reintroduction to this country of burial practices by the pagan Vikings. Presumably the Late Saxon swords in the British Museum found in such graves had been obtained by trade or looting (i.e. Wensley, Sancton, Ardvonrig and Burneston).

Another factor might be the custom of the sacrificial deposition of weapons in rivers (Wilson 1965, 50–1, Appendix A). The large number of swords and seaxes found in rivers, to which recent discoveries are still adding, is difficult to account for, although Alcock (1975, 345) points out that many battles were recorded as having been fought at river crossings. The sword from the Thames at Kew (reg. no. 1891, 9–5, 3) has only recently been reidentified from registration details and is added to the list while the sword from Lough Gur, Ireland (reg. no. 1864, 1–27, 30), might be included in the same category. A large number of the late seaxes too come from rivers which suggests that the sacrificial river deposits, if such they were, were made by both pagan Vikings and Christian Saxons.

6.   Conclusions

A radiographic survey of the Anglo-Saxon and Viking swords and seaxes in the British Museum was carried out. Examination of the radiographs leads to the following conclusions:

1)   Most British Museum swords have relatively simple patterns, compared with Continental swords and even compared with other English swords examined elsewhere. The patterns are based on two or three twisted rods or rod composites, with some straight sections. Eight groups showing variations of these factors have been distinguished.

2)   A few swords have patterns which do not fit into these categories; two of these have Continental counterparts (Hurbuck with an Anglo-Saxon sword from Borgstedt, Schleswig-Holstein and Waterbeach with Inversheim and Waal-bij-Nijmegen). The two-band continuous twist pattern was popular both in England and on the Continent.

3)   Many Continental patterns have curving patterns, resulting from grinding away the surface. In the British Museum such a pattern is only present on part of one sword, from Crundale Down. It seems likely that most of the British Museum swords were finished by hammering rather than grinding and are therefore probably the products of a local technological tradition which has developed differently from that on the Continent.

4)   Socio-economic changes were reflected by the decreasing number of swords which were interred during the seventh century. The increased proportion of pattern-welded swords indicated that only the wealthier, more important men were buried with their swords.

Three more general conclusions may also be mentioned.

5)   At present there is insufficient evidence to determine whether pattern-welding was primarily for strengthening or decoration, but it is clear that the latter was very important.

6)   The survey further underlines the richness of society in Kent.

7)   The chronology and distribution of find sites reflects the changes in religious practices, with the disappearance of swords in Anglo-Saxon graves after the late seventh century, and the appearance of the river sacrifices, mainly in the ninth–tenth centuries, made, it would seem, by both Anglo-Saxons and Vikings.

Acknowledgements

The authors would like to thank their colleagues Leslie Webster, Katherine East and Susan Youngs in the Department of Medieval and Later Antiquities and Dr M.S. Tite and Dr Paul Craddock in the British Museum Research Laboratory for their help and advice. They are very grateful to Professor V. Evison for invaluable dating information in advance of her report on the excavation of the Dover (Buckland) cemetery which has been published since this paper was submitted for publication; the dates given in the present study are necessarily provisional. Also they would like to thank J.D. MacDonnell and Brian Gilmour for most fruitful discussions and permission to mention some of their as yet unpublished work, and to thank Sonia Chadwick Hawkes for her encouraging support and allowing them to see and comment upon some of her important comparative material, and Lena Thalin-Bergman for her help in making available the work of Sten Modin of the Swedish Metallurgical Institute, to whom they are extremely grateful. They would particularly like to thank Dr R. Davis and the staff at the Royal Marsden Mammography Unit for the xeroradiographs.

Table 7.1

T   Inscription
O   No pattern
I   Inlay, non ferrous metal
P   Pattern, but not clear enough to be categorised or not in one of the categories.
S   Seax

* See section on inscriptions

Registration	Culture	Date AD	Location of find	Type, Features
AL 116/775	AS	9	Thames, Westminster	B1 2 layers
Oliver's Battery (on loan)	AS	7	Hampshire	IS
Lyle 236 (Not in BM)	AS	10	Thames, Westminster	T
Yorkshire Museum	AS	6–7	Acklam	P
Tr 169		9	?Nottingham	P
Tr 173	AS	9–10	No provenance	O
Tr 174	V	E10	Nottingham	T
OA 321	AS	No Details		O
OA 324	AS	9–10	No provenance	O grooves
OA 6609	AS	5–7	Gt Chesterford	O
OA 6610	AS	5–7	Barnet, Herts	C2a
OA 6568	AS	5–7	?Kent	O
557	AS	5–6	Mucking, Essex	O
618	AS	5–6	Mucking, Essex	O 3 plain
682	AS	5–6	Mucking, Essex	O
776	AS	5–6	Mucking, Essex	O
769	AS	5–6	Mucking, Essex	O
951–70	AS	E6	Faversham, Kent	P
952–70	AS	E6	Faversham, Kent	B2b
953–70	AS	6	Faversham, Kent	B1 2 layers
954–70	AS	c.525–600	Faversham, Kent	B2a 2 layers
956–70	AS	5–7	Faversham, Kent	B2a + B2b 2layers
957–70	AS	6	Faversham, Kent	B2a + B2b 2 layers
958–70	AS	5–7	Faversham, Kent	O
1839 10–29 144b	AS	(6)–7	Chartham Down, Kent	B1
1839 10–29 144a	AS	(6)–7	Chartham Down, Kent	A
1848 7–27 1	AS	L5	Battle Edge, Burford, Oxford	B2a
1848 10–21 1	AS	10	Lincoln	T
1850 2–7 1	AS	9–10	Thames	I
1853 4–12 89	AS	6–7	Barham Downs, Kent	B1
1853 4–12 90	AS	6–7	Barham Downs, Kent	B1 (probably fragments of same sword as 1853 4–12 89
1854 11–7 12	AS	L9–10	Norwich	C1
1855 10–18 1	AS	5–6	Ashdown, Berks	O
1856 7–1 1404	V	10–11	Thames, Temple	T

Registration	Culture	Date AD	Location of find	Type, Features
1856 7–1 1405	AS	L9	London	A
1856 7–1 1408	AS	9–10	London	PS
1856 7–1 1409	AS	9–10	London	OS grooved
1856 7–1 1410	AS	9–10	London	OS grooved
1856 7–1 1411	AS	9–10	London	OS grooved
1856 7–1 1412	AS	9–10	Finch Lane, London	OS grooved with plaited Cu/Au
1856 7–1 1413	AS	9–10	Honey Lane, London	IS inlaid line of alternating bronze + copper wire set in herringbone pattern
1857 6–23 1	AS	L9	Battersea	IS non-ferrous twisted wire inlay runic inscription
1857 6–23 2	–	9–10	Battersea	IS bands
1859 1–22 12	AS	9–10	Thames, London	IS plaited Cu/Au
1862 7–19 5	AS	6–7	Milton Field, Berks	OS
1862 7–19 6	AS	L6–7	Long Wittenham, Oxon	OS grooved
1864 1–27 3	V	10	Loch Gur, Co. Limerick, Ireland	I
1867 7–29 150	AS	c.500	Chessell Down IOW	B2a
1867 7–29 152	AS	6	Chessell Down IOW gr.84	O
1868 9–4 24	AS	9–10	Thames, London	OS grooved
1869 3–15 1	A	5–6	Waterbeach, Cambs	P
1869 10–11 13	AS	E6	Chessell Down IOW gr.26	B1 + straights on edges
1869 10–11 14	AS	L5–6	Chessell Down IOW	O
1869 10–11 15	AS	L5–6	Chessell Down IOW	O
1869 10–11 16	AS	L5–6	Chessell Down IOW	B2B
1869 10–11 17	AS	L5–6	Chessell Down IOW	B1
1869 10–11 18	AS	L5–6	Chessell Down IOW	O
1869 10–11 55	AS	L5–6	Chessell Down IOW	O
1873 6–2 104	AS	7	Tissington, Derbys	B2b
1875 3–10 40	AS	6	Long Wittenham, Oxon	C2a
1875 4–3 169	AS	L9	Burneston, N Yorks	T
1876 2–12 30	AS	L5–6	Lakenheath Fen, Suffolk	O
1876 2–12 46	AS	L5–6	Barrington, Cambs	O
1879 12–9 2078	AS	7	Lowick, Northumberland	SO
1850 5–21 1	AS	6	Longbridge, Warwicks	B1
1880 8–9 1	AS	L5–6	Barrington, Cambs	O
1881 6–23 1	AS	9–10	Sittingbourne, Kent	IS Cu or Au letters, strip and plaits
1883 7–26 1	AS	L9	Santon, Norfolk	O Viking grave
1883 12–12 1	AS	9–10	Little Bealings, Suffolk	PS grooved
1883 12–13 612	AS	6	Sittingbourne, Kent	B2a
1883 12–13 613	AS	6	Sittingbourne, Kent	O
1883 12–13 614	AS	6	Sittingbourne, Kent	O

Registration	Culture	Date AD	Location of find	Type, Features
1883 12–13 621	AS	6	Sittingbourne, Kent	B2b
1883 12–13 622	AS	6	Sittingbourne, Kent	O
1883 12–13 646	AS	6	Faversham, Kent	C2a
1883 12–13 647	AS	6	Faversham, kent	O
1883 12–14 4	AS	E7	Taplow, Bucks	C2a
1847 2–9 1	V	10–E11	Temple London	B2b
1888 7–19 57	AS	5–7	unprovenanced	B2a two layers
1890 9–2 1	AS	6?	Lyminge, Kent	B1 + B2b two layers
1891 3–23 1	AS	L5–6	E Shefford, Berks	O
1891 6–24 75	AS	6	Kempston, Beds	O No pattern
1891 6–24 78	AS	6	Kempston, Beds	B1
1891 6–24 79	AS	L5–6	Kempston, Beds	P
1891 6–24 80	AS	5–7	Kempston, Beds	P
1891 6–24 103	AS	6–7	Kempston, Beds	OS
1891 6–24 131	AS	9–10	Kempston, Beds	O
1891 9–5 3	V	10	Kew, Thames	T
1894 8–3 87	AS	L5–6	?Strood, Kent	C2a
1894 11–3 1	AS	M7	Crundale Down, Kent	B2a 2 layers ground away cruciform pattern at tip
1894 12–16 4	AS	E7	Broomfield, Essex	B2a 2 layers
1895 3–13 10	AS	6	Croydon	O
1895 6–13 22	AS	9	Ardvonrig, Barra	A 2 opposed layers
1896 5–22 5	AS	6–7	Thames	O
1902 7–22 171	AS	L5–6	Droxford, Hants	A
1902 7–22 172	AS	L5–6	Droxford, Hants	O
1902 7–22 173	AS	L5–6	Droxford, Hants	O
1902 7–22 174	AS	L5–6	Droxford, Hants	O
1902 7–22 175	AS	L5–6	Droxford, Hants	P
1902 7–22 176	AS	L5–6	Droxford, Hants	O
1902 12–16 2	AS	E6	Windmill Hill, Bucks	B1
1906 6–12 1	V	9–10	Farnden ,Notts	P
1912 7–23 1	AS	L9	Hurbuck, Durham	B1 2 layers
1912 7–23 2	AS	9–10	Hurbuck, Durham	PS whorl patt. inlayed Cu/Au plait
1912 12–20 2	AS	L7	Twickenham, Surrey	B1
1913 7–17 1	AS	7	Barlaston, Staffs	F
1915 5–3 2	AS	L5–6	Herringswell, Suffolk	B2a
1915 5–4 1	V	L9–E10	Edmonton, Middx	T
1915 12–8 353	AS	5–6	Astwick, Beds	B2b
1918 7–8 13	AS	L5–6	Howletts, Kent	O
1929 2–6 1	V	10–11	Windsor, Berks	P
1936 5–11 54	AS	L5–E6	Howletts, Kent gr.16	B2a 2 layers
1936 5–11 75	AS	6	Howletts, Kent gr.19	C2b
1936 5–11 76	AS	E6	Howletts, Kent gr.20	P

Registration	Culture	Date AD	Location of find	Type, Features
1936 5–11 99	AS	6	Howletts, Kent gr.25	B2a
1936 5–11 132	AS	6	Howletts, Kent gr.36	0
1936 5–11 164	AS	5–6	Howletts, Kent	A(S)?
1936 5–11 166	AS	5–6	Howletts, Kent	B1
1939 10–10 95, 19–29	AS	E7	Sutton Hoo, Suffolk	C2b 2 layers
1963 11–8 124	AS	L5–E6	Dover, Kent gr.22	B2a
1963 11–8 128	AS	E7	Dover, Kent gr.27	B2b
1963 11–8 174	AS	E7	Dover, Kent gr.33	B1
1963 11–8 281	AS	6–E7	Dover, Kent gr.41	B2a
1963 11–8 340	AS	L6–E7	Dover, Kent gr.56	B2a
1963 11–8 416	AS	E7	Dover, Kent gr.71	A
1963 11–8 469	AS	6	Dover, Kent gr.91	B2b
1963 11–8 483	AS	6	Dover, Kent gr.93	A
1963 11–8 493	AS	6–7	Dover, Kent gr.94B	B2a
1963 11–8 502	AS	E7	Dover, Kent gr.96A	A
1963 11–8 509	AS	E7	Dover, Kent gr.96B	A
1963 11–8 511	AS	6	Dover, Kent gr.98	F2b
1963 11–8 603	AS	E7	Dover, Kent gr.131	B2b
1963 11–8 751	AS	525–600	Dover, Kent gr.90	B2a
1963 11–8 782	AS	6–7	Dover, Kent	A
1963 11–8 783	AS	6–7	Dover, Kent	B2a
1964 7–2 381	AS	6	Gt Chesterford, Essex	B1
1965 7–3 1	AS	L9	Wensley, Yorks (old)	C2a

References

Addyman, P.V. 1964: A Dark Age Settlement at Maxey, Northamptonshire, *Medieval Archaeology* 8, 20–73.

Alcock, L. 1975: *Arthur's Britain*, 345.

Anon 1851: Antiquities and Works of Art Exhibited, *Archaeological Journal*, 8.

Anstee, W.J. and Biek, L. 1961: A Study in Pattern-Welding, *Medieval Archaeology* 5, 71–93.

Anteins, A.K. 1966: Im Ostbaltikum gefundene Schwerter mit damaszierten Klingen II, *Waffen und Kostumkunde*, 111–126.

Anteins, A.K. 1968: Structure and Manufacturing Techniques of Pattern Welded Objects found in the Baltic states, *Journal of the Iron and Steel Institution*, June, 563–570.

Belaiew, N.T. 1918: Damascus Steel, *Journal of the Iron and Steel Institution* 97, 417–574.

Belaiew, N.T. 1921: Damascene Steel part II *Journal of the Iron and Steel Institute* 104, 181–186.

Brady, C. 1979: Weapons in *Beowulf*: an analysis of the nominal compounds and an evaluation of the poet's use of them, *Anglo-Saxon England* 8, 79–141.

Brodribb, A. 1972: *Excavations at Shakenoak Farm, Wilcote, Oxon.* Pt. 3.

Brown, P.D.C. & O'Leary, T. (forthcoming): The Bath 'Ulfberht' sword, in B. Cunliffe's report (forthcoming) on the Bath excavations.

Bruce-Mitford, R.L.S. 1953: Some recent results of the application of laboratory techniques to antiquities of the Anglo-Saxon period in Britain, *Congrès International des Sciences Préhistoriques et Protohistoriques*. Actes de la IIIe. Session, Zurich 1950, 321–323.

Bruce-Mitford, R.L.S 1978: *The Sutton Hoo Ship Burial* Vol. 2 (BMP).

Calissendorff, K, 1979: Linguistic Evidence for Early Iron Production, in *Iron and Man in Prehistoric Sweden* ed. Helen Clark (Jernkontoret).

Cleere, H. 1983: The Organisation of the Iron Industry in the Western Roman Provinces in the Early Empire with Special Reference to Britain, *Offa* 40, 103–114.

Cramp, R. 1957: *Beowulf* and archaeology, *Medieval Archaeology* 1, 57–77.

Crew, Peter 1984: Bryn y Castell, Ffestiniog. A Late Prehistoric Working Centre, *Symposium of the Comité pour La Sidérugie Ancienne* (Belfast).

Crossley, D.W. 1981: Medieval Iron Smelting in *Medieval Industry* ed. D.W. Crossley (CBA Research Report No. 40).

Davidson, H.R.E. 1962: *The Sword in Anglo-Saxon England. Its Archaeology and Literature* (Oxford).

East, K., Larkin P. and Winsor P. 1985: The Chertsey Ulfberht sword, *Surrey Archaeological Collections* 76.

Emmerling, J. 1972: Technologische Untersuchungen an Eisernen Bodenfunden, *Alt-Thüringen*.

Emmerling, J. 1978: Technologische Untersuchungen an Kaiserzeitlichen Schwertern aus Buchhain, *Alt-Thüringen* 15, 92–102.

Emmerling, J. 1979: Zur Technologie Zweier Schwerter und einer Lanzenspitze aus Wolkow, *Alt-Thüringen* 16, 120–126.

Evans, A.C. 1978: In *The Sutton Hoo Ship Burial* Vol. 2, ed. R. Bruce-Mitford (BMP).

Evison, V.I. 1967: A sword from the Thames at Wallingford Bridge, *Antiquaries Journal* 124, 160–189.

Evison, V.I. 1987: Dover: The Buckland Cemetery.

France-Lanord, A. 1949: La Fabrication des épées damassées aux époques mérovingiennes et carolingiennes, *Le Pays Gaumais* 10, 1, 2, 3.

France-Lanord, A. 1952: Les techniques de la metallurgie du fer de la préhistoire au temps des Grandes Invasions, *Revue de Metallurgie* 49, 411–422.

Goodway, M. 1987: Phosphorus in Antique Iron Music Wire, *Science* 236, 927–932

Haglund, K. 1978: Rod-shaped and Scythe-shaped currency bars, *Excavations at Helgö*, V: 1, 38–45.

Haslam, Jeremy 1980: A Middle Saxon iron smelting site at Ramsbury Wiltshire, *Medieval Archaeology* 24, 1–68.

Hill, D. 1981: *Atlas of Anglo-Saxon England* (Oxford).

Hodges, R. 1985: Beginnings of the Medieval Iron Industry in Western Europe in *Medieval Iron in Society* (Symposium Stockholm).

Holdsworth, P. 1980: *Excavations at Melbourne Street, Southampton 1971–76* (Southampton Archaeological Research Committee Report, CBA).

Kirpichnikov, A.N. 1966: Drevnerusskoye oruzhiye (vyp.I). Mechi i Sabli, IX–XIII vv. *Arkheologiya SSR* (Svod Arkheologicheskikh Istochnikov), E1–36.

Kirpichnikov, A.N. 1969: Russiske-Skandinaviske forbindelser i IX–XI århundrede, illustreret ved våbenfund, *Kuml*, 1969 (Årbog for Jysk Arkaeologisk Selskab) 165–189 (Copenhagen).

Koch, U. 1977: *Das Reihengräberfeld bei Schretzheim* (Germanische Denkmäler der Völkerwanderungszeit, Serie A, 13. Berlin).

Lang, J.R.S. 1984: The Craft of the Blacksmith. *Symposium of the Comité pour la Sidérurgie Ancienne* (Belfast).

Lang, J.R.S. and Price, J. 1976: Iron tubes from a Late Roman Glass-making site at Merida, *Journal of Archaeological Science* 2, 296–298

Leppäaho, J. 1964: *Späteisenzeitliche Waffen aus Finnland. Schwertinschriften und Waffenverzierungen des 9–12. Jahrhunderts*. (Suomen Muinaismuistoyhdistyksen Aikakauskirja/Finska Fornminnesforeningens Tidskrift 61. Helsinki).

Liestøl, Aslak 1951: Blodrefill og Mål, *Viking, Tidsskrift for norrøn arkeologi* 15 (Oslo).

Lorange, A.L. 1889: *Den Yngre Jernalders Svaerd. Et Bidrag til Vikingetidens Historie og Teknologi* (Bergen Museum).

Martens, H. Irmelin 1983: The Norwegian Bloomery Furnaces and their Relation to the European Finds, *Offa* 40, 119–124.

Maryon, H. 1948: A Sword of the Nydam type from Ely Fields Farm, near Ely. *Journal of the Cambridge Antiquarian Society* 41, 73–76.

Maryon, H. 1950: A sword of the Viking period from the River Witham, *Antiquaries Journal* 30, 175–9.

Maryon, H. 1960: Pattern Welding and Damascening of Sword Blades *Studies in Conservation* 5, 25–36, 52–59.

McGrath, J.N. 1973: A report on the Metallurgical Examination of 5 fragmentary Early Iron Age sword blades from Llyn Cerrig Bach, *Journal of Arms and Armour Soc.*, 71.

Menghin, Wilfried 1974: Ein Langobardisches Kriegergrab in Germanischen National Museum Nürnberg, *Archäologisches Korrespondenzblatt* 4, 251–256.

Menghin, Wilfried 1983: *Das Schwert im Frühen Mittelalter* (Nürnberg).

Modin, Sten: unpublished report.

Müller-Wille, M. 1970: Ein neues ULFBERHT-Schwert aus Hamburg, *Offa* 27, 65–88.

Müller-Wille, M. 1977: Krieger und Reiter im Spiegel früh-und hochmittelalterlicher Funde Schleswig-Holsteins, *Offa* 34, 40–74 (Neumünster).

Müller-Wille, M. 1982: Zwei Karolingische Schwerter aus Mittelnorwegen, in H-J. Hässler *et al.* (eds), *Studien zur Sachsenforschung* 3, 101–154 (Hildesheim).

Neumann, B. 1927–8: Romanische Damastahl, *Archiv für das Eisenhüttenwesen* (Düsseldorf).

Oakeshott, R.E. 1951: An "Ingelri" sword in the British Museum, *Antiquaries Journal* 31, 69–71.

Oakeshott, R.E. 1960: *The Archaeology of Weapons* (London).

Page, R.A. 1964: The inscriptions, Appendix A in Wilson (1964), 67–90.

Panseri, C. 1963: Damascus steel in Legend and Reality, *Gladius* 4, 5–66.

Petersen, J. 1919: De Norske Vikingesverd. En typologisk-Kronologisk studie over vikingetidens vaaben, *Skrifter utgit av Videnskaps-selskapet i Kristiania*. II.Hist.-Fil.Klasse 1919. No. 1.

Piaskowski, J. 1961: Metallographic investigations of ancient iron objects from the territory between the Oder and the basin of the Vistula River *JISI*, July 1961.

Pleiner, Radomir 1969: Eisenschmiede im frühmittelalterlichen Zentral Europa, *Archäologischer Anzeiger*, Heft I, 79–92.

Read, C.H. 1915: A Viking sword found in the Lea near Edmonton, *Proceedings of the Society of Antiquaries of London*, 2nd ser. 27 (1914–15), 215–217.

Rogers, J.E.T. 1865–6: *A History of Agriculture and Prices in England from 1259*, 2 Vols. (Oxford).

Rollason, E.C. 1978: Metallurgy for Engineers.

Rosenqvist, Anne 1967–68: Sverd med Klinger ornert med figurer i kopperlegeringer fra eldre jernalder, i Universitetets Oldsaksamling Oslo, *Unversitetets Oldsaksamling Årbok* 1967–1968, 143–200.

Salin, E. 1957: *La Civilisation Mérovingienne* (iii).

Schultz, E. H. and Pleiner, R. 1965: Untersuchungen an Klingen eisener La Tène Schwerter, *Technische Beiträge zur Archäologie* 2, 38–50.

Schürmann, Eberlard 1959: Untersuchungen an Nydam Schwertern, *Archiv für das Eisenhüttenwesen* 30.3, 121–120.

Shetelig, H. 1940: *Viking Antiquities in Great Britain and Ireland. Pt.IV. Viking Antiquities in England* (Oslo).

Smith, C.S. 1957: A Metallographic Examination of Some Japanese Sword blades, Symposeum *La Tecnica di Fabbricazione delle Lame di Acciaio Presso gli Antichi*, ed. C. Panseri, Quaderno II, 41–64.

Smith, C.S. 1960: *A History of Metallography* (Univ. Chicago Press).

Stalsberg, A. 1981: Zu Datierungen der frühen wikingerzeitlichen Funde Skandinavischer Herkunft in der alten Rus, *Les Pays du Nord et Byzance (Scandinavie et Byzance)*. Actes du colloque d'Upsal 20–22 avril 1979. (Acta Universitatis Upsaliensis, Figura, Nov. ser. 19), 53–62.

Tebbutt, C.F. 1982: A Middle-Saxon Iron Smelting site at Millbrook, Ashdown Forest, Sussex, *Sussex Archaeological Collections* 120, 19–35.

Tylecote, R.F. 1962: *Metallurgy in Archaeology*.

Tylecote, R.F. 1976: *A History of Metallurgy* (The Metals Society).

Tylecote, R.F. and Gilmour, B. 1986: *The Metallography of Early Ferrous Edge Tools and Edged Weapons* (BAR 155, Oxford).

Wadsworth, J. and Sherby, Oley D. 1979: On the Bulat (Damascus Steels) *Bull. Metals Museum Japan* 4 Sept, 7–23.

Webster, G. 1982: in *The Archaeology of Canterbury vol I – Excavations at Canterbury Castle* – P. Bennett, S. Frere and S. Torr, (Kent Archaeological Society) 184–190.

Wegeli, R. 1902–5: Inschriften auf mittelalterlichen Schwertklingen, *Zeitschrift für Historische Waffenkunde* 3, 177–183 and 218–225 (Dresden).

Williams, J.H. 1979: *St Peter's Street Northampton. Excavations 1973–6.*

Wilson, D.M. 1964: *Anglo-Saxon Ornamental Metalwork 700–1100 in the British Museum* (British Museum, London).

Wilson, D.M. 1965: Some neglected late Anglo-Saxon swords, *Medieval Archaeology* 9, 32–54.

Wilson, D.M. 1969: Medieval Britain in 1968, *Medieval Archaeology* 13, 230–87.

Wilson, D.M. and Hurst D.G 1965: Medieval Britain in 1964, *Medieval Archaeology* 9, 170–220.

Yater, W.M 1983–4: The Legendary Steel of Damascus, *The Anvil's Ring*, 11, 4 pp. 2–17.

Ypey, J. 1960–1: Een aantal vroeg-middeleeuwse zwaarden uit Nederlandse musea, *Berichten van de Rijksdienst voor het Oudheidkundig Bodemonderzoek* 10–11, 368–394.

Ypey, J. 1973: In *Reallexikon der Germanischen Altertumskunde* (ed. J. Hoops, Berlin).

Ypey, J. 1982: Europäische Waffen mit Damaszierung, *Archäologisches Korrespondenzblatt* 12, 381–388.

Ypey, J. 1983: Rekonstruktionsversuch der Schwertklinge von Sutton Hoo. *Archäologisches Korrespondenzblatt* 13, 495–498.

Ypey, J. 1984: Einige wikingerzeitliche Schwerter aus den Niederlanden, *Offa* 41, 213–225.

Chapter 8

Anatomical Interpretations of Anglo-Saxon Weapon Injuries

S. J. Wenham

The bodies of the slain were one of the inevitable end-products of Anglo-Saxon warfare. Whatever their date, such bodies can shed light on aggression at that time; but unfortunately ancient bodies survive for study only rarely. Therefore, the paleopathologist must turn to the bones of the slain to study injuries resulting from ancient aggression.

The study of bones rather than whole bodies has obvious limitations, since it was the complete injury, including soft tissue injuries, which had its effect upon the victim. Indeed, many injuries never contact the bone and hence are 'lost' since all evidence of them has disappeared (Inglemark 1939).

The main concern of this study has been the investigation of Anglo-Saxon skeletal material from the cemetery at Eccles, Kent, with some comparative study. From the cemetery as a whole, a high percentage namely six, skeletons, show evidence of fatal edged weapon injury. One of the aims of the study was an accurate anatomical description of each injury, leading to a reconstruction of the entire injury, including its soft tissue component. The reconstruction allows a consideration of the effects of the injury on the victim and hence of possible causes of death.

The study also aimed to describe and to investigate experimentally the macro- and microscopic behaviour of bone when subjected to edged weapon injury. This led to the development of diagnostic criteria which allowed the positive identification of such injuries. Finally, the study attempted to relate the Eccles skeletons to Anglo-Saxon weapons and their mode of use.

The Skeletons

All six of the skeletons studied were male, although a seventh injured skeleton, now lost, was possibly female. All six showed edged weapon injury to the cranium, with two of the six cases showing more than one blow to the head. In addition, one skeleton also shows a projectile injury to the lumbar spine and another shows multiple post-cranial injuries. The state of preservation of the skeletons was generally good, although in several cases the cranium was fragmented.

The identification numbers given to the skeletons on excavation were considered to be

123

too unwieldy to be used conveniently during this study. Each skeleton was therefore assigned a number I to VI for the purposes of this project.

The numbers were given as follows:

Excavation No.	Project No.
J0114	I
0 in P171	II
Burial G	III
L46	IV
JP151	V
KP153/4	VI

The skeletons will be referred to throughout by their project numbers. In the cases of skeletons showing multiple injuries, each injury is identified by a numbered suffix, e.g. II/13.

The skeletons have previously been described in the Eccles Skeletal Report (Manchester 1984), which is as yet unpublished. This report gives the age, sex and stature of the individuals and these have not been reassessed.

The injuries were examined in increasing detail from gross anatomical to light and scanning electron microscopical (SEM) level, photographing injuries at each level of examination and producing both a written and standardised visual record of the position and characteristics of each injury.

The injuries were as follows:

Victim I (Fig. 8.1)
This individual was a male, aged 25–35 years and height 163 cm. He has a single linear cranial injury 16 cm long to the frontal and parietal bones, slightly to the left of the midline. The plane of the injury is almost vertically downwards.

Victim II (Figs. 8.2, 8.3, 8.4)
Victim II was a male aged 20–25 years and height 170 cm. He shows overwhelming multiple cranial and post-cranial injuries. Thirty bone injuries have been catalogued which represent a minimum of seven cranial and eleven post-cranial blows. The injuries appear to fall into three broad groups: blows to the head (injuries II/1 to II/16); blows to the back of the trunk (injuries II/17 to II/27); and blows to the arms (injuries II/28 to II/30).

Victim III (Fig. 8.5)
Victim III was a male aged 35 + and height 176 cm. He has a single cranial injury and a projectile injury to the lumbar spine. The cranial injury is to the right side of the back of the head, showing a long, curved cut on the cranial vault and two small wounds to the inner surface of the skull. The latter show that the blade passed right through the brain to contact the bone lying below it.

The projectile injury is to the third lumbar vertebra. On excavation, this vertebra was found to show deep iron staining which corresponded exactly with a corroded iron projectile point lying beneath the spine (Manchester 1984). The projectile point was to the victim's left, indicating that it entered the body from his right. Its long axis is virtually perpendicular to that of the vertebral column. The spinal cord was not damaged.

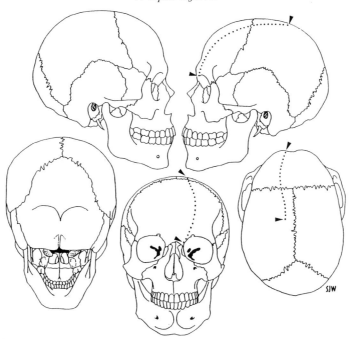

Fig. 8.1 Right, left, back, front and top of human skull showing injury of victim I, arrowed.

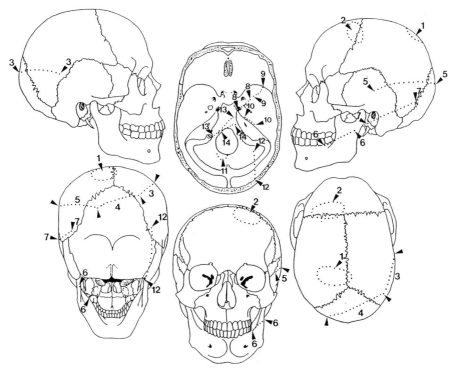

Fig. 8.2 Human skull with cranial injuries of victim II (1 to 14), arrowed.

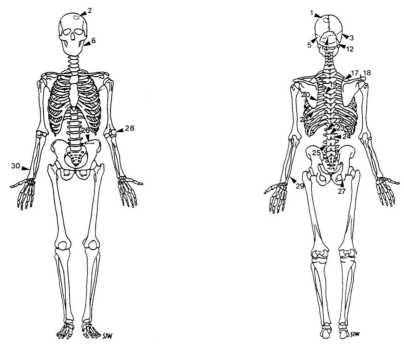

Fig. 8.3 Front view of human skeleton showing
post-cranial injuries of victim II, arrowed.

Fig. 8.4 Back view of human skeleton showing
post-cranial injuries of victim II, arrowed.

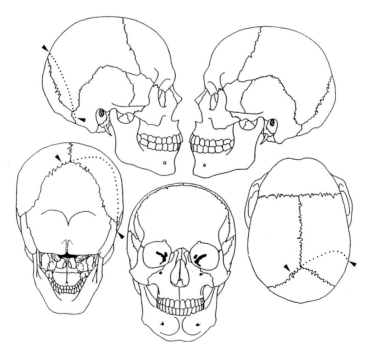

Fig. 8.5 Human skull showing injury of victim III.

Victim IV (Fig. 8.6)

Victim IV was a male, aged 25–35 years and height 179 cm. He shows three cranial injuries. The first lies over the left eye (IV/1), the second (IV/2), is a linear injury 13 cm long to the left temporal and parietal bones and the third (IV/3), is a small injury to the left parietal bone.

Victim V (Fig. 8.7)

Victim V was a male aged 25–35 years and height 172 cm. He has a single linear cranial injury, 13 cm long, to the left frontal and parietal bones. The plane of the injury is at 45° to the horizontal.

Victim VI (Fig. 8.8)

Victim VI was a male aged 20–25 years and height 165 cm. He has a single linear cranial injury, 12 cm long, to the frontal and parietal bones just left of the midline. The plane of the injury is almost vertical.

Positive Identification of Injuries

One of the major problems facing this study was that of pseudopathology. Can the injuries listed above genuinely be termed edged weapon injuries, or could they possibly be the result of other events; for instance, post-depositional fracture?

This problem was overcome by the development of a set of diagnostic criteria which allowed the positive identification of an edged weapon injury. The criteria were initially based on a common-sense assessment of the appearance of bone when cut by a very sharp, fast-moving blade. The criteria were then tested by the experimental cutting of bone by a variety of blades and were found to be valid.

The criteria were the following:

1. Linearity, without large irregularities in the line of the injury.
2. An edge to the injury which was well-defined and clean.
3. A cut bone surface which was flat and smooth and in some cases polished.
4. The presence of parallel scratch marks on some cut bone surfaces.

In addition, the length of a proposed injury was taken into account, as was the pattern of detachment of bone of the outer and inner skull surfaces surrounding the injury. Marks on the bones were regarded as injuries until they failed to meet the above criteria.

If the diagnostic criteria are applied, all except three of the injuries listed above are found to be genuine. Two of victim II's multiple injuries are slightly doubtful, but their removal from the catalogue of damage does not change the overall pattern of the injury. Also, the long cranial injury of victim I does not meet the criteria particularly well, but its length and position argue for it being genuine.

Assuming, therefore, that the Eccles injuries were indeed produced by edged weapons, it remains to consider when in the history of the skeletons these injuries occurred. Because injuries received immediately before and immediately after death cannot be distinguished from each other (McWirr, Viner & Wells 1982; Ortner & Putschar 1981), could the Eccles injuries have been produced post-depositionally? Brothwell (1971) points out that bone injuries of a clean-cut appearance can be produced only when the bone has its full organic matrix, i.e. when it is alive or newly dead. When decomposition is advanced and the bone more brittle, "the vault would have collapsed into many pieces before the cuts could have been produced". This seems to rule out post-depositional trauma as a source of the Eccles injuries and indicates that they occurred at some time when the bone was fresh.

Soft Tissue Injuries and Their Effects

Close examination of a bony injury reveals the presence or absence of healing processes related to the injury. If the injury shows signs of healing then the victim must have survived for some length of time, whereas if there are no signs of healing or any other reaction it can be concluded that the victim died soon after receiving the injury.

The injury of living or freshly dead bone produces well-defined clean-cut surfaces. If the injury is survived, the process of healing begins and the bone is gradually re-modelled. As this process continues, the clean-cut edges are reshaped and the well-defined edges become progressively blurred (Revell 1986). In addition, the bone can become marked with signs of inflammation or infection. It follows that if an injury shows well-defined surfaces it was not survived for long enough for the healing process to begin. Revell (1986) suggests that healing is visible on the bone after five days, although this will vary between individuals.

Thus, completely unhealed injuries are termed 'perimortal' since they were received close to the time of death. Injuries received soon after death will obviously also be unhealed and so cannot be distinguished from those received soon before death.

None of the Eccles injuries shows any evidence of healing or infection and it must be concluded that they are perimortal. However, the position of the injuries on the body makes them almost certainly pre-mortal.

It therefore seems probable that the injuries which the Eccles skeletons show represent the cause of death of the individuals concerned, although there may have been other injuries which failed to contact the bone and so went undetected. Reconstruction of the total injury sheds light on the immediate and delayed effects of the injury upon the individual.

Whilst recognising the limitations to a precise replication of injuries inflicted on one individual onto tissue obtained from another, a reconstruction of the soft tissue injuries of each victim was made, based upon the description of the bone injury already prepared. These reconstructions were made with reference to standard anatomical tests and to dissections of the appropriate regions. The injury to the brain associated with each cranial injury was reconstructed experimentally by mapping the position of each injury onto a human brain.

The cranial injuries of all six individuals showed a similar pattern of soft tissue damages. In all cases, the scalp, the meninges which surround and protect the brain, the brain itself and the blood vessels associated with these three structures would have been injured. The immediate effects of the blows to the head would have been profuse bleeding, especially from the scalp and almost certainly loss of consciousness, due to the force of the blow to the head and its associated shock to the brain. Death may have followed almost immediately from shock to the central nervous system or from blood loss. Certainly victim II would have died from the first of several blows which severed his brainstem, causing the cessation of vital functions. It is possible that the other individuals may have survived longer, though

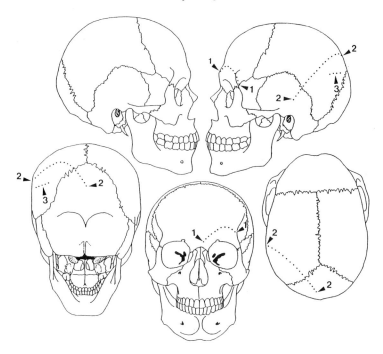

Fig. 8.6   *Human skull showing injuries of victim IV, 1, 2 and 3.*

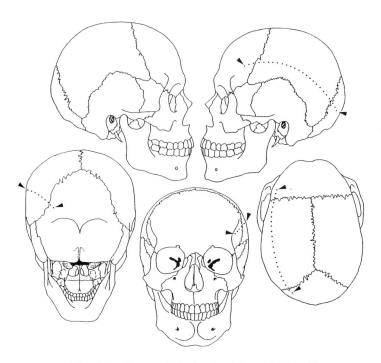

Fig. 8.7   *Human skull showing injury of victim V.*

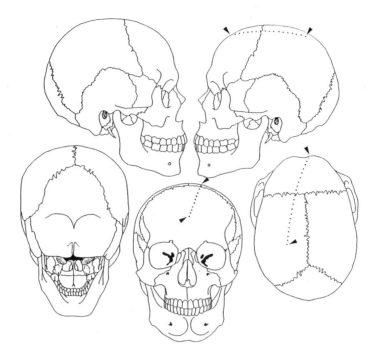

Fig. 8.8   Human skull showing injury of victim VI.

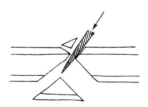

Fig. 8.10a   Cross-section of a typical edged weapon injury showing the blade entering the bone and the pattern of bone detachment.

Fig. 8.10b   Schematic cross-section of injury showing acute and obtuse edges.

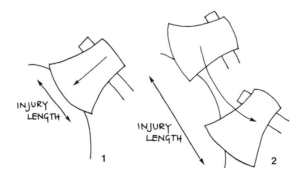

Fig. 8.14   1. Blow of a 'chopping' type, producing a short injury.   2. Blow of a 'slicing' type, producing an injury longer than the weapon itself.

probably never regaining consciousness. If this was the case they succumbed in hours or a few days, either due to infection or to deteriorating central nervous system function.

It is impossible to reconstruct the effects of these injuries in any greater detail since edged weapon injuries to the head are, fortunately, extremely rare today and hence the effects of such injuries are virtually undocumented.

Surprisingly, some head injuries of the extent of those seen in the Eccles skeletons were survived in antiquity (McWhirr, Viner & Wells 1982). However, if such injuries are survived in the long term, there can still be a variety of severe residual defects including epilepsy, chronic headaches, problems with sight and movement, memory loss and a variety of psychological problems.

Only two skeletons (II and III) show post-cranial injury. The projectile injury of victim III did not damage the spinal cord and probably avoided other important structures. However, the injury was probably disabling and may have contributed to the individual's death. Of the multiple post-cranial injuries of victim II, those to the arms best repay study since they reveal that this individual was rendered almost unable to defend himself. Injury II/30, to the right radius (forearm) severed the flexor muscles which allow the forming of a fist or the gripping of any object in the hand, so that the right hand would have been rendered virtually useless. Injuries II/28 and II/29 were to the left arm. II/28 cut across the front of the elbow, having almost the same disabling effect on the left hand. Injury II/29, to the left ulna (forearm) is particularly interesting since its position is such that if this individual was ever carrying a shield he must at this point have lost it. With both arms badly disabled, unable to grip a weapon and without a shield, it is not surprising that victim II succumbed to terrible blows to the head and body.

Weapons and The Injuries They Produce

The characteristics of any injury are to some extent governed by the object or objects which produced it. The bony injury produced by an edged weapon is no exception and the injury reveals a good deal about the weapon which made it.

All the edged weapon injuries encountered in this study show a set of common characteristics which is independent of the type of blade used. The minimum characteristics of cranial injuries are outlined in the diagnostic criteria above; and illustrated in Figure 8.9. The more detailed elements are shown in Figures 8.10 and 8.11, 8.12 and 8.13.

1. At least one side of the injury shows a smooth, flat surface cut by the blade. If the blade entered the bone roughly at right angles then both surfaces may be of this kind. However, if the blade enters the bone at another angle, as shown in Figure 8.10, then it is only the obtuse-angled side which shows a smooth cut surface. The acute-angled side shows a broken surface as in (2) below.

2. On the acute-angled side, the outer surface of bone is detached from the underlying bone as thin flakes. In ancient material. the flakes themselves are normally lost, only the underlying broken surface remaining. In the experimental bone injuries carried out in this study, the flakes remained held in place by the tough membrane which surrounds the bone.

3. Injuries also frequently show large areas of bone broken away from beneath the blade as it passed through. This bone detachment takes the form of large chunks rather than smaller flakes described in (2) above. The detached bone is driven in front of the blade into the underlying meninges and brain. This type of bone detachment does not always occur and it appears to be independent of the angle at which the blade strikes the bone.

These characteristics are common to all the injuries encountered in this study, other than one distinctive type of axe injury where the bone is crushed and fractured rather than cut. We must therefore look to other features of the injury to distinguish between different types of blades. Whilst the mode of use of a weapon may affect the areas of the body it tends to injure, it is the physical characteristics of the blade which are mirrored in the injury. The features of the blade which are important in this respect are its length, its thickness and its sharpness.

The length of a blade is a basic but very useful consideration when distinguishing weapon injuries. An injury cannot be produced by a blade shorter than its own length unless the injury is made by the blade moving in a 'slicing' rather than a 'chopping' fashion (Fig. 8.14). If the injury shows the use of a longer blade this obviously suggests the use of a sword (or long seax) rather than an axe. For instance, with respect to the "so-called Neolithic [actually Saxon] skeleton Q1 from Maiden Castle", for one injury "The length of the incision across the base of the skull would exclude any form of weapon with a cutting edge of less than 110 mm. In other words, it is unlikely that an axe has been used to produce at least this injury" (Brothwell 1971). By this estimation, all the major cranial injuries in the Eccles material, excepting injury II4 at 5 cm long, were produced by a blade at least 8 cm long; the injuries of victims I, V and VI respectively require blades of at least 16 cm, 13 cm and 12 cm long. Thus, the length alone of the major cranial injuries of the Eccles material suggests that they were produced by swords.

However, experimental cutting of human bone showed that an axe which was not particularly sharp could produce injuries almost identical to the Eccles injuries in even their detailed characteristics. The only major differences in the axe injury was the length (5–7 cm) and the presence of fractures extending from the ends of the injury. These, termed terminal fractures, often lie in the same line as the injury proper and are split fractures, apparently resulting from the blade behaving as a wedge. The ability of a blade to behave as a wedge is determined by its thickness: the thicker the blade behind its cutting edge, the greater the splitting potential. Thus, the presence of terminal fractures in a cranial injury indicates that it was made by a thicker blade. The experimental cutting of bone with a variety of blades has shown that axe injuries are very much more likely to show terminal fractures than are sword injuries.

Of the Eccles cranial injuries, only one (injury VI) shows possible terminal fracturing but this may be the result of post-depositional damage. This absence of terminal fractures also points to the Eccles injuries having been inflicted by a sword.

One type of injury enountered in this study can undoubtedly be distinguished as being produced by an axe. This injury is of additional interest since it demonstrates that one weapon can produce very different injuries, i.e. a sword-like injury but with terminal fractures and, if landing with less force, a crushing and fracturing injury.

This second injury type is unlike any seen in the Eccles material but was produced on

Fig. 8.9 The cranial injury of victim III to show the criteria for identification of an edged weapon injury – a clearly defined edge (single arrow) and a flat smooth surface (double arrow). Scale in mm.

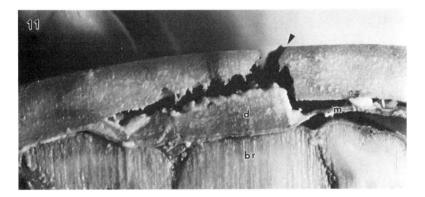

Fig. 8.11 Cross section of experimental axe injury. Arrow indicates direction of blow. d = detached bone driven inwards; br = brain; m = meninges.

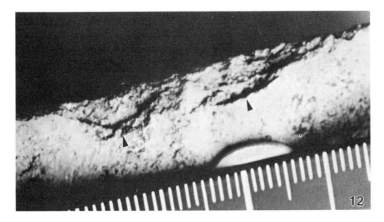

Fig. 8.12 Flaking of the outer table (arrowed) on the "acute" side of injury. Victim IV. Scale in mm.

Fig. 8.13 Axe and experimental second injury to the cranial vault.
sw = sword injury; c = cut surface; b = broken surface; d = detached bone driven inwards.

Fig. 8.15 Ancient unprovenanced axe injury to skull
A66 of the Walmesley Collection, Belfast. × 1

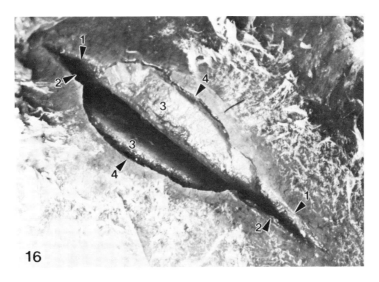

Fig. 8.16   Experimental axe injury × 1. 1. Tapered terminal regions; 2. Crushed bone of terminal regions; 3. Fractured bone driven inwards; 4. Fracture outline producing wide central region of injury.

Fig. 8.17   A scanning electron micrograph of a resin replica of the surface of a cut on the occipital bone of victim II. Note the coarse and fine parallel scratches (arrowed), visible even at very high magnification.
(× 900)

Fig. 8.18   Experimental sword injury, scanning electron micrograph of actual bone specimen, showing parallel scratches (arrowed).   × 12.5

Fig. 8.19   Scanning electron micrograph of a resin cast of the edge of a replica Anglo-Saxon sword. The edge of the blade is marked by an arrow, the star indicates a dent in the edge, a possible cause of scratches on cut surfaces.   × 60

experimental bone cutting and also shown in an ancient but unprovenanced skull in the Walmsley Collection, Queen's University, Belfast (Figs. 8.15 and 8.16). The experimental injury barely penetrated the bone surface and owed more to sudden localised compression than to cutting. The ends of the injury showed crushed bone with an outline matching the profile of the blade. The central region shows two plates of bone, detached and driven inwards by the blade. In the ancient injury, the central region shows a large hole where such a fractured plate of bone has been lost.

In addition to the macroscopic features of edged weapon injuries, this study has investigated the microscopic appearance of the cut bone surfaces. This initially involved light microscopy, but scanning electron microscopy (SEM), which gives high resolution images of surface structures, proved a more valuable technique. Both the bone itself and resin replicas of injuries were studied by SEM.

The most striking feature of cut surfaces is the presence on most of them of parallel scratch marks (Figs. 8.17 and 8.18). Experimental bone cutting demonstrated that these marks indicate the direction in which the blade was moving as it cut the bone and therefore they are almost certainly produced by irregularities in the edge of the blade (Figure 8.19). The cut surfaces of experimental injuries showed parallel scratch marks almost identical to those seen on the Eccles material. This further confirms that the Eccles injuries were produced by edged weapons and it seems likely that the use of SEM will prove valuable in the future diagnosis of edged weapon injuries. Interpretation of the surface structure of cut surfaces using SEM also has the potential to reveal much about the structure of the weapons which made them.

Cranial Injury and Fighting Patterns

The pattern of combat, which occurs during an armed conflict, influences the areas of the body which are injured (Inglemark 1939; Manchester 1983). Thus, by considering the positions of the Eccles injuries it is possible to gain insight into the kind of conflict which resulted in the death of these individuals.

All of the Eccles injuries were probably produced by swords. Single combat between swordsmen followed an almost formalised pattern and tended to produce a clearly defined pattern of injuries. A right-hander would hold the shield on the left arm and the sword in the right hand. The adversaries faced one another and blows were dealt by each in turn, with a slight pause between each blow (Frontispiece). Blows were aimed downwards onto the head, shoulders and arms. In most cases the literary sources describe a cutting stroke, although thrusting strokes are occasionally referred to (Davidson 1962).

This kind of single combat produces a distinctive pattern of injuries (Inglemark 1939; Manchester 1983). The easiest blow to the head from a right-handed attacker lands on the left side of the opponent's head or body. As a result, the majority of cranial blows fall to the front of the left side of the head (left fronto-parietal region). It is of interest that the effectiveness of blows to the head was recognised by the Anglo-Saxons, as indeed it had been for much of antiquity (Davidson 1962, Courville 1948).

In contrast, multiple blows and blows aimed by attackers standing to the side of or behind victims, are a result of less formalised fighting. Such blows "have probably been struck at warriors who had fallen, were retreating, or were attacked from behind" (Inglemark 1939).

The six Eccles skeletons fall into two clear groups. Skeletons I, V and VI show single injuries in the left fronto-parietal region, and as such these individuals were almost certainly killed by a right-handed opponent who was facing them. It is misleading to state that these individuals died in single combat since, whilst this may have been the case, there is no evidence that they were able to defend themselves. This being the case, their deaths are as likely to have resulted from the efficient dispatch of an ill-defended individual as from single combat proper.

The remaining skeletons, II, III and IV show multiple injuries. Of fifteen major cranial blows in the Eccles material, only four are to the right side of the head (II/3, II/4, II/12 and III) and all occur on the multiply injured skeletons, as do all the blows which were delivered from the side (II/1, II/2, and IV/1). This supports the hypothesis of Inglemark (1939) that multiple blows tend to be the result of disorganised fighting when the position of blows to the head varies.

Victim II, who falls into the multiply injured group, does show signs of having defended himself. The injuries to his arms, discussed above, suggest that his arms were at least raised in self-defence, although the blows they received would have effectively disabled them. It is likely that, following this disablement, victim II was felled by blows to the head, which partially decapitated him. The multiple injuries to the back (at least eight separate blows) were almost certainly delivered after the individual had fallen.

In the absence of stratigraphic information, it is impossible to say whether the six Eccles skeletons represent one or several violent incidents. Certainly the material presents what appears to be a clear group of single and multiple sword injuries, with a single projectile injury, although additional individuals may have died of injuries not detectable on the skeleton. However, if the six skeletons represent a single incident it is clear that a variety of fighting styles was being used.

Acknowledgements

I am grateful to Dr M. Shackley and Dr J. Wakely for supervising this project during my year as an Intercalated B.Sc student in the Department of Anatomy, University of Leicester. I also wish to thank Mr D.H. Adams and Mr G.L.C. McTurk for tuition and technical assistance. Dr Alec Detsicas excavated the Eccles Skeletons on behalf of the Eccles Excavation Committee, and it is by his permission that they feature here as the subject of this study. Dr K. Manchester and Miss C. Roberts of the Calvin Wells Laboratory kindly loaned me the skeletons from Eccles and have given me unlimited advice and assistance. Professor K. Carr and all the staff of the Anatomy Department, Queen's University made me welcome in their Department and allowed me to study their collection of skeletal material. I thank Dr P.M. Mason, H.M. Inspector of Anatomy in connection with the experimental studies. Many thanks to the members of the Dark Ages Society for useful discussions and loan of the replica sword and to all in the Departments of Anatomy and Archaeology at Leicester who contributed by their interest and encouragement.

References

Brothwell, D.R. 1971: Forensic aspects of the so-called skeleton Q1 from Maiden Castle, Dorset, *World Archaeology* 3, 233–241.

Courville, C. 1948: War weapons as an index of contemporary knowledge of the nature and significance of craniocerebral trauma, *Medical Arts and Sciences* (July), 2:3.

Davidson, H.R.E. 1962: *The Sword in Anglo-Saxon England*. (Oxford University Press, Oxford).

Inglemark, B.E. 1939: The Skeletons, *Armour from the Battle of Wisby 1361*, ed. Thordeman, B. (Stockholm, Sweden).

Manchester, K. 1983: *The Archaeology of Disease*. (Bradford University Press, Bradford).

Manchester, K. 1984: Eccles Skeletal Report. Unpublished.

McWhirr, A., Viner, L. & Wells, C. 1982: *Romano-British excavations at Cirencester*. (Cirencester Excavation Committee, Cirencester, Gloucestershire).

Ortner, D.J. & Putschar, W.G.J. 1981: *Identification of Pathological Conditions in Human Skeletal remains*. (Smithsonian Institution Press, New York).

Revell, P.A. 1986: *Pathology of Bone*. (Springer-Verlag, London, Heidelberg, New York).

Chapter 9

Did the Anglo-Saxons have warhorses?

R. H. C. Davis

A warhorse was no ordinary horse. Not only did it have to be trained for battle, but it had also to be large enough and strong enough to give its rider a real advantage over foot-soldiers. Finding a horse of the right size was not easy, because the indigenous horse of N.W. Europe and Britain was no larger than a Shetland pony (8–10 hands). To produce a larger horse it was necessary to embark on selective breeding. During the Middle Ages this became a major industry. We do not know the average height of the Normans' horses, though we might guess it was about 12 hands, but there can be no doubt that at the time they were considered magnificently large, and that subsequent breeders succeeded in producing beasts that were still larger. By the fourteenth century 'great horses' stood at 16 or 18 hands, a size which was subsequently reckoned too large for use in cavalry.

Did the Anglo-Saxons also attempt to produce horses large enough for service in war? The horseshoes and equine bones discovered so far have indicated only small horses, but at any period of the Middle Ages the majority of horses would have been small, being used as packhorses or peasant workhorses. Warhorses would have been much larger, but they would have been rarely seen except on battlefields or in specialized stud farms. The purchase price of a good horse could easily be twenty or thirty times as much as that of a horse which was only just rideable, and the cost of its upkeep was also very much greater.

Fodder is never cheap, but it is one of the most important factors in breeding for size and strength. A mare which is left in the open to find what little grazing exists will be half-starved in the winter months when she is carrying her offspring which, in consequence, will be born weak and small. The improvement to be observed when the mare is fed with hay and oats throughout the winter is very great indeed. It can be compared with the remarkable rise in the height of children in Great Britain as a result of the nationwide provision of special foods (milk, cod-liver oil, fruit juices etc.) in the years after the Second World War.

A further expensive requirement for selective breeding is the segregation of the better mares, so as to ensure that they are covered only by the best stallions. In the Middle Ages this was effected by keeping the mares in parks surrounded by fences sufficiently tall and strong to keep all other horses out. A selected stallion would then be put in with the mares and left there until he had had the opportunity of covering them all. His efforts would have been in vain if some other male horse had broken through the park fence and anticipated him. Consequently the maintenance of park fences was of the utmost importance, even though it was expensive.

We know that the Anglo-Saxons had stud farms by the end of the tenth century, because they are mentioned in wills from then onwards. Since specially fine horses are mentioned much earlier, the 'royal' horse which King Oswine (644–51) gave to St Aidan being a particularly good example,[1] it must be suspected that kings or rich nobles had some sort of stud farms from an early date. A clue to their form of organization comes from a charter of King Ceolwulf of Mercia, dated 875, in which he freed 'the whole diocese of the Hwicce [i.e. Worcester] from the feeding of the king's horses and those who lead them.[2] If this 'farming out' of the horses onto religious houses had been a general rule, it would help to explain how it was that in the ninth century the Danish invaders had relatively little difficulty in finding horses for themselves; they had only to seize the relevant churches and hold them and their occupants to ransom until horses were produced. The Alfredian Chronicle makes a point of stating where the Danes 'horsed' themselves, referring twice over to the shameful fact that in 876 they had succeeded in doing so within Alfred's own Kingdom at Wareham where, it will be recalled, there was a notable minster church. Subsequently the Chronicle records how the Danes obtained horses in Flanders (881), lost their horses at Rochester (885), shipped horses to England from the continent in 892 and lost most of then at Buttington-on-Severn in 893.

The Chronicle also refers, from 877 onwards, to the English army *riding* in pursuit of the Danes and in 896 to new royal officials called 'horse-thegns'. Some thirty years later decrees of Alfred's grandson, King Athelstan (929–39), declared that every landowner should provide two well-mounted men for every plough in his possession, and that no horse should be sent overseas except as a present.[3] Both these decrees are similar to, and probably inspired by, Frankish laws of the late eighth and ninth centuries, and suggest that the organization of the English army may not have been unlike that of the Franks.

Nonetheless, even though the English were clearly capable of riding to war on horseback, it remains uncertain whether they also fought on horseback or dismounted for the battle. The question has been debated endlessly and remains unresolved, but some progress may be made if we concentrate on the availability of the right sort of horse. In later centuries it was axiomatic that a knight needed one horse for battle and another for riding. Quite apart from the fact that a trained warhorse would be unlikely to give a comfortable ride, it would have been too tired to perform well in battle if it had already been ridden for several hours. Consequently it was normally led by a squire who would have been mounted on a less valuable horse, while a servant looked after the packhorse which would have been carrying the knight's armour and other luggage. Every knight, in short, required two horses for himself, a third for his squire and a fourth for the luggage. By the thirteenth century he often required two more for armed assistants.

The number of horses required by the more important Anglo-Saxons can be deduced, at any rate from the middle of the tenth century, from the heriots mentioned in their wills. The number is usually three or four, and in the eleventh century it begins to be stated that only half the horses were to be saddled[4] (e.g. the Will of Alfwold Bishop of Crediton, c. 1008–12). This situation was formalized c. 1023 in the laws of King Cnut which laid it down that an earl's heriot included 8 horses (4 saddled and 4 unsaddled) with 4 helmets, 4 coats of mail and 4 swords with 8 spears and shields, while a King's thegn's heriot included only 4 horses (2 saddled and 2 unsaddled) with 2 swords, one helmet, one coat of mail and 4 spears and shields. In each case the attendants leading the unsaddled horses seem to have been provided with a spear and shield, while each of the warriors proper had two horses, presumably one warhorse and one riding horse.[5]

Another fact which suggests that the English army was becoming increasingly cavalry-minded is the introduction of the office of staller. This has recently been discussed by Kathrin Mack[6] and by Pamela Nightingale,[7] but neither of them questions the thesis of L.M. Larson, which Stenton also adopted, that the office was 'Norse in name and origin and that it came into England with the Danish host of King Cnut', deriving its name from a 'stall' or important seat in the King's hall, so that a 'staller' was 'anyone with a permanent and recognized position in the King's hall'.[8]

Larson's theory depended on much material which was not contemporary, notably the *Formannasaga*, *St Olaf's Saga* and the *De Inventione Sancte Crucis ... Waltham*, and the late F.E. Harmer established that it was not supported by the record evidence which suggests, rather, that the office of staller was introduced into England by King Edward the Confessor at the beginning of his reign (1042).[9] Since Edward had spent the previous twenty-nine years of his life in Normandy, it is surely likely that the office which he was introducing was one with which he had become familiar there, and that the word 'staller' was simply an Anglicization of the Franco-Norman constable or *comes stabuli*. This was what almost all etymologists and historians had believed before Larson, but subsequently they had become unwilling to believe that any Anglo-Saxon King could have needed a military officer whose control of the stables suggested the existence of a cavalry force.

In fact five of the eight known stallers can be shown to have exercised military functions, to have been concerned with the King's stables or horses, or to have been described after 1066 as 'constable'. To judge from their attestations in charters, there were probably three stallers in office at any one time. The list of them is:

1. Osgod Clapa. Though he attested several charters for King Cnut as *minister* and *miles*, he appears as *stallere* only in the D version of the *A.S.C.* for 1046 (*recte* 1045). Exiled in 1045, he returned at the head of 29 ships in 1049 in an attempt to raid or invade the Kingdom.
2. Ælfstan occurs in Robertson, *Charters* no. 101, after Christmas 1145.
3. Esgar, cccurs in a writ of Edward the Confessor c. 1042 (*Writs* no. 75), and in Robertson's *Charters*, nos. 114, 115, 117. He survived till about 1066, being a principal *antecessor* of Geoffrey de Mandeville (e.g. *D.B.* i.132 where he is specifically styled staller). As 'Ansgar' he also figures prominently in the *Carmen de Hastingae Proelio* which credits him with the defence of London against William the Conqueror. It is likely, however, that the *Carmen* is no earlier than the twelfth century, and the importance which it attributes to Ansgar may have been due to a desire to support the claims of Geoffrey de Mandeville II to exercise a similar influence in London: during the reign of King Stephen.
4. Leofyng or Lyfing occurs c. 1053–5 in Robertson, *Charters* nos. 114, 115.
5. Raulf c. 1053–68/70 figures in Robertson, *Charters* 114, 115, 117, and in Domesday Book in Lincs., Norf., Suff. and Cornwall. In Lincolnshire five of his manors owed a total of 300 *s*. for fodder for (the King's) horses (*ad victum equorum*) (*D.B.* i.347b–348).
6. Robert (Fitz-Wimarc) c. 1053–68. Harmer, *Writs* 83, 85; *Reg.* i no. 23 (1068). The *Vita Edwardi*, p. 70, refers to him as *Robertus regis palatii stabilitator* (*recte* stabiliarius).
7. Eadnoth c. 1053–67. Harmer, *Writs* 85; *Reg.* i no. 7 (1067). He held land T.R.E. in Berks. as *Ednod stalre* (*D.B.* i.58b) and in Wilts. as *Ednod dapifer* (*ibid.* i.69), and was

killed in battle in Somerset resisting Harold's sons who had landed there in 1067 (*A.S.C.* (D) 1067).

8. Bondig c. 1061–67. Robertson, *Charters* no. 117, *Reg.* i no. 23 (1067). T.R.E. held lands in Bucks. and Beds. as *Boding constabularius* (*D.B.* i.151 *bis*) and *Bondi stalrus* (*D.B.* i.218b).

In this list I have not included *Thored steallare*. Larson gave him great prominence since he appears as a witness in an alleged charter of King Cnut (Robertson, *Charters* 85 (Sawyer 981)), but it is now recognized that this charter is spurious and its witness-list chronologically impossible.

Notes

1. Bede, *Historia Ecclesiastica* Bk. iii, ch. 14.
2. *English Historical Documents*, i, ed. Dorothy Whitelock, no. 95 (Sawyer no. 215).
3. II Athelstan, 16 and 18 (*English Hist. Docs.* i no. 35, p. 384).
4. Will of Ælfwold Bishop of Crediton (1008–12), *The Crawford Collection of Early Charters*, ed. A.S. Napier and W.H. Stevenson (Oxford, 1895), no. 10 (Sawyer no. 1492).
5. *English Hist. Docs.* i no. 50, clauses 71, 71a, 71.1. See also N.P. Brooks 'Arms, Status and Warfare in Late-Saxon England' in *Ethelred the Unready*, ed. David Hill (*B.A.R.* British Series, 59 (1979)), 81–103.
6. *Journal of Medieval History* 12 (1986), 123–34.
7. *English Historical Review* 102 (1987), 564–6.
8. L.M. Larson, *The King's Household in England before the Norman Conquest* (Madison, 1904), 146–52.
9. F.E. Harmer, *Anglo-Saxon Writs* (Manchester, 1952), pp. 50–52.
10. Abbreviations used in these notes are:
    A.S.C.: *Anglo-Saxon Chronicle*
    Robertson, *Charters*: A.J. Robertson, *Anglo-Saxon Charters*, 2nd ed. (Cambridge, 1956)
    Carmen: *Carmen de Hastingae Proelio*, ed. Catharine Morton and Hope Muntz (Oxford Medieval Texts, 1972) and my own critique in *E.H.R.* 93 (1978), 241–61
    Harmer, *Writs*: as in n. 9 above
    Reg. i: *Regesta Regum Anglo-Normannorum*, ed. H.W.C. Davis (Oxford, 1913)
    Vita Edwardi: *The Life of King Edward the Confessor*, ed. Frank Barlow (Nelson's Medieval Texts, London, 1962)
    D.B.: Domesday Book

References

Davis, R.H.C. 1987: The Warhorses of the Normans, *Anglo-Norman Studies*.
Davis, R.H.C. 1989: *The Medieval Warhorse: Origin, Development and Redevelopment* (Thames & Hudson).

Chapter 10

The Place-Name Burton and Variants

Margaret Gelling

The compound of the nominative case of *burh*, 'fort', with *tūn*, the commonest Old English settlement-term, is found in 47 examples of Burton, 11 of Bourton, one of Boreton and 7 of Broughton. (It should be noted, however, that Broughton is more frequently derived from *brōc–tūn* 'brook settlement' than from *burhtūn*.)

The term *byrhtūn*, from the genitive of *burh*, is found in 3 examples of modern Burton (one of which is Burton on Trent), 2 Buertons in Cheshire, and Bierton in Buckinghamshire.

A third form, *byrigtūn*, from the dative of *burh*, gives rise to 7 examples of Berrington, one of Burrington, and 3 of Burton. This form is the most westerly, occurring in Gloucestershire, Herefordshire, Worcestershire, Shropshire and Somerset.

There are 4 eccentric modern developments: Humberton (Yorkshire), Barton (Isle of Wight), *Norbelton* (Sussex) and Boreham (Wiltshire). The first 3 are from *burhtūn*; Boreham is from *byrigtūn*. *Norbelton* in Hellingly, Sussex, is lost a name, recorded in that form in the 14th century, but as *Norburton* in 1287. A few other names included in the above statistics are also those of vanished settlements.

It has hitherto been assumed that these place-names could arise from three separate situations, which were:

a) the proximity of a *tūn* to an ancient fort;
b) the proximity of a *tūn* to an earlier or more important settlement with a name ending in *burh*;
c) the existence of a particular type of settlement known as a *burhtūn*.

The experiment of plotting these names on a map has suggested, however, that they may all arise from the same situation, and that in Mercia they may refer to a system of defence posts which remained operative until the Danish wars of the late ninth century. The proximity of some of the places to prehistoric forts, and to settlements with names like Aldborough (Yorkshire), Tutbury (Staffordshire), Tenbury (Worcestershire), does not seem to be a more marked phenomenon than can reasonably be ascribed to coincidence when the number of names to be considered is eighty-seven.

Several interesting and unexpected points are brought out by the mapping of these names. The distribution is not even throughout the country. They are mainly characteristic of Mercia and southern Northumbria. There is a notable series in the West Saxon shires of Wiltshire and Dorset, but they are absent or very rare in the rest of Wessex, and in the whole of East Anglia, Kent, Sussex and the area which may have belonged to an early kingdom of Middlesex (Fig. 10.1).

In some counties the names are very evenly spaced. See, for example, the three in the eastern part of Warwickshire, and the three south of Lincoln, in Kesteven. It was this characteristic, of there being two or three to a county in parts of the midlands, which first suggested that it would be worth while plotting them on a map. But there are also some heavy concentrations, the most notable of which is in the Welsh Marches.

Also in the Welsh Marches is the major concentration of names containing Old English *burhweard*, 'fort guardian'. I have noted 9 occurrences with common place-name generics in the whole country, and apart from Buscot in Berkshire and an obsolete name in Kent they are all in Cheshire, Shropshire and Herefordshire. The seven names in the Marches are Burwardsley and Brewer's Hall in Cheshire; Broseley and Burwarton in Shropshire; a Domesday manor called *Burwardestone* which lay partly in Cheshire and partly in Flintshire; another Domesday *Burardestune* which can be firmly identified with Bollingham House in Eardisley, Herefordshire; and Treverward in the parish of Clun (Shropshire), which is *Treboreward* in 1284, an obvious Welsh version of Burwarton, as Trebirt in Llanfair Waterdine is an obvious Welsh rendering of Burton. There is also Burslem Staffordshire, which is probably 'estate near Lyme forest belonging to a *burhweard*'.

Burhweard in these place-names has always been explained as a personal name, but the highly specialised distribution suggests a more significant interpretation. There is no record of an official with the title *burhweard*, but this does not seem to me conclusive evidence against the existence of such an office in Mercia in the ninth century. Buscot in Berkshire may be specially significant. The use of the generic *cot* in this name has always seemed surprising, as the estate was assessed at 40 hides in the time of King Edward. There is no other settlement in Buscot parish, and the surrounding land-units are all named in the Domesday survey. If the impression given by the distribution map of a heavy defence of this area at some period be correct, this could have led to the granting of a hitherto humble settlement called *Cote* to an official who was put in charge of the local defences, and this could have resulted in the development of the estate, subsequently called *Burgweardescote*. A likely time for such events would be between 779, when King Offa of Mercia re-occupied the debatable land on either side of the R. Thames, and the mid-ninth century, when Berkshire finally reverted to Wessex.

The other category of names shown on the map consists of four instances of *burh-ēg*, 'fort island'. The three along the Thames (Laleham Burway, Borough Marsh near Sonning, and Burroway near Bampton) are remarkably evenly spaced. The fourth is Burway near Ludlow, Shropshire. There is a prehistoric fort called Burroway Castle at the site near Bampton, Oxfordshire (Lambrick 1984), and the name may mean simply 'island with an ancient fort'; but the possibility of re-use in the eighth and ninth centuries deserves consideration.

The Welsh Marches emerges on the map as the most-heavily defended region in the country. As regards concentrations of Burton names in Northumbria, the series which runs from Scarborough towards Spurn Head looks like a carefully planned coastal defence, though it is curious that the line does not continue to the north of Scarborough. The series which runs up the R. Ure in the North Riding covers the main route across the Pennines, and the more widely-spaced series running up the R. Trent into the midlands also makes good strategic sense.

In Wessex, the names cluster on the Dorset/Wiltshire/Somerset border, where the forest of Selwood was the boundary between Saxon and British lands in the mid-seventh century.

Bourton in the northern tip of Dorset is adjacent to Penselwood, which may be the place (*æt Peonnum*) where the West Saxons defeated the Britons in 658. When I presented this thesis to a seminar at Leicester University it was pointed out to me that I ought not to claim a date between 600 and 650 as the likely one for the origin of a group of Burton names, as we have good evidence that *tūn* was not much used in place-name formation till about 750. I acknowledge the difficulty. But *burhtūn* could have been in the language as an appellative from the earliest date of the organisation of the kingdoms, and the appellative could have replaced earlier place-names at a date, perhaps in the eighth century, when functional names in *tūn* became fashionable. The *burhtūns* were probably established at pre-existing settlements, and earlier names doubtless dropped out, as they must have done at all the Prestons, Charltons and Kingstons. In order to associate the 5 *burhtūn* names near Penselwood with events of the seventh century, it would be necessary to assume that this was still felt to be border territory between ancient Wessex and Wessex beyond Selwood throughout the eighth century, and that the defence points were maintained after the victory of 658.

There is a marked difference in status between the Mercian and Northumbrian names and those in Wessex. In Mercia and Northumbria, though only Burton on Trent became a town, a very high proportion of the examples are parishes or townships and/or Domesday manors. In Wessex, while there are some Domesday manors, the majority of the names belong to subsidiary settlements, many of them not recorded till the 13th century. (Bourton in north-west Berkshire can be counted as a Mercian, rather than a West Saxon, example.) The superior status of the places with these names in Mercia and southern Northumbria could be due to the postulated defence system surviving longer there than in Wessex. In Wiltshire and Dorset it was perhaps rendered obsolete by the reorganisation which created the shires sometime in the eighth century.

Anglo-Saxon charters from the late eighth century onwards commonly include a statement that the land granted is to be free from all secular dues except the obligation to provide men for work on bridges, work on fortifications, and service in the army. Sir Frank Stenton (1971, p. 292) considered the implications of *burhbōt* ('fortress repair'), but concluded that there was no reason to suppose that this obligation related to local fortifications which were part of a national scheme of defence. He believed that such a system was organised for the first time in England by King Alfred, as a response to the Danish invasions. It may not be unduly fanciful, however, to see the remains of an earlier system in my distribution map. I suggest that these place-names refer to fixed military centres of the pre-Viking period. The forts could be mentioned in place-names without all being operative at the same time. Berrington and Boreton in Shropshire are so close that a replacement may reasonably be suspected, perhaps Berrington superseding Boreton, since that seems to be the later form of the name. If a substantial number of the forts were functioning contemporaneously it might be conjectured that they were too numerous, and the units manning them too small, to be effective against a highly mobile invasion.

If such centres existed, as mustering places for the *fyrd* and as refuges for villagers whose homes were destroyed by war or other disasters, it is hardly conceivable that the system did not operate in East Anglia and the Home Counties, where these names are rare or absent. (Burtonwood Fm in Great Chesterford, Essex, is a possible instance). It is more probable that in these areas there was a less uniform terminology for the local fortresses. Several other place-names might be considered. These include *burh-steall*, *byrh-steall* (Birstall Yorks. W.

Riding, Burstall Yorks. E. Riding and Suffolk, Birstal Leics., Borstal Kent, Boarstall Bucks.); *burh-stede* (Bursted Kent, Birstead Essex); *burh-stōw* (Burstow Surrey). A compound of *burh* with *hām* (or possibly *hamm*) gives Burpham Surrey and Sussex, and Burham Kent. The Sussex Burpham is one of the forts of the Burghal Hidage, and the defences, which form a promontory fort projecting into the alluvium of the R. Arun, are well-preserved. This may be one of the few instances in which the rulers of Wessex re-used an older fort during the Danish wars. It would, however, be unwise during this early stage of hypothesising to cast the net too widely in a search for names which may be analogous to those from *burhtūn*.

There is a single occurrence of the word *burhtūn* in a literary source. This is in a poem known as *The Wife's Lament*. The woman uttering the lament appears to be homeless and living in the open, and she compares her lodging in a cave to *burgtūnas* which are overgrown with briars and *wīc* (usually translated 'dwellings') which are empty of joy. This establishes that *burhtūn* was a compound appellative in Old English, but it does not give much help with the quest for a precise meaning. It would, at least, be consistent with the interpretation of *burhtūn* as 'place of refuge'.

When this paper was presented in Oxford, Professor Nicholas Brooks commented that the names plotted on my map might reflect the strengthening of settlement-defences by individual landowners whose estates were in dangerous territory, rather than being evidence of a coherent defence system established by rulers of Anglo-Saxon kingdoms. This is obviously possible; but in view of the charter-provision for work on fortresses, we are entitled to look for officially-designated defence posts of the pre-Viking era.

The main aim of this paper is to present a list of place-names in which Old English *burh* is compounded with *tūn*, and to draw attention to the distribution of these and of names containing *burhweard*. If the names are adjudged to be no more than a reflection of unstable conditions in certain areas, they will still be of some interest to students of Anglo-Saxon military history. They are commended to the attention of local historians. It would be gratifying if relevant archaeological evidence were to be found at one of them.

References

Lambrick, G. 1984: Clanfield: Burroway, *South Midlands Archaeology* (CBA Group 9 Newsletter) 14, 104–5.
Stenton, F.M. 1971: *Anglo-Saxon England*, 3rd edn. (Oxford).

Place-Names derived from OE Burhtūn, Byrhtūn, Byrigtūn

Mercia

Berkshire
1. Bourton, parish on N.W. county boundary. Not in DB, but recorded in a spurious Anglo-Saxon charter which copied place-name spellings from pre-Conquest sources.

Buckinghamshire
1. Bierton, N.E. of Aylesbury. DB manor. Bierton with Broughton is a parish. From *byrhtūn*.
2. Bourton, a mile E. of Buckingham. DB manor.

Cheshire
1. Burton near Tarvin, township and DB manor.
2. Burton in Wirral, parish, first recorded in 1152. The name has been considered to refer to a promontory fort on Burton Point.
3. Buerton, E. of Audlem. Township and DB manor. From *byrhtūn*.
4. Buerton, N.E. of Aldford. Township, first recorded c. 1230. From *byrhtūn*.

Denbighshire
1. Burton, parish, near Cheshire border, first recorded in 1315.
   (There is another parish in Pembrokeshire, first recorded in 1291; this must be a post-Conquest name, and is probably transferred from one of the English Burtons.)

Derbyshire
1. Burton in Bakewell. DB manor. The name has been associated with the fortification at Bakewell which King Edward the Elder ordered to be constructed and manned in 924.
2. *Burton* in Abney. A lost settlement, to which there are a few references starting in 1319.

Gloucestershire
1. Bourton on the Hill, parish and DB manor.
2. Bourton on the Water, parish and DB manor, first recorded in a charter of 949. The name has been considered to refer to the prehistoric earthwork called Salmonsbury, which is near the village.
3. Berrington Mill in Chipping Campden. Marked on 19th-cent. O.S. map ½ mile E. of Chipping Campden. The name is first recorded in 1205, and is from *byrigtūn*.

Herefordshire
1. Burrington, parish and DB manor beside R. Teme. From *byrigtūn*.
2. Berrington Hall, N. of Leominster. First recorded 1223. From *byrigtūn*.
3. Burton Court in Eardisland, W. of Leominster. Mr B. Coplestone-Crow has supplied a good series of 12th–14th cent. spellings.
4. Burton Court in Linton, E. of Ross. Mr B. Coplestone-Crow has supplied *Biriton* 1280, *Buriton* 1282. From *byrigtūn*.
5. Burton Hill in Weobley. Mr Copelstone-Crow supplies *Buriton* 1355, *Buryngton* 1426. From *byrigtūn*.

Leicestershire
1. Burton on the Wolds, near the N. County boundary. Parish and DB manor.
2. Burton Lazars, S.E. of Melton Mowbray. DB manor. Burton and Dalby is a parish.
3. Burton Overy, about half way between Leicester and Market Harborough. Parish and DB manor. The 1″ map marks 'ancient earthworks' beside the church.

Lincolnshire

1. Burton upon Stather. Beside the R. Trent, N. of Scunthorpe. Parish and DB manor.
2. Gateburton. Beside R. Trent, S. of Gainsborough. Parish and DB manor. 2½ miles downstream from West Burton Notts.
3. Burton, N.W. of Lincoln. Parish and DB manor.
4. Brant Broughton, E. of Newark on Trent. DB manor. Brant Broughton and Stragglethorpe constitute a parish.
5. Burton Pedwardine, S.E. of Sleaford. Parish and DB manor.
6. Burton Coggles, S.E. of Grantham. Parish and DB manor. From *byrhtūn*.

Northamptonshire

1. Burton Latimer, S.E. of Kettering. Parish and DB manor.

Nottinghamshire

1. West Burton, S. of Gainsborough, on W. bank of Trent, 2½ miles upstream from Gate Burton Lincs. Parish and DB manor, but very little remains of the village, and this looks a good site for archaeological investigation.
2. Burton Joyce, on N. bank of R. Trent, 5 miles N.E. of Nottingham. Parish and DB manor. The 1″ O.S. map shows earthworks surrounding Burtonwood Fm, N.W. of the village.

Oxfordshire

1. Bourton, N. of Banbury. The parish contains the settlements of Great and Little Bourton. The name is first recorded c. 1210.
2. Black Bourton, N.W. of Bampton. Parish and DB manor.

Shropshire

1. Broughton, 7 miles N. of Shrewsbury. Parish and DB manor, but there is no village.
2. Broughton in Claverley, 5 miles E.S.E. of Bridgnorth. A hamlet, first recorded in 1191.
3. Broughton in Lydham, 1 mile N.W. of Bishop's Castle. Two hamlets (Upper and Lower), the name first recorded in 1255.
4. Berrington, 4 miles S.E. of Shrewsbury. Parish and DB manor. From *byrigtūn*.
5. Boreton, on the opposite side of Cound Brook from 4. DB manor.
6. Bourton in Much Wenlock parish. DB manor.
7. Trebirt in Llanfair Waterdine. Early spellings are *Treburt* 1284, 1381, *Trefburt'* 1345, and this is an obvious Welsh rendering of Burton. Upper and Lower Trebirt are about ½ mile W. of Offa's Dyke. Treverward (a Welsh rendering of Burwarton) is less than 2 miles N.E., on the English side of the Dyke.

Staffordshire

1. Burton on Trent. First mentioned in a document of A.D. 1002–4. From *byrhtūn*.
2. Burton in Castlechurch. This place is shown on the 19th-cent. O.S. map, 2 miles S. of Stafford. DB manor.
3. Broughton, 1½ miles S. of Ashley. This is *Burghton* 1281, *Borghton* 1327, and is a likely candidate for DB *Hereborgestone*, which has *here* 'army' as first element.

Warwickshire

1. Burton Hastings, 3 miles S.E. of Nuneaton. Parish, first mentioned in document of 1002–4.
2. Bourton on Dunsmore, 5 miles S.W. of Rugby. Parish and DB manor.
3. Burton Dassett, 8 miles N.W. of Banbury. Originally a settlement in Dassett, first recorded in 1327. Probably from *byrigtūn*.

Worcestershire
1. Burton Court in Lower Sapey, 10 miles N.W. of Worcester. First recorded in 1293.
2. Berrington, 1½ miles W. of Tenbury Wells. DB manor. From *byrigtūn*. Burford Shrops, 1 mile E. on the north bank of the R. Teme, is *burh-ford*. Little Hereford Shrops, 1 mile W., also on the north bank, means 'army ford'.

Northumbria

Lancashire
1. Broughton in Manchester. Township. First recorded 1177.
2. Burtonwood, N.W. of Warrington. Township. First recorded 1200.

Westmorland
1. Burton in Kendal. Parish and DB manor.
2. Burton in Warcop, first recorded in 1265. An interesting moorland site at GR NY 744186. The 19th-cent. O.S. map shows a Hall and some buildings which are not on modern maps. A mountain 2½ miles N.E. is called Burton Fell, and there seems little doubt that Burton has been a village. There is a rectangular banked enclosure called Howgill Fold immediately W. of Burton Fm which was classified by the Royal Commission on Historical Monuments as 'an ancient village settlement'.

Yorkshire, East Riding
1. North Burton or Burton Fleming. Parish and DB manor.
2. Burton Agnes. Parish and DB manor.
3. Brandesburton. Parish and DB manor.
4. Hornsea Burton. DB manor in the parish of Hornsea.
5. Burton Constable, W. of Aldbrough. DB manor.
6. Burton Pidsea, S. of Aldbrough. Parish and DB manor.
7. Bishop Burton and Cherry Burton, adjacent parishes W. of Beverley, both DB manors.
8. Burton Fields, immediately E. of Stamford Bridge. Recorded as *pratis de Burtuna* in the 12th cent.

Yorkshire, North Riding
1. Humberton, N.E. of Boroughbridge. Township and DB manor.
2. Burton on Yore, E. of Masham. Township and DB manor. An adjacent township is called Aldburgh.
3. Constable Burton, E. of Leyburn. Township in the parish of Finghall, first recorded c. 1280.
4. West Burton, township in Aysgarth parish. DB manor.
5. Burtondale in Scarborough, first recorded in 1210. This is the most northerly of a line of names down the east coast.

Yorkshire, West Riding
1. Burton Leonard. Parish and DB manor. This is one of a series of names up the R. Ure; the others are catalogued as 1–4 under the North Riding.
2. Burton Hall, 3 miles S.W. of Selby. DB manor, first recorded c. 1030.
3. Kirkburton and Highburton, S.E. of Huddersfield. Kirkburton is a township, both are DB manors. From *byrhtūn*.
4. Burton in Lonsdale. Township and DB manor.

Wessex and the South

Dorset
1. Bourton, in the northern tip of the county. Parish and large village, first recorded in 1212.
2. Burton near Dorchester. A hamlet, N. of the R. Frome. First recorded in 1212.

3. Burton near Stalbridge. First recorded in c. 1250. The place is not shown on 1″ maps, and the symbol on the map has been placed at Stalbridge.
4. East and West Burton, 6 miles W. of Wareham. East Burton is a fairly large village. First recorded in 1212.
5. Long Burton, S. of Sherborne. Parish and large village. First recorded in 1285.

Hampshire
1. Burton, N. of Christchurch. Village. First recorded 1316.
2. Barton Manor in Whippingham parish, in the N. tip of the Isle of Wight. First recorded in 1274. It is possible that two names, one from *beretūn* and one from *burhtūn*, have coalesced, but a great many of the early spellings point to the existence of a *burhtūn* here.

Kent
1. Great and Little Burton in Kennington, N.E. of Ashford. The 19th-cent. O.S. map shows Burton House where the modern map has Spearpoint Corner. First recorded in 1219, probably from *byrhtūn*.

Somerset
1. Bourton near Wick St Lawrence, N.E. of Weston super Mare. A hamlet, first recorded in 1274.
2. Burrington, 4 miles N.E. of Axbridge. Village, first recorded *c.* 1190. From *byrigtūn*.

Sussex
1. Westburton in the parish of Bury, N. of Arundel. First recorded in 1230. This has been explained as 'farm to the west of and belonging to Bury', but it is much more likely to be a *burhtūn* distinguished by the prefix West- from another *burhtūn* which may not have survived long enough to be recorded. The name of the nearby parish of Burton has a different derivation.
2. *Westburton* in Friston, W. of Eastbourne. this is *Westbortone* in DB, and is last recorded in 1677. It is known to have been part of Crowlink Fm. The reason for the prefix West- is no more apparent than in the preceding example. It does lie slightly to the west of the next example, but 'south' would have been a better description.
3. Broughton in Jevington. A DB manor, not on modern maps, but known to have lain between Crane Down Bottom and Folkington Park.
4. *Norbelton*, a lost place in Hellingly, N. of Hailsham. First recorded as *Norburton* in 1287. Probably 'north *burhtūn*'. It is the most northerly of the three examples in East Sussex.

Wiltshire
1. Burton Hill, S. of Malmesbury. First recorded in 1248. The place lies immediately across the R. Avon from Malmesbury; cf. the position of the second Dorset example in relation to Dorchester.
2. Burton in Nettleton parish, a village beside the Wilts/Glouc border. First recorded in 1204.
3. Bourton in Bishop's Canning parish, N.E. of Devizes. Hamlet, first recorded in 1279.
4. Bourton Fm in Maddington, first recorded in 1327. The name does not appear on 1″ maps, and the symbol has been placed at Maddington.
5. Burton, E. of Mere. A hamlet, first recorded in 1204. This and no. 6 should be considered in conjunction with the three examples in north Dorset.
6. *Burton*, now Boreham, E. of Warminster, first recorded in 1241. From *byrigtūn*. The most northerly of a group of five examples.

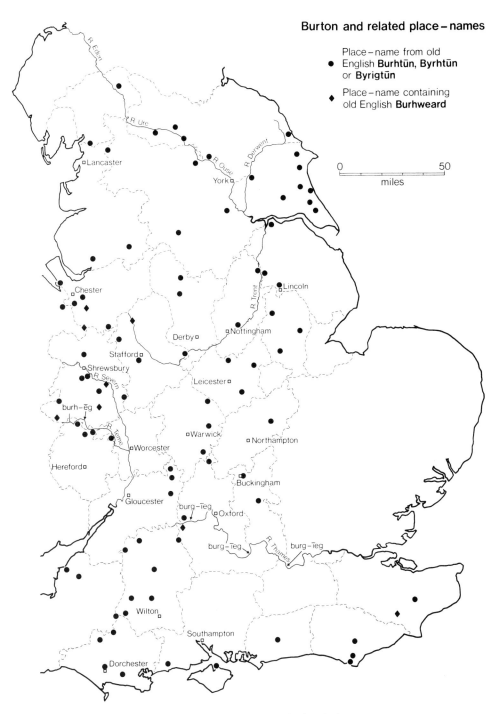

Fig. 10.1   Distribution of Burton and related place-names

Chapter 11

Anthropology and the Study of Pre-Conquest Warfare and Society: The Ritual War in Anglo-Saxon England

Guy Halsall

Archaeologists, especially those studying prehistoric societies, have long been aware of the value of anthropological work in broadening horizons or in providing alternative models to explain given sets of data. In the historical periods, however, such an approach has not been as widely adopted. Anthropological studies may nevertheless be a very valuable aid to our understanding of the nature of pre-conquest warfare. We may, if we take notice of the essential warnings provided by, for example, Professor Ucko (Ucko, 1969), use such data to open up new fields of debate in the study of Anglo-Saxon warfare and society. In this paper I should like to make a brief survey of anthropological work on conflict in pre-industrial societies – the varying levels of violence, the division of war into different phases and the reasons for, and purposes and results of, such warfare. Then, applying the model so created to the data from pre-Conquest England, I would like to examine one particular area in which anthropology may help increase our knowledge of the character of Old English warfare and possibly open up one new area for debate.

Part One[1]

In many early societies anthropological work has shown that violence is clearly divided into various levels, with warfare, as it is usually understood in the twentieth-century West, occupying only the very top rung. An example of this from one comparatively undeveloped society might be sought among the Yanomamö of the Brazilian-Venezuelan border (Chagnon, 1963). Here the lowest order of violence between members of different groups is the chest-pounding duel, in which the antagonists deliver, and receive, an equal number of fearsome punches on the chest, until one side feels unable to go on or decides to escalate the combat to the next scale – the side-slapping duel. This operates on similar principles to the chest-pounding duel but is more dangerous since the blows can lead to unconsciousness. If desired, one side may sue for the use of the flat sides of machetes or axes to raise the intensity of the duel. The next stage, if the dispute still cannot be settled or if tempers rise further (as they frequently do), is the club fight, in which the participants strike each other about the head (or in the heat of action more usually the arms and shoulders) with long clubs.

155

Needless to say, this often results in bloodshed and there are occasional fatalities. Most Yanomamö males carry scars on their heads from such duels. Chagnon likens some scarred male pates to road maps! If tempers flare higher but the protagonists do not wish to enter open war then violence may escalate to spear-throwing fights. These cause mainly flesh wounds but the old and infirm, who are not agile enough to dodge the missiles, can be killed. As might be expected, this usually seems to lead to the commencement of warfare. Yanomamö wars involve constant raids and counter-raids with the objective of killing one or more of the enemy in revenge for any deaths previously caused among the raiding tribe. If any raiders are killed the raid is *always* deemed a failure. Where such situations have not resolved the causes of violence there are occasional outbursts of *Nomohoni* – massacres brought about by treachery. It can be seen that the Yanomamö have been called 'the Fierce People' with good reason but for present purposes the main point is the existence of several clearly defined levels of violence.

The same phenomenon can be seen among more settled peoples such as the Dugum Dani of Western New Guinea (Heider 1970), where a progression from brawl to feud to war can be seen. Here there is a distinction between 'endemic' or 'ritual' warfare, which can go on for decades between rival alliances, subject to clear rules, and 'non-ritual' wars usually between members of an alliance, which break out every decade or twenty years and which are much more bloody. Dani ritual war can often be seen as a kind of game, whereas the last recorded instance of non-ritual war, before the imposition of the *Pax Hollandia*, resulted in more deaths in a few weeks than could be expected in several years of endemic fighting. In such attacks all the norms of ritual war are ignored and we may liken this, in part, to the *Nomohoni* of the Yanomamö.

Further examples of endemic or ritual warfare can be found around the globe. The Nuer of southern Sudan wage wars which appear to be governed by a number of social mores. The raids and counter-raids of the North American Plains Indians are another example and further instances can be found among the Chimbu of New Guinea (Brown 1975), the Bantu of Africa (Sangree in Gibbs (ed.), 1965), the Maori (Buck 1962), and others. For us it is important to note the frequency of these wars (hence the term endemic), their government by norms of behaviour and their clear distinction from other levels of violence. These other levels of violence may be smaller scale, such as the feud which occurs in very many societies, or may be larger scale warfare. This latter can be traced among many peoples, whether or not it has been discovered to be such a distinct category of conflict as amongst the Dugum Dani and whether or not it has been dubbed 'non-ritual' or 'Warfare of Conquest'. Buck (1962) clearly sees that Maori wars could differ in scale, and Brown (1975) notes that the large Chimbu battles described by earlier observers were obviously different from the normal small raids which she witnessed.

Having established that violence is clearly graded in a number of pre-industrial societies and that 'ritual' or 'endemic' inter-tribal warfare occupies a distinct position in this gradation of conflict we may ask why these peoples undertake so many wars since it is 'perhaps to the surprise of the archaeologist [that the] state of war is so common wherever people and conditions facilitate it' (Orme 1981, p. 195). The participants themselves usually attribute a state of warfare between one group and another to some personal factors. Among the Dani, the theft of pigs is the most common cause of conflict, with women who leave a husband for another group second and land rights 'a poor third' (Heider 1970, p. 100). A similar pattern can be seen among the Chimbu. Paula Brown tabulated the causes of Chimbu conflict and here too pig theft was prominent, followed by disputes over women (adultery seems to be more common than among the Dani) and finally killings and accusations of sorcery (incidentally, the main initial cause of warfare among the Yanomamö). Land disputes do not apparently enter into it (Brown 1975, p. 64). The avenging of these kinds of personal affronts – theft, trespass, murder, kidnapping of women, insults and adultery – are commonly expressed as the reasons why a war started but endemic warfare is fuelled by the deaths inflicted during its course as both sides try to avenge their own dead or to create an even greater deficit among the enemy.

But regardless of the expressed motives of the warriors themselves the underlying reason for warfare is land and population pressure, as Marvin Harris has shown (Harris 1971 & 1978). As population reaches its carrying capacity arguments between people are more likely to occur, and Brown indeed noted this among the Chimbu (Brown 1975, pp. 63–4). In origin at least warfare, especially endemic warfare, serves as a population regulating mechanism (commonly in association with female infanticide) which, though wasteful, is probably preferable among pre-industrial peoples to the other alternatives of general infanticide or abortion or of allowing the population to reach such a high level that a natural disaster (plague or famine) is brought about (Harris 1971, pp. 228–31). One might suggest that the sporadic outbursts of non-ritual warfare or 'wars of conquest' are, among other things, back-up mechanisms to ease population pressure when the deficiencies of the ritual war mechanism are felt after periods of a decade or more.

Besides this latent major reason for warfare, conflict also serves a number of purposes. The first of these may be termed 'War as Solidarity'. Certain societies are very amorphous and intra-group feuding is common. Here, the establishment of an out-group will help unify members of the tribe. An example of this can be found among the Nuer. It has been suggested that were it not for the existence of the neighbouring, and very similar, Dinka as perpetual enemies, Nuer society would break up (Evans-Pritchard 1940; Orme 1981, pp. 195–6). Chimbu clans appear to fight wars to ensure solidarity within the unit (though here the enemies are usually other Chimbu clans, Brown 1975, p. 57). In modern times, the Nazis' establishment of the Jews as an out-group, as a means towards the unification of German society, is a further example of this.

Marvin Harris has shown that warfare can be used to ease pressures within a society by distracting attention from intra-group tensions (the British and Argentine experience in the Falklands may be said to be an example of this) and one way in which this is manifested is in the concept of, to use Harris' own phrase, 'War as Play'. Endemic warfare can be seen as a kind of 'overenthusiastic football' (Orme 1981, p. 196) – a sport for certain members of society. Dr Orme has pointed out, quite rightly, that we may be surprised that pre-industrial warfare is not always 'a totally awful state of affairs for the participants' (Orme 1981, p. 195). The warriors experience the thrill of battle and the excitement of combat, but without a great risk of serious injury, if they are careful. Dugum Dani battles involve a large element of farce. If the weather is too hot both sides might fall back, rest and exchange insults with each other, particularly witty remarks being greeted by great laughter *from both sides*. On one occasion a particularly slow battle was disrupted when both sides broke off to throw sticks and stones at a passing cuckoo dove (Heider 1970, p. 111). Nonetheless, as in other cultures, these battles serve to bring potential leaders to the fore, can act as a kind of initiation for young males as well as bringing 'many people together in a game they enjoy' (Orme 1981, p. 199).

In connection with the mention made above of the use of warfare to bring out new leaders, it must also be said that conflict of this kind is a means of personal aggrandisement. A man's personal reputation could be earned by *counting coup* among the Cheyenne, or by the number of heads he had taken among the Nagas (Fürer-Haimendorf 1966) or Kiwai Papuans (Landtmann 1927). This in turn leads on to another economic motive for warfare besides that of underlying land or population pressure – that of the acquisition of resources or prestige goods. Bantu raids, and the wars of several other African tribes, aimed at the acquisition of cattle, the addition of which to the family herds increased prestige. Horses, after the arrival of the Europeans, played a similar role among the Plains Indians, and gaining pigs is the object of a succcessful raid in some parts of the New Guinea highlands. Among the Yanomamö, who practice female infanticide, raiders aim to bring back women wherever possible.

The results of endemic warfare are various and examination of these is important for our purposes. The most noticeable thing to arise is the exaltation of the warrior. In Maori society, although it is appreciated that a provider of food will acquire more lasting importance than a warrior, most songs and stories are concerned with the exploits of famous heroes. Among the Yanomamö it is essential for males to be fierce, and Kiefer has said of the Tausug of the Philippines that 'to be Tausug is to be capable of fighting; a man must fight because he is a Tausug' (Kiefer 1972, p. 55). Bantu young adult males boasted of their military exploits, especially in front of young women, and an age group's lasting reputation was acquired while it occupied the warrior grade (Sangree in Gibbs (ed.), 1965, p. 46, 70). A number of other peoples also place much stress on boasting of, or singing about, warfare, among whom we might cite here the Nagas of southern Asia (Fürer-Haimendorf, 1966) and the Chimbu. In such societies the paraphernalia of conflict acquires symbolic importance. Among the Maori a chief's spiritual power 'and the ritual (as well as the physical) wellbeing of the community' can be tied up with weapons (Orme 1981, p. 196). Maori weapons thus gain a ceremonial value. Similarly, the eight or nine foot Chimbu spear becomes a 'highly symbolic object' used in dances and processions and carried by public speakers (Brown 1975, pp. 57–8). Both the Kiwai and the Dani of New Guinea attach a great deal of importance to arrows which have wounded a member of the group. In some cultures the head-hunting cult is born. The Nagas are 'addicted to head-hunting' and heads as trophies play an important part in Kiwai life. Though introduced by Europeans, scalp-hunting played a similar role among the Plains Indians.

Besides the creation of a warrior cult, endemic fighting has various other results. We have seen that it can keep a population within limits , unify a society and provide both a welcome relief from 'the monotony of life' and a means of personal elevation. Long periods of conflict between groups can lead to a greater dispersion of settlements and the creation of 'No Man's Lands' in between. They can also, oddly enough, bring about the solidification of the warring tribes into a permanent alliance or confederation. Dr Orme quotes, as an example of this, the Bushongo kingdom of Africa. 'The contact which warfare engenders can stimulate the development of larger political units through or with a parallel increase of personal authority and without the conquest of one group by another' (Orme 1981, p. 200). Paul Bohannan, in his interesting examination of warfare (Bohannan, 1969) underlines that in a multi-centric system warfare creates common understandings and, in the absence of communication, is the only way in which such a system can continue to function. Though the Leagues of Five Nations and of Four Nations in early colonial North America may also be examples of confederations brought about by endemic warfare, this remains a rare phenomenon. As Bryony Orme has said, in most cases people remain content in separate and warlike divisions.

Non-ritual wars or wars of conquest are brought about when the tensions not fully resolved by endemic conflict become too great, or when there is an imbalance and a strong group is able to conquer, expel or eliminate a weaker one. These wars, occasionally motivated by religious zeal, lead to more permanent transfers of land and property, greater loss of life and more noticeable changes in the political system and the distribution of population.

Deeper more unfortunate consequences of the endemic or ritual war, and which have been termed 'maladaptive aspects' by Harris (1971 pp. 228–31), can be seen with particular reference to the Yanomamö. Here the centuries of perpetual fighting and the subsequent exaltation of warriors and of 'fierceness' have resulted in the reduction of the population to well below its carrying capacity: on the edges of the Yanomamö area settlements are greatly dispersed, and horticulture is adversely affected. It has been estimated that 33% of Yanomamö adult male deaths result from raids and ambushes. The product of this obsession with conflict has been that the Yanomamö have become so easy to anger, so ready to fight, that they frequently cannot get along with their own family and fellow villagers. Group fission appears to be common, and males live under constant threat of attack. Similar maladaptive consequences can be seen in many other societies which practice endemic warfare. The Maori were also dominated by fear of attack, ambush or revenge killings and around 29% of Dugum Dani men die of wounds. Though the Dani seem to have remained curiously jovial even in battle, the Tausug, the Chimbu, the Nagas and the Maoris all demonstrate the fierce pride and quickness to take offence as is shown by the Yanomamö.

Part Two

When applied to the data from Anglo-Saxon England the anthropological model arising from the discussion in Part One (Fig. 11.1) reveals some very interesting points. I would like to begin the second part of this paper by asking three preliminary questions. Firstly, is it possible to see different levels of violence in Old English society, in a general sense? Secondly, do the narrative sources we have present anything like a complete picture of the incidence of war in pre-conquest society, and thirdly, can we see differing scales or levels in Anglo-Saxon warfare? From there we will move on to follow the model outlined above, looking at the reasons for, and purposes and results of, Old English warfare.

Can we define distinct levels of violence in Anglo-Saxon society? I believe that we can. The first or lowest stage would be brawls and wayside robberies or killings. If the aggressor could be identified, this might lead to the next level, the feud. Within a settlement we may doubt, given the degree to which people living in the same hamlet were probably related, that feuds were very costly in life and they were probably ended by blood payments relatively quickly. If the guilty man came from another settlement, however, feuds were likely to be much more serious. The feud, although vital in Old English life and the pre-conquest concepts of violence (King Edmund devoted an entire law-code to limiting it – clearly, like the Lombard Rothari, he felt unable or unwilling to stop it) will unfortunately have to be largely left out of this discussion through lack of space. For our purposes, though, it is useful to note the part which anthropology has played in increasing awareness of the conceptions and purposes of the feud (Gluckmann 1965; Wallace-Hadrill 1966). However, I will return briefly to the subject of the feud in later parts of this paper.

I now come to my second preliminary question, which is 'do the narrative sources available to us present a complete picture of the incidence or frequency of warfare in pre-conquest England?' To answer this we must, paradoxically, turn first to the Anglo-Saxon poetic and hagiographical sources. The *Maxims*, which are surely to be seen as fairly realistic statements of the Old English philosophy on the proper 'order of things', are probably as good a place to start as any. These make it clear that warfare was regarded as a central part of the way of life of at least some classes of society. 'Good comrades must encourage a young nobleman to war-making and to ring-giving' (Maxims II).[2] 'Majesty must go with pride, the daring with the brave; both must wage war with alacrity. An earl belongs on a charger's back. ... In the man, martial warlike arts must burgeon' (*Maxims* I). The *Gifts of Men* and the *Fortunes of Men*, which as S.A.J. Bradley notes are to be seen in close connection with the *Maxims* (Bradley, 1982), underline the very real presence of warfare in Old English life. 'One the spear shall spill; one warfare shall destroy. ... To one glory in war and battle mastered' (*The Fortunes of Men*). 'One is hardy in warfare, a man skilled in fighting, when shields resound' (*The Gifts of Men*). For kings the evidence is yet more plentiful: 'Many a time Scyld Scefing dispossessed the throngs of his enemies, many nations, of their seats of feasting and struck awe into men of stature, ... until each one of his neighbours across the whale-traversed ocean had to obey him and yield him tribute. He was a good king' (*Beowulf*). The Anglo-Saxon image of the first Christian emperor and thus of a model king was of 'a just king, his people's defence in war', 'the protector of princes, the warriors' ring-giver', 'lord defender of warriors', 'the people's surety, hardy in battle and daring with the spear' (*Elene*).

In prose we can find support for the idea of warfare as dominating the lives of the nobility in Felix's *Life of Guthlac*. Guthlac, when he reached the age of fifteen, gathered about him a troop of warriors and spent the next nine years raiding, burning and looting. There is no apparent model for this[3] and we may assume that Felix was describing what, to his audience, was a reasonable course of action for a young aristocrat. In earlier Merovingian hagiography we can detect a similar praise of warlike skills as befitting a noble layman (Irsigler in Reuter (ed.), 1979). Unfortunately for us, a change in conventions towards extolling more pacific, saintly virtues was well under way by the time such sources become common in England. Nevertheless, some early lives, such as the two *vitae* of Cuthbert, do show youths engaged in games which appear to be training for warfare; wrestling, running and so on. In archaeological terms, the use of weaponry as symbols of social status must also support the idea that warfare was an integral part of the life of certain social strata.

When, however, we turn to the narrative sources such as the *Anglo-Saxon Chronicle* and its derivatives, which stem from traditions current in the late ninth century, a very different picture appears. Fig. 11.2 shows the recorded incidence of wars waged between the three major kingdoms of the Heptarchy between c. 600 and 850. These have been gleaned from as many of the sources as possible. As can be seen, the *Chronicle's* compilers were not aware of the great bulk of military actions outside Wessex, especially after about 700 and the end of Bede's history. It is even clear that some West Saxon actions were not remembered. Most of the other instances have been filled in from Bede, the 'Continuation' of Bede, the *Annales*

Scales of Violence

Brawl → Feud → Warfare

Scales of Warfare

Frequent, small scale warfare, obeying certain rules of conduct (*Endemic* or *Ritual War*).

↓

Periodic outbursts of serious, large scale conflict, in opposition to usual norms of behaviour (*Non-Ritual* or *Secular War*, or *War of Conquest*).

Reasons for War

Ritual War		Non-Ritual War
Expressed	'Real'	
Avenging insult, or injury against a person or his/her family/clan.	Pressure for land and resources means that population must be kept down. Limited war is a means of doing so.	Ritual wars have not resolved tensions completely, or have not solved population pressure problem. Occasionally a religious motive.

Purposes of War

Ritual War	Non-Ritual War
Solidarity within clan/tribe/kingdom. (enemy or out-group defined) Acquisition of critical resources. Personal aggrandisement (wealth). War as Play (leads to:) Initiation for males. Personal aggrandisement (prestige). Leaders brought forward. Communication between components of a political system.	

Results of War

Ritual War	Non-Ritual War
Socio-economic purposes fulfilled. Warfare and weapons gain importance in everyday life and tribe's culture. Quickness to quarrel becomes characteristic. Fear of attack/ violent death. Population well below carrying capacity. Agriculture/ horticulture affected. Settlements dispersed/ No Man's Lands. Occasional solidification of warring tribes into political confederation.	Change in the political balance. Major redistribution of land and/or people. Sometimes complete conquest, absorption or annihilation of weaker group by stronger.

Fig. 11.1   Warfare and society: an anthropological model.

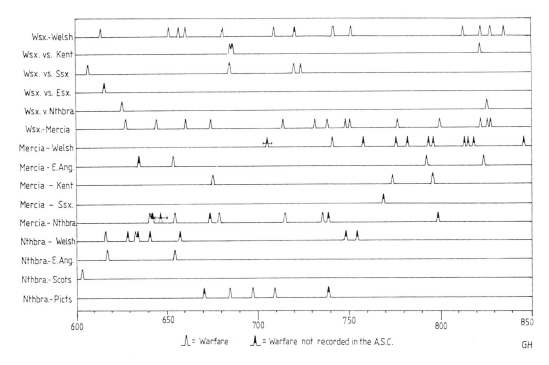

Fig. 11.2   Warfare in the heptarchy, 600–650.

Cambriae and the *Chronicle's* derivatives, especially Simeon of Durham, but one or two come from saints' lives (the Lives of Guthlac, for the Mercian Welsh war of 704–9; and of Wilfrid, for the Northumbrian Pictish war of 671). Some Scottish actions of the later seventh century, recorded in the Annals of Ulster, may have involved the Northumbrians but, as we have no way of being sure, these have been omitted.

What emerges from this is that the major kingdoms of the Heptarchy, Wessex, Mercia and (up to around 750) Northumbria fought each other and their other important neighbours, the Welsh, only once every twenty years or so. Mercian-West Saxon wars occur every 17.85 years on average; West Saxon-Welsh wars every 19.23 years; Mercian-Welsh wars every 22.72 years, and Mercian-Northumbrian wars every 25 years. Over the whole of England during these 250 years, excluding civil wars and Viking raids, which may be taken as unusual, 82 campaigns are recorded: that is one for every three years or so.[4]

From Fig. 11.2, and from the examples cited above of wars which were not recorded in the *Anglo-Saxon Chronicle*, it can be seen that this source provides an incomplete record of warfare up to 850. In places this is clear even from its own testimony. Under 757 and the accession of Cynewulf of Wessex we are told that this king fought many great battles with the Welsh – yet none of these merited an individual entry. Even when one has analysed all the chronicles, some wars have been forgotten, namely those noted only by near-contemporary hagiographers. This is underlined if we look at what kind of military actions

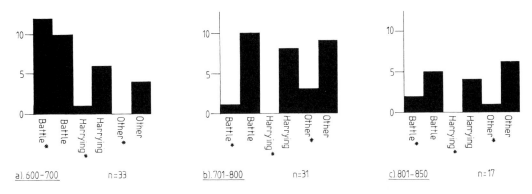

* = Involving the death of a king or ætheling.

Fig.11.3 English warfare 600–850: changing patterns or changing traditions?

were recorded. Figure 11.3 shows that the further back in time one goes from the writing of the *Chronicle*, the more the number of battles increases, especially those involving the death of a prominent person (ætheling or king). This may well represent in part a change in the patterns of Anglo-Saxon warfare, with seventh century conflicts being more concerned with set-piece battles and the fates of individual leaders, but surely it also indicates that from further back in time only major engagements were remembered – harryings, except those which were particularly devastating, and other actions were not.

All this would appear to support the idea that there was much more fighting going on in Middle Saxon England than the chronicles indicate. Even if we count all of the campaigns shown in Fig. 11.2, and some were almost certainly fairly minor,[5] is one battle every three years over all England or one battle every six years for Mercia (with forty-two recorded actions the most bellicose realm) enough to create an obsession with the warrior cult as outlined above? Assuming that every man of the 'warrior castes' went on every campaign, and that a warrior's active service life was from 15 to 40 (both fairly generous assumptions) a 'young nobleman' might see action four times in his life, or five if he was – if this is the word – lucky. Can we assume from this that this was what was meant by the *Maxims*, the *Fortunes of Men*, *Beowulf*, and the rest? I would suggest not.

Thus, to come to the third and final of those questions which need to be answered before we can progress further, I would suggest that the evidence adduced above allows us to envisage two scales of Anglo-Saxon warfare. The engagements recorded in the narrative sources surely represent those which formed a 'large-scale' phase. The much more frequent fighting which we can postulate from the other sources was 'small-scale' and thus did not find its way into the traditions upon which the *Chronicle's* compilers drew. We have seen that the *Chronicle* and the other narrative sources, even given the obvious caveats about taking their dating too precisely, place battles between important neighbours on average once every twenty years, or perhaps once per generation. In the light of the anthropological work discussed in Part One, we might expect these outbursts to be different not simply in scale, but in character too.

At this point we need to consider our terminology for these phases. From an anthropological point of view (such as Orme's), the terms 'endemic', for the small-scale, and 'War of Conquest', for the large-scale, might be expected to be applicable. Alternatively the terms 'ritual' and 'non-ritual' (or 'secular') might be used to differentiate the two. The applicability of these terms, and the precision with which we can use them will be discussed below. For immediate purposes, though, I propose to call the small-scale warfare 'endemic warfare' in the sense that it was integral to the society of the times.

Having suggested the existence of an endemic warfare, the individual actions of which were usually not remembered by the compilers of the later *Chronicle*, we must define what kind of actions we understand to be embraced by the term. These wars probably comprised raiding actions to acquire booty, either by loot or tribute, the ravaging of enemy lands and small battles between armies made up largely, if not totally, of aristocrats and their retainers. Such at any rate is the impression of these wars which we can glean from our information (*Beowulf*, the Laws of Ine and of Hywel Dda, the Life of Guthlac, etc). How frequent were such conflicts? This is difficult to establish but it will be useful to recall that the laws of Hywel Dda allowed for the king to lead plundering raids each year. In Middle Saxon England it may well be that the king or his ealdormen undertook small campaigns most years too. Most Nuer men take part in a raid on the Dinka once every two or three years at most and it may not be unreasonable to suppose that healthy English thegns and higher nobles of fighting age, with their retinues, saw service with a similar frequency.

If we are to use the term 'ritual war' we must look for some evidence that the practice of war was governed by normative rules of conduct. Firstly, Old English topography may provide some clues. Dr Della Hooke points out a route known as *Fyrdstraet* in the West Midlands (Hooke 1985) and there are of course two Herefords. These two terms, which might loosely be translated as 'Militia Street' and 'Raiders' Ford'[6] could indicate that pre-Conquest armies followed certain well-defined routes. This is supported to some extent by the evidence that armies entering a country could expect to be met by a royal official who would ask them their business. Hrothgar's thegn fulfils this role in *Beowulf* and Brihtric of Wessex had at least one reeve, Beaduheard at Dorchester, charged with the same task. Clearly these officials did not expect to be killed out of hand – hence the outrage at Beaduheard's killing by the Vikings (only later sources, perhaps arguing from the practices of their own day, add that he thought they were traders) – and this may be another of the 'rules of war'.[7] Other mores governing warfare may have included allowing poets or bards to live, as in *Y Gododdin* ('of all that hastened out after the choice drink none escaped but three, through feats of sword-play ... and I too, streaming with blood, by grace of my brilliant poetry' [trans. K. Jackson]). Godsons of the victors would also be spared, as in the *Chronicle*, *sub-anno* 757, where Ealdorman Osric's godson was allowed to live, and *sub anno* 893, where the sons of Haesten were set free since one was Alfred's godson and the other Ealdorman Ethelred's. In 613, when Chlothar II invaded Austrasia, the only one of Theuderic's sons whom he spared was Merovech, his godson (Fredegar IV.42).

One might also expect to be given a fair fight. Regardless of the comments of modern military historians, the Maldon poet showed no surprise that Byrthnoth allowed the Danes onto the mainland to fight. Dr Metcalf, at the January conference, argued convincingly that the payment of a 'geld' to the enemy seems to have been an accepted military 'move', and this in no way started with the Danish invasions (this volume, p. 179 ff.). In 655 Oswy only gave battle to Penda when he had failed, in Wallace-Hadrill's memorable phrase, to 'buy the old savage off' (Wallace-Hadrill 1975), and the same king is recorded by the *Annales Cambriae* as having 'come and taken tribute' (*Annales Cambriae* s.a. 658). To this we may add the exchange of hostages and swearing of oaths of friendship as devices to get out of a tight spot (cf. *ASC* 874, where both sides appear to be aware of such practices). Two further possible rules may be noted. The first is the custom of the 'hazelled field' beyond which an army may not pass until the issue has been decided in battle, but this is recorded only in late sources such as *Egil's Saga*, where the reference is apparently to Brunanburh. The second is Felix's statement that Guthlac returned one third of the loot he took on his campaigns. This would not be entirely unexpected from an anthropological viewpoint but, though Guthlac's *Life* must have been plausible to the Old English, as noted already, we may suspect that Felix included this purely to exonerate Guthlac and show his sanctity. Nevertheless the returning of some booty taken in endemic war remains possible.

From this it can be argued that Old English warfare was hedged about with rules of conduct, but to use the term 'ritual war' as an alternative to 'endemic war' in describing the small-scale conflicts of the period we need to know that the large-scale battles were different. Now, of the evidence quoted above, only the late reference to Brunanburh, and possibly the tale about the battle of Maldon, may be said to involve a serious, large-scale engagement. Only one of the other items comes from a reference to a major battle in the narrative sources before the late ninth century (after which time the *Chronicle* may be said to be more or less contemporaneous and to present a fuller picture of warfare). That exception is the story about Oswy taken from Bede, but here the point is surely that in a serious war, the accepted option of paying geld was not allowed. We have a little more evidence to suggest that these rules were not followed in the large-scale conflicts. Bede's references to Cadwallon of Gwynedd and Penda of Mercia wishing to exterminate the population of Northumbria (*Ecclesiastical History* II.20, III.24) and to the West Saxon conquest of Wight, which apparently involved a substantial slaughter of the inhabitants and their replacement by *Gewissae* settlers (*ibid.* IV.16), may be indications of this. We will see below that large-scale wars may also have differed in that they could result in the political transfer of land. Thus, as we would expect on anthropological grounds, we may not be unjustified in distinguishing the endemic small-scale and the large-scale conflicts of Anglo-Saxon England as 'ritual' and 'non-ritual' respectively.

In connection with this discussion of the rules of war we might look at the location of Anglo-Saxon battles. Fig. 11.4 shows the results of a locational analysis of the 28 battles named in English sources, excluding civil wars and Viking attacks, between 600 and 850. It can be seen that of those battles whose location can be reasonably plausibly established, almost all are by river crossings or 'ancient monuments'. The only exception, Degsastan, may in fact also conform if we take 'Degsa's Stone' to be some kind of pre-English monument. These monuments include prehistoric hillforts, barrows, Roman cities (probably, as recent research has shown, deserted at the time of the battles) of Chester (c. 613), Cirencester (628) and York (634)), dykes, other earthworks and Hadrian's Wall. There are three possible explanations for this distribution. The first may be termed tactical and would argue that the nature of these sites represents the desire for battlefield defences on the part of the Old English or Welsh. This seems to be the least likely explanation. If fortifications were so important to the Anglo-Saxons it remains a puzzle why we have so little evidence for the renovation of old hillforts in Middle Saxon England, or for the construction of any kind of fortified site before the Burh system of Alfred the Great. The Burton names may be indicative of such building activity, and the establishment of the duty of 'fortress-work' towards the end of the Middle Saxon period (Brooks, 1971; Gelling, this

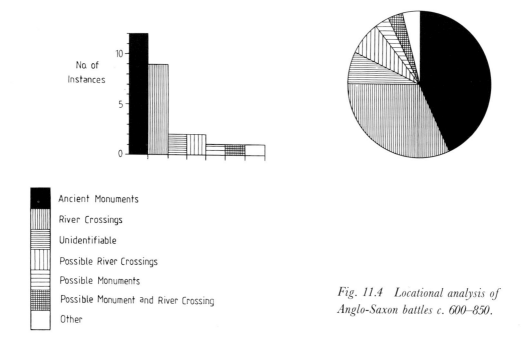

Ancient Monuments

River Crossings

Unidentifiable

Possible River Crossings

Possible Monuments

Possible Monument and River Crossing

Other

Fig. 11.4   Locational analysis of Anglo-Saxon battles c. 600–850.

volume, 145–53) certainly suggests it, but it is significant that only one battle, Burford (752), contains the *burh-* element, and that may be a 'ford battle'. Also, if fords were chosen for their defensive value this does not explain why a tenth century commander should be expected to allow the enemy to cross one and fight on equal terms. 'Holding the ford' may have formed an initial phase of fighting (cf. Maldon and Stamford Bridge) but it is difficult to see how decisive results could be obtained where the two sides were separated by a major obstacle. Neither would be willing to cross one such because of the loss of cohesion, so important in shield-wall warfare, which that would cause.

The second possibility may be termed strategical and is the most satisfactory. Briefly, in the days before extensive and systematic scouting made the location and bringing to battle of an enemy easier, surely the best way to bring about an engagement was to occupy a well-known landmark as a challenge and await the arrival of the enemy. This is supported by the *Chronicle's* entry for 1006 where a Danish army camped at the famous monument of Cwichelmslow, Ashdown, Berks. (a barrow, significantly) for two weeks and then marched away when, to the shame of the English, no army arrived to take up the challenge. This, although most of our named examples are probably non-ritual battles, may have applied to ritual engagements too. Perhaps certain kinds of site were set aside as 'places of fear' – as in New Guinea – and this leads us to our third explanation, which can be called sacrilegious. With reference to the 'Ancient Monument' battles we will recall the importance attached by the Old English to relics of bygone ages. The poetry refers to them as 'the work of giants' (*The Ruin, Maxims* II) and Germanic cemeteries are frequently sited by them, probably because of their ritual connotations.[8] Given the probable non-ritual nature of these battles and the character of such outbursts among other pre-industrial peoples, deliberately going against the norms of society, may we not suggest that the choice of 'ancient monuments' as sites shows just how serious these conflicts were? This, we must admit, remains less likely than the strategical explanation and, unless there was a cult of water in England (as Salin 1952, p. 14, & 1959, pp. 50–52, suggested for Merovingian Gaul) or of crossing places, it does not explain the 'ford' battles, but it nonetheless remains an intriguing possibility.[9]

This digression over, we may conclude the preliminary section of this part of the paper by making two propositions. Firstly, violence was clearly graded in Old English society. Secondly, this grading divided warfare into two scales or phases. On the one hand was small-scale, endemic or ritual fighting, taking the form of raids and counter-raids, and occuring more or less every year except in times of strictly enforced peace. On the other were outbursts of serious, large-scale 'non-ritual' or 'secular' wars, which broke out, it seems, between major neighbouring kingdoms once every generation or so. Having put these notions forward, we can now turn to apply the anthropological model to the Anglo-Saxon data, looking first at the fundamental reasons for, and origins of, pre-conquest warfare, then at the reasons for war given by the Old English, and finally at the purposes for and results of conflict in this period.

The origins of the Old English systems of war are in part to be sought in the forests and hills of North Germany and Celtic Britain, outside the scope of this paper, but we may reasonably argue that they were founded in the problems of population or land pressure (it would in this connection be interesting to know if archaeological cemetery evidence suggested female infanticide in any way[10]). So the endemic war was probably well established by the time of the *Adventus Saxonum*. In the fifth and sixth centuries during the formation of the Anglo-Saxon kingdoms such warfare was probably very similar to that in other early societies, taking the form of feuds between villages. It is, of course, precisely in this period that weaponry occurs so frequently as a symbol in funerary rites.

However, as the small tribes and villages coalesced into larger states, and as political organisation progressed beyond the tribal stage, changes occured. It was probably impossible for kings to eradicate the deeply ingrained concepts which had given rise to these scales of violence – and indeed continuing the practices of feud and endemic war was useful to them socially and politically (see Wallace-Hadrill 1966, for the feud, and below in this paper for the small-scale war). Early English kings do, however, seem to have tried to limit them. We have already noted that they worked at limiting the feud throughout the pre-Conquest era (above, p. 159) and they also adapted the notion of endemic warfare to their purposes. By Ine's time, the king was passing laws to limit wars to those which had royal backing.[11] It has recently been proposed that Ine's code was formulated at the same time as Wihtred of Kent's when the two rulers ended the war between them[12] and if this is so the significance of the titles which appear to be limiting warfare is increased. It was probably in the period of state formation, too, that the right to fight became limited to certain classes of society, as shown by Professor John (John 1966, though, given the two-tiered nature of Old English warfare, we need not accept his thesis in its hard-and-fast entirety). This too may, I think, be seen as a result of the limiting of endemic warfare by Anglo-Saxon kings. These limitations led to certain fundamental differences between Middle and Late Saxon warfare and that practiced by other, tribal, societies. The royal initiatives could not, however, entirely remove the deep-seated concepts of war and so there are still numerous points of reference with the anthropological model outlined in Part One.

Whatever the origins of Old English war and the basic reasons for its existence, the reasons given by the Anglo-Saxons themselves are worth examination for they tally closely with those given in other early societies. J.E. Cross discussed this in an excellent analysis of the ethic of war in this period (Cross 1971) and there is little to add here. It will suffice to say that, with a few exceptions where land is mentioned, the majority of the recorded causes of wars stress human grievances or insults. The war in Beowulf between the Geats and the Swedes can be seen as a series of 'just' revenge attacks sparked off by one 'unjust' incident.

As in the first part of this paper we may distinguish the reasons for war, the incidents or latent pressures which spark off conflicts, from the purposes which, once started, such warfare fulfils. Using the same categories as outlined in our anthropological model, we begin with 'War as Solidarity'. There is little hard evidence for this but it is interesting to note that the Magonsætan on the Welsh border retained their tribal identity well into the eleventh century, by which time most of the other early folk-units of the *Tribal Hidage* had disappeared. The Hwicce, on the Mercian-West Saxon border, had clearly defined enemies and these too kept their identity longer than most of the other constituent nuggets of Mercia. The endemic wars ease stress in a kingdom. It is perhaps significant that Northumbria lapsed into its anarchic period after a succession of pacific or boy kings and that after the long reign of Edgar the Peaceable (we may suspect that the epithet was more grudging than has hitherto been suspected) the English kingdom began to be troubled by internecine disputes. Similarly, the reign of the peace-loving Edward III 'the Confessor' saw serious outbreaks of civil strife. The conclusion may be drawn that we should see stress in Anglo-Saxon England not in warlike periods but in peaceful ones!

The concept of 'War as Play' finds little or no support in the data from pre-Conquest England. Whereas Dani weapons and tactics are clearly undeveloped in directions that would lead to greater killing power (Heider 1970), nothing can furnish a finer example of an efficient pre-industrial killing instrument than the Anglo-Saxon long-sword. On the other hand we should not entirely dismiss this concept. Though undoubtedly bloodier than, for example, Dani battles, an Anglo-Saxon struggle between shield-walls need not have been too dangerous so long as cohesion was maintained, as the work of the Dark Ages Society[13] has shown. We can identify the side-effects of 'War as Play' too. Warfare was certainly used to bring forward new leaders. Posts such as that of ealdorman could be given to renowned warriors and at times it is likely that a significant proportion of the Old English aristocracy received the lands which supported their noble status as rewards for military service. In literature it is mainly Beowulf's martial exploits which bring him the kingship of the Geats. Skill in war was also seen as the mark of a man in some social strata, as the quotes from the *Maxims*, given above, demonstrate. In this connection it is worth noting that Alfred, in his will, refers to the male side of his family as 'the spear side'.[14]

The economic purpose of warfare must not be underestimated. Treasure was vital at all levels of early medieval politics (James 1982, p. 132–3) and its acquisition and redistribution to followers was a major concern of any ruler, as the Old English poetry reveals. Work in recent years has shown how the kings took great trouble to control trade and thus the distribution of prestige items but the less peaceful side of this preoccupation with the control of wealth has received less attention. Endemic war actions could provide slaves (they were probably a main source of such a commodity; see Pelteret 1981), cattle (Hywel Dda's laws make it clear that the acquisition of cattle was a major aim of his endemic raids), horses and other forms of liquid wealth. When times were hard, restricting trading activity, such actions were probably the only way a lord could maintain his power.

	PEACEFUL	VIOLENT
UNICENTRIC SYSTEM	LAW OR AVOIDANCE	FEUD OR 'EXECUTIONS'
MULTICENTRIC SYSTEM	DIPLOMACY | RITUAL WAR	NON RITUAL WAR

Fig. 11.5 Settlement of differences in Anglo-Saxon England.

We can imagine that such objects changed hands frequently in raid and counter-raid, and that thus the state of endemic warfare between realms could be seen as beneficial to the rulers of both, so long as a balance was maintained.

This point leads to 'War as Communication'. If we adapt Bohannan's table of the solution of grievances to Anglo-Saxon England the results can be shown in Fig. 11.5. A unicentric system may be a kingdom or a shire, while a multicentric system would be the Heptarchy, or a kingdom in unsettled times when fragmentation into a number of territory- or leader-centred units occurred (as in Edward the Confessor's time). Now, on this table endemic warfare can be shown as semi-violent. This is because its effects were limited both by behavioural norms and, where parity existed, by the fairly rapid turnover in the items sought in war (as shown in the last paragraph). If Guthlac's return of a proportion of the booty taken was, in general terms, common this point is underlined. Where 'diplomatic' communication did not exist the endemic war was the best way of keeping the Heptarchy functioning as a system. It was usually beneficial to the ruling classes of both sides, as outlined with relationship to the purposes of war above; involved little real change in the political situation; created, as Bohannan said, 'common understandings', and thus facilitated communication.

The reasons for large-scale wars were similar to those given for other pre-industrial peoples. Endemic warfare eases tensions but it does not remove them, and eventually the cumulative deficit can only be resolved by serious secular phases of conflict. This, the absence of a small-scale war phase, or the failure of endemic wars to fulfil their purposes, governed the frequency of major wars. The transfer of land also seems to have been a major aim and result of such wars among the Old English. Borderlands in the upper Thames seem to have changed hands as a consequence of serious battles between the Mercians and West Saxons, whilst Lindsey changed hands in 674 and 679 following major engagements. The conquest of Wight and the massacre and replacement of at least part of its inhabitants have already been mentioned, and, in the chapter preceding his account of this, Bede tells us that the Kings of the West Saxons held the kingdom of Sussex for some years, following the defeat of its king (*Ecclesiastical History*, IV.15). Oswy was king of the northern part of Mercia for a few years after his victory at Winwaed, and the defeat of Eadbert Praen led to the kingdom of Kent passing briefly to his conqueror, Cenwulf of Mercia, and then to the latter's brother. This aspect – the seizure of territory from, or even the kingship of, an

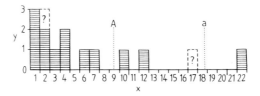

x – Number of years after a change of king in Mercia
    or Wessex within which a major campaign was fought.

y – Number of instances of campaigns within x years of
    a change of king.

A – Average number of years between changes of king in
    either realm.

a – Average number of years between campaigns.

Fig. 11.6   Incidence of Mercian West Saxon warfare in relation to changes of king in the two realms.

enemy – is probably one way in which the large scale wars differed from the norms of warfare, and is therefore a reason for us to use the ritual/non-ritual distinction.

Kings might instigate 'secular' wars to alter the balance of power. In the 770s the battles of Otford and Bensington were almost certainly brought about as a result of Kentish and West Saxon desires to throw off Mercian hegemony in the south – a hegemony built up through ritual conflicts over twenty years.[15] The Brunanburh campaign came about because the Scots, Welsh and Danes wished to end the 'Imperial' supremacy of Athelstan, as is shown by the *Armes Prydein.* Here again, Athelstan had built up his power without a serious battle. Another cause of serious conflict might be the escalation from a small-scale war, just as a 'non-ritual' war might be defused by the payment of a large geld or by a series of small battles (as in the Year of Battles, 871). Finally, events which might potentially damage the *status quo* could lead to major conflict. Such an event might be, most obviously, a change of king. If we look at the incidence of serious warfare between Mercia and Wessex (Fig. 11.6) we see that most battles were fought within four years of a change of ruler in one kingdom or the other. Given that a change of king in one of the two realms took place only once every eight and a half years on average, this might well be significant, and could represent either the new king wanting to show his worth or the ruler of the other kingdom testing his mettle or trying to use the potential instability surrounding a change of king to alter the balance of power in his favour. In this case, especially given the Mercian invasion of Wiltshire on the very day of Ecgbert's election in 802, the latter may be more likely.

In general, however, it can be argued that kings were expected to be involved in major military actions fairly soon after their accession. Fig. 11.7 shows this with reference to the rulers of Mercia from Penda to Wiglaf, and of Wessex from Ceolwulf to Ecgbert. The Mercian example is particularly good, which may result from better recording of military actions, including ritual ones. The only instance of a king taking more than six years to undertake a campaign is that of Æthelbald, whose first recorded action is his attack on Somerton in 733. However, we can probably take the *Chronicle's* notice under 716 of the death of Osred of Northumbria 'south of the border' as being in battle and in Æthelbald's reign. If this is so this king can be argued to have fought an action within a year of his accession. The other 'possible' dates represent the Welsh attack on Mercia recorded by Felix only as 'in the reign of king Cenred'. The West Saxon example is less pleasing. Cynewulf's first recorded battle is Bensington, twenty-two years after his accession, but since the *Chronicle* records, under the year of his succession to the throne, that he fought many battles with the Welsh we may argue that he went on campaign much sooner than that. Brihtric spent his entire sixteen-year reign without a specified military action but, again, the *Chronicle* later says that he and Offa drove Ecgbert, later Brihtric's successor, out of his kingdom of Kent, and this probably implies a military undertaking. In both realms a king's first military engagement was usually against one of his country's major enemies; the Welsh, the West Saxons or, before 716, the Northumbrians, for Mercia, and the Welsh or the Mercians for Wessex. In early medieval Ireland we can also see the idea that a king must raid his enemies soon after his accession (ó Corráin 1972, p. 37) and this must all surely be taken in connection with the idea of the king as war-leader (Chaney 1970).

With regard to the results of Anglo-Saxon warfare it is again useful to look at this in relation to the anthropological model outlined in the first part of this paper. The creation of a warrior cult in England is obvious. The Old English poetry, like that of the Maoris, is principally concerned with warriors, heroes and stylised battle accounts and even biblical and religious models are adapted to fit in with the stereotyped battle description (cf. *Exodus, Elene, Judith* etc.). Christ is described as a 'young hero ... firm and unflinching' (*Dream of the Rood* trans. in Wilson 1971). The artefacts of war gained especial importance in Anglo-Saxon society. In the cemeteries of Early Saxon England weapons obtained a particularly strong symbolic value. The spear seems to be used to represent all free males, and more complete weapon sets those who came from higher classes theoretically liable to take part in war, regardless of the physical ability of the deceased to fight (cf. Härke, this volume, pp. 49–61). The riddles, poetry and later sagas all show us that characters were ascribed to weapons. They were held to be imbued with the success of their users, success which might

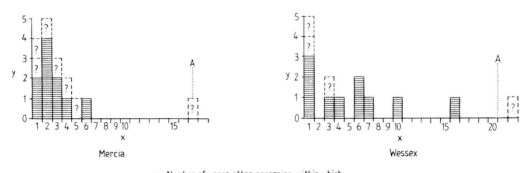

x- Number of years after accession, within which first recorded campaign was fought.

y- Number of kings who fought their first recorded campaign within x years.

A- Average length of reign.

Beornred and Ecgfrith of Mercia, and Sigiberht of Wessex have not been included as they only reigned for one year or less.

Fig. 11.7 Number of years between accession and first recorded campaign.

rub off on later wielders. We even come across magic weapons. All this evidence for the exaltation of the warrior caste can only have come about in a society where warfare was more common than the narrative sources (up to the later ninth century) would have us believe. Even without the data which suggests that there were Middle Saxon wars which were not recorded in the chronicles, this obsession with warriors and weapons would be reason enough for us to suspect the existence of endemic warfare in pre-Conquest England.

The effects of ritual warfare on settlement are difficult to assess. Much more work is required before we will ever be able to suggest greater dispersion in warlike areas, or 'No Man's Lands'. The question of the fortification of settlements is vexed. Given that the lower classes of Anglo-Saxon England were not warriors, we would not expect their dwellings to be fortified. The *Burton* placenames (Gelling, this volume, pp. 145–53) may simply indicate the presence of refuges. The residences of the ruling strata might well be different, however. The *Chronicle, sub anno* 757, implies that Cynewulf's burh was fortified, and perhaps the fortress work required in the charters refers to the defence of lordly dwellings. However, excavated sites like Cheddar (Rahtz 1979) and Yeavering, yield no conclusive evidence of fortification. Only the late sites of Goltho, Sulgrave and possibly Portchester seem to hint at such defences. It is worth repeating the suggestion made by Philips in the Ordnance Survey's map of *Britain Before the Norman Conquest* (p. 21) that the term *burgheat* used to define thegnly status, may have meant the right to fortify a residence. We may also tentatively suggest, however, that 'halls', where a lord and his retainers were concentrated, played some defensive role, as do the men's houses of the Nagas.

The political results of endemic warfare have largely been mentioned already – transfer of land or wealth, underlining or strengthening of the political status quo, and communication between realms. Non-ritual wars might lead to more important changes in the balance of power. There is no clear evidence of the fusion of political units through endemic warfare, as among the Bushongo, but this is an interesting possibility which might profitably be explored in relation to the origins of the confederation-like kingdom of Mercia.

The maladaptive aspects of ritual warfare seem to have been limited, probably by the fact that unlike that in many early societies, warfare in pre-Conquest England was usually the business of males of the upper strata only (cf. John 1966). Thus, as we have seen, the settlement pattern was not adversely affected to any great degree. On the other hand, among the warrior classes, the quickness to quarrel characteristic of almost every society which practises endemic warfare can be traced. 'From one, an irascible ale-swiller, a man full of wine, a sword's edge will thrust out the life upon the mead-bench; previous to that his words will have been too hasty' (*The Fortunes of Men*). Fear of attack was great, as is shown by the *Charm for a Safe Journey*. Boasting of, and pride in, warlike deeds were common. One need look no further than *Beowulf* for support of this. We do not have any figures to help us examine the extent to which warfare kept down the population level. Traces of wounds from excavated cemeteries would give a negligible figure but, again, we may suspect that such effects were felt mainly by the warrior nobility. However, it is worth noting that in the ninth century no fewer than ten West Saxon ealdormen (from the shires from Kent to Devon) died in warfare and this may represent a significant percentage of the men who attained that rank in that kingdom. Nevertheless, maladaptive aspects of war do not seem to have been as pronounced as among the Celts, whose inability to agree or unite for any length of time was notorious.

It will now be advisable to head off an obvious criticism of the approach used here. It can be argued that the societies which we discussed in Part One were generally simpler, in terms of political development, than the Anglo-Saxon kingdoms of the period from 600 onwards. This is true, even for the Tausug who were at least nominally ruled by a Sultan. On the other hand, it can be argued that the feud is practiced in these societies and is remarkably similar to that practiced in early medieval Europe, regardless of political development. The feud probably had its origins in an earlier, prehistoric, acephalic period when there was no higher authority to enforce law, but early medieval kings, while they tried to restrict the feud, did not stop it since it served a purpose for them. We may see warfare in a similar light. We have argued above that the origins of the Anglian systems of war must be sought partly in the periods before the English came to Britain, and that they later developed from inter-tribal feuding in a way which paralleled the growth of kingdoms. Old English kings could occasionally suppress the tendency towards ritual war, as Edgar did, but the result of such royal initiatives was generally the limitation of endemic war, not its extinction. It can be seen from the arguments above that it was politically useful for the king to continue to lead 'ritual' actions in the old style. After the close of the period under review the aristocratic ritual war can be seen to have continued in the form of the baronial struggles, and the rules of war fossilised in the notion of chivalry are a further indicator of the fact that endemic or ritual war among the upper social strata did not end with the coming of the Normans.

We can see that it is very likely that in common with many other societies the Old English knew of two types of war. The first was small-scale and is indicated by some snippets in the narrative, hagiographical and poetic sources. The Anglo-Saxon obsession with warriors and weapons, and boastful pride and readiness to quarrel must also, on anthropological analogy, have been brought about by the practice of endemic warfare. The other level of warfare was large-scale, comprising major battles between the armies of kingdoms, and particularly severe harryings. It was only these conflicts which were remembered by the time the Chronicle was written down. Such encounters can be shown to have occurred between neighbours only once every twenty years or so, which tallies quite closely with the Dani evidence.

We may term the smaller scale 'ritual war' since there is evidence that there were behavioural norms governing its conduct, or 'endemic war', since the purposes which it served made it integral to Old English society. The large-scale conflicts can be termed 'non-ritual' or 'secular' since we can find some, albeit not much, evidence that they did not follow the usually accepted rules of conduct. Although the actual conquest of one group by another was rare in Middle Saxon England, the transfer of land seems to have been a common result of such major wars so the term 'War of Conquest' may be partly applicable. In the end, though, we must admit that the Old English probably did not have clearly defined terms for these two kinds of war, even if they recognised their existence, and in this connection we should note that the Dani call both of their kinds of war *wim*.

It is hoped that the realisation of this distinction into two scales of warfare will help our understanding of Anglo-Saxon conflict. In the debates over the size of pre-Conquest armies, or over what social classes had the right to fight – both debates characterised by the wishes of the contenders to show that their interpretation of the facts applied across the board – we can see that this removes the necessity to argue that all Old English armies were of this or that order of size, or that all Anglo-Saxon armies did or did not comprise of nobles only or of levies of all the free classes. If we recognise that warfare in Anglo-Saxon society had this dual nature then we can see that army size and composition might vary from one scale of war to the other. The ambiguous evidence on these subjects, which has kept these debates alive for so long, probably confirms this.

Before we can really understand the specific details of pre-Conquest warfare it is necessary to set that warfare in its context both in the whole of Old English society and in the Anglo-Saxon concepts of the scales of violence. It is hoped that this paper may have gone some way towards doing so.

Acknowledgements

I should like to express my thanks to Drs Tania Dickinson and Edward James of the University of York for their help in preparing this paper. I am grateful to Mr Patrick Wormald of Glasgow University, Mr Steve Roskams of the University of York, Dr Sam Newton and Mr Simon Barton who also read the rough drafts of this paper and made valuable suggestions. Finally, I owe to Miss Vicky Thompson and to my father the eradication of my more serious misuses of the English language. For any errors that remain, in spite of the attentions of the above, I must claim all the credit.

Notes

1. This section of this paper owes a great deal to the writings of Bryony Orme (1981) and Marvin Harris (1971, 1978). Indeed it was reading Dr Orme's *Anthropology for Archaeologists* which set the present writer onto the trail which led to the production of this paper.
2. Except where stated, all translations of Old English verse are those of S.A.J. Bradley.
3. St Martin also joined the army at fifteen (Vita S. Martini, II.5) but whereas Sulpicius makes this explicit, Felix says that Guthlac was twenty-four when he left the warrior life, and that he had been a warrior for nine years. We are left to make the deduction ourselves, and hence I do not think that Sulpicius provided a model here.
4. The frequency of warfare between any two kingdoms is expressed here as the result of dividing 250 (the number of years between 600 and 850) by the number of battles between those kingdoms recorded in the sources. This method was used to circumvent the obvious problems involved in using the dating in the *Chronicle* and its derivatives too precisely. Here we simply count the number of conflicts remembered over this 250–year period and find the average. The problem of having to rely on precise dates is thus avoided. This methodological problem resurfaces, with more justification, when we come to look at the incidence of battles in relationship to changes of king. Here precise dates for the accession of rulers have been used but it was felt that the *Chronicle's* sources for such events, that is to say regnal lists, would be quite accurate in establishing this for the period after 600 AD. The average lengths of reigns have therefore been calculated by dividing the number of years between the accession of the first king and the death of the last by the number of kings under consideration.

    The problem of using the exact dates given for battles remains, however, probably giving the results of such a survey only a suggestive value. These problems led to the limitation of the period under study to that after 600 AD. While it is possible to argue that the dates given in the *Chronicle* for events in the seventh to ninth centuries would be broadly accurate (given the evidence of Bede for the earlier part of this period), and more or less precise after this work becomes contemporaneous in the 880s, before 600 recent work has shown that this source cannot be used with any precision.
5. I have also been fairly generous in what I have called a military action. For instance, I have assumed

that the slaying of Osred of Northumbria 'south of the border' was in battle (Boniface's letter to Æthelbald of Mercia [Whitelock 1979, doc. 177, pp. 818–819] unfortunately sheds little more light on the circumstances of his death – but if I am right that it was in battle with the Mercians, Boniface would have had no need to spell this out), and that Offa's killing of Aethelbert of East Anglia in 794 involved some kind of military action, although in this case later sources, both hagiographic and narrative state the contrary. I have put the Mercian Northumbrian campaigns of 737 (*A.S.C.*) and 740 (*Continuation of Bede*) as two events when they may have been one and the same; and assumed that the *Continuation of Bede's* statement, under 750, that Cuthred rose up against Æthelbald of Mercia to imply military action, when it might, of course, simply refer to the battle of Burford in 752).

6. These loose translations adopt the apparently usual connotations of the words *fyrd*, as a defensive force, and *here*, as an offensive, raiding force. Thus the Chronicle usually talks of Danish invaders as comprising a *here*, whereas the English usually oppose them with a *fyrd*.

7. The Merovingian kings of France also posted guards on their borders (cf. *Gregory of Tours Libri Historiarum* VI.19, Liber Historiae Francorum 45). The fact that officials like Beaduheard were also involved in the regulation of merchants crossing the border, as Sawyer points out (Sawyer 1981), underlines the fact that trading and raiding could be different sides of the same coin (Polanyi 1978).

8. Despite recent persuasive arguments that many of the henges and other early monuments will have been ploughed or eroded away by Anglo-Saxon times, some certainly were not, and there remain, in Germany, certain sites associated with prehistoric landmarks (the Galgenberg most obviously [Böhme 1973]) and, in England, cemeteries by abandoned Roman cities (cf. Markshall and Caistor-by-Norwich). In France the siting of cemeteries in 'Roman ruins' is very much the rule. There are a great number in Lorraine (Berthelming, Gondrexange, Bettborn, St Ulrich, Wiesviller and others in the *Département* of Moselle alone) and the phenomenon can be seen in other parts of France too (Delahaye 1982 and Percival 1976, chs 8 and 9). These monuments were all certainly visible at the time.

9. Finally, mention must be made of Sims-Williams' theory that some of the monument battles of the *Anglo-Saxon Chronicle* were invented to show West Saxon claims to areas of Southern England (Sims-Williams 1983). This theory seems very plausible but we must remember that it relates to the *Chronicle's* entries before 600, whereas this discussion is mainly concerned with those between 600 and 850, when some other explanation is probably required. I am grateful to Dr Tania Dickinson for reminding me of this.

10. We would not expect the victims of female infanticide to receive formal burial in a cemetery but physical anthropological studies might show a disproportionately small number of females surviving infancy, as may have been the case at Lavoye (Meuse) in France (see Young 1984).

11. Ine 13.1 appears to be limiting the size of personal retinues, on pain of being considered as an enemy, while Ine 16 seems to outlaw participation in raids which did not have royal approval, punishing offenders with the loss of their *Wergild*.

12. I should like to thank Patrick Wormald for allowing me to refer here to the excellent lecture he gave at the 'Early Medieval Kingship' conference at Leeds in July 1987. There, he also suggested that the laws of Hlothere and Eadric were formulated at a time when the rivals were at peace. The promulgation of law as part of the process of formal peace-making would tie in neatly with the thesis proposed here that warfare between kingdoms was very much the norm and that Royal efforts to forbid it altogether, rather than to limit it, were few and far between.

13. For information on this, the best of modern reconstruction societies, contact Alan Baxter at 2 Wideham Cottages, West Stow, Suffolk, IP28 6EZ.

14. My thanks to Simon Barton for drawing my attention to this.

15. The harrying of the Hastings region in 770, the only recorded action in this series of events, is only reported in a later source, but the charter evidence makes it clear that Offa had gained supremacy over Cynewulf of Wessex and Ecgbert of Kent.

References

Alcock, L. 1971: *Arthur's Britain* (Harmondsworth).

Alcock, L. 1977: Her ... gefeaht wip Walas: aspects of the warfare of Saxons and Britons, *Bulletin Board Celtic Studies*.

Arnold, C.J. 1982: Stress as a stimulus for socio-political change: Anglo-Saxon England in the seventh century, in *Ranking, Resource and Exchange* ed. C. Renfrew and S. Shennan (Cambridge).

Arnold, T. (ed.) 1879: *The History of the English by Henry, Archdeacon of Huntingdon* (London, Rolls Series).

Bachrach, B. (trans) 1973: *Liber Historiae Francorum* (Lawrence, Kansas).

Bohannan, P. 1969: *Social Anthropology* (London).

Böhme, H.W. 1976: Der Galgenberg bei Cuxhaven-Sahlenburg, in *Führer v.-u. frühgesch. Denkmal.* Band 31 (Mainz).

Bradley, S.A.J. 1982: *Anglo-Saxon Poetry* (London).

Brooks, N.P. 1971: The development of military obligations in eighth and ninth century England, in Clemoes and Hughes (eds).

Brooks, N.P. 1978: Arms, status and warfare in Late Saxon England, in *Ethelred the Unready*, ed. D. Hill (British Archaeological Reports, British Series, no. 59. Oxford).

Brooks, N.P. 1979: England in the ninth century: the crucible of defeat, *Trans. Royal Hist. Soc.*

Brown, P. 1975: *The Chimbu. A Study of Change in the New Guinea Highlands* (London).

Buck, P. 1962: *The Coming of the Maori* (Wellington).

Campbell, A. (ed. and trans.) 1962: *The Chronicle of Æthelweard* (London).

Chagnon, N.A. 1963: *Yanomamö. The Fierce People* (New York).

Chaney, W.A. 1970: *The Cult of Kingship in Anglo-Saxon England* (Manchester).

Clemoes, P. and Hughes, K. (eds) 1971: *England Before the Conquest* (Cambridge).

Colgrave, B. and Mynors, R.A.B. 1969: *Bede's Ecclesiastical History of the English People* (Oxford).

Colgrave, B. (ed. and trans.) 1927: *The Life of Bishop Wilfrid by Eddius Stephanus* (Cambridge).

Colgrave, B. (ed. and trans.) 1940: *Two Lives of Saint Cuthbert* (Cambridge).

Colgrave, B. (ed. and trans.) 1956: *Felix's Life of Guthlac* (Cambridge).

ó Corráin, D. 1972: *Ireland Before the Normans* (Dublin).

Cross, J.E. 1971: The ethic of war in Old English, in Clemoes and Hughes (eds).

Delahaye, G.-R. 1982: Observations sur la formation des nécropoles mérovingiennes riches en sarcophages, *Association Française d'Archéologie Mérovingienne. Bulletin de Liaison*, no. 7.

Dornier, A. (ed.) 1977: *Mercian Studies* (Leicester).

Ellis Davidson, H.R. 1962: *The Sword in Anglo-Saxon England* (Oxford).

Ellis Davidson, H.R. 1972: *The Battle God of the Vikings* (York University Medieval Monographs No. 1. York).

Evans Pritchard, E.E. 1940: *The Nuer* (Oxford).

Farrell, R.T. 1981: *Beowulf* and the northern heroic age, in *The Vikings* ed. R.T. Farrell (Chichester).

Fürer Haimendorf, C. von 1966: *South Asian Societies. A Study of Values and Social Controls* (London).

Gelling, M. 1979: *Early Charters of the Thames Valley* (Leicester).

Gibbs, J.L. 1965: *Peoples of Africa* (New York).

Gordon, E.V. (with Scrag, D.G.) 1976: *The Battle of Maldon* (Manchester).

Gluckmann, M. 1965: The peace in the feud, in *Custom and Conflict in Africa* (Oxford).

Harris, M. 1971: *Culture, Man and Nature. An Introduction to General Anthropology* (New York).

Harris, M. 1978: *Cannibals and Kings. The Origin of Cultures* (London).

Heider, K. 1970: *The Dugum Dani. A Papuan Culture in the highlands of New Guinea* (Chicago).

Hennessey, W.M. 1887: *The Annals of Ulster* (Dublin).

Hill, D. 1981: *An Atlas of Anglo-Saxon England* (Oxford).

Hodges, R. 1984: The Anglo-Saxon Migrations, in *The Making of Britain: The Dark Ages*, ed L. Smith (London).

Hooke, D. 1985: *The Anglo-Saxon Landscape. The Kingdom of the Hwicce* (Manchester).

Irsigler, F. 1979: On the aristocratic character of early Frankish society, in Reuter (ed.).

Jackson, K. 1969: *The Gododdin* (Edinburgh).

James, E. 1982: *The Origins of France* (London).

Jarman, A.O.H. 1981: *The Cynfeirdd* (Cardiff).

John, E. 1964: *Land Tenure in Early England*. Leicester.

John, E. 1966: English feudalism and the structure of Anglo-Saxon Society, in *Orbis Britanniae and Other Studies* (Leicester).

John, E. 1977: Warfare and Society in Tenth Century England: The Maldon Campaign, *Trans. Royal Hist. Soc.*

Keynes, S. and Lapidge, M. (ed. and trans.) 1983: *Alfred the Great* (Harmondsworth).

Kiefer, T.M. 1972: *The Tausug. Violence and Law in a Philippine Moslem Society* (New York).

Landtmann, G. 1927: *The Kiwai Papuans of British New Guinea* (London).

Morris, J. 1980: *Nennius. The British History and the Welsh Annals* (Chichester).

Ordnance Survey 1973: *Britain Before the Norman Conquest* (Southampton).

Orme, B. 1981: *Anthropology for Archaeologists* (London).

Owen, A. 1841: *Ancient Laws and Institutes of Wales* (London).

Owen, G.R. 1981: *Rites and Religions of the Anglo-Saxons* (London).

Palsson, H. and Edwards, P. 1976: *Egil's Saga* (Harmondsworth).

Pelteret, D. 1981: Slave raiding and slave trading, in *Anglo-Saxon England*, 9.

Percival, J. 1976: *The Roman Villa. An Historical Introduction* (London).

Polanyi, K. 1978: Trade, markets and money in the European early Middle Ages, *Norwegian Archaeological Review*, Vol. 11, no. 2.

Rahtz, P.A. 1979: *The Saxon and Medieval Palaces at Cheddar* (British Archaeological Reports, British Series, no. 65. Oxford).

Reuter, T. (ed.) 1979: *The Medieval Nobility* (Amsterdam).

Salin, E. 1952: *La Civilisation Mérovingienne*, Vol. 2 (Paris).

Salin, E. 1959: *La Civilisation Mérovingienne*, Vol. 4. (Paris).

Sangree, W.H. 1965: The Bantu Tiriki of Western Kenya, in Gibbs (ed.).

Sawyer, P.H. and Wood, I.N. (eds) 1977: *Early Medieval Kingship* (Leeds).

Sawyer, P.H. 1977: Kings and merchants, in Sawyer and Wood (eds).

Sawyer, P.H. 1981: Fairs and markets in early Medieval England, *Danish Medieval History: New Currents*, d. N. Skyum-Nielsen and N. Lund (Copenhagen).

Sawyer, P.H. 1982: *Kings and Vikings* (London).

Sims-Williams, P. 1983: The settlement of England in Bede and the Chronicle, in *Anglo-Saxon England*.

Stevenson, J. (ed.) 1953–9: *The Church Historians of England* (London).

Thorpe, L. 1974: *Gregory of Tours. History of the Franks* (Harmondsworth).

Ucko, P.J. 1969: Ethnography and the archaeological interpretation of funerary remains, *World Archaeology* 1, no. 2 (October).

Wallace-Hadrill, J.M. 1960: *The Fourth Book of the Chronicle of Fredegar* (London.)

Wallace-Hadrill, J.M. 1966: The blood feud of the Franks, in *The Long Haired Kings* (London).

Wallace-Hadrill, J.M. 1975: War and peace in the Early Middle Ages, *Trans. Royal Hist. Soc.*

Whitelock, D. (ed. and trans.) 1979: *English Historical Documents. Volume 1, c. 550–1042*. 2nd edition (London).

Williams, I. (ed.) 1975: *The Poems of Taleisin* (Dublin).

Williams, I. and Bromwich, R. 1982: *Armes Prydein* (Dublin).

Williamson, C. 1983: *A Feast of Creatures. Anglo-Saxon Riddle-Songs* (London).

Wilson, D.M. 1971: *The Anglo-Saxons* 3rd Edition (Harmondsworth).

Wilson, D.M. (ed.) 1976: *The Archaeology of Anglo-Saxon England* (London).

Young, B.K. 1984: *Quatre Cimetières Mérovingiennes de l'Est de France* (British Archaeological Reports, Supplementary Series 208. Oxford).

Chapter 12

Large Danegelds in Relation to War and Kingship. Their Implications for Monetary History, and Some Numismatic Evidence.

D. M. Metcalf

Historians have from time to time wondered whether the recorded figures for danegelds were not much exaggerated, or whether they could be accepted at face value, and if so whether they offered useful evidence for the widespread availability of cash in early medieval France and England. The levying of gelds by *mansi* in France, and on a hidal basis (probably) in England seems to imply that cash could be demanded from the people of every village and that they were expected to be able to find it. The question to which this chapter is addressed is whether the demands were reasonable, in the political sense of whether they were reasonably adjusted to what people could in general be expected to pay, on a once-only basis, without thereby becoming hopelessly impoverished or disaffected. This is tantamount to asking, not just whether there was cash in the rural economy, but whether there was plenty of cash in the rural economy.

As an approach to assessing the extent to which the rural economy was monetized, it is a line of argument beset by vagueness. More straightforwardly, one could base one's case on the twofold argument that a) the amount of cash in existence, as calculated by die-estimation from the coinage, was large; and b) stray finds of single coins accidentally lost are scattered widely through the countryside, forming a topographical pattern which has great strength as evidence, in so far as it is based on random information. But there are weaknesses in this line of argument too. The average output of a coin die, which is very exactly documented from the thirteenth century onwards by a long series of official statistics, was variable and was not necessarily, or certainly, the same in the ninth to eleventh centuries. And the stray losses, which one can map so interestingly, are not necessarily a fair reflection, as regards their numbers, of the division of the currency between town and country. Perhaps (the counter-argument might run) there was a large currency, but it was essentially associated with towns and trade, and did not spill over into the countryside to anything like the extent that the stray finds seem to imply. Given the force of these objections,[1] the evidence of danegeld for a monetized rural economy may, after all, deserve to be weighed in its own right. We therefore need to consider carefully the scepticism that has been expressed to the effect that the figures recorded by chroniclers may well be exaggerated or fanciful. And we need to establish a clearer understanding of the reasonableness or otherwise of the sums demanded. Of course, reasonable or not, if they were paid then the silver must have been there with which to pay them, and the degree of pain caused to those who had to surrender their wealth is in a sense only a matter of subjective colouring. Grierson has argued that the length of time sometimes taken to collect the sums promised, or even the eventual failure to do so, are evidence that large quantities of silver sometimes simply were not there; and this may have been the case when a region had been impoverished (Grierson 1981).

The Edict of Pîtres gives us numerous glimpses of what impoverishment meant – already by 864 – at a local, day-to-day level: for example, it says that people who could not pay legal fines because of the ravages of the Northmen are not to be treated harshly. The edict condemns as being eventually destructive the selling of byrnies, weapons, and horses at low prices to meet ransom demands. The ownership or holding of land changed under pressure of poverty: peasants sold their hereditary holdings and retained only the homestead. In worse straits, people mortgaged or sold themselves into slavery, or sold their children into slavery in time of famine. Many simply fled from regions that had been ravaged by the Northmen, and lived in other regions – where, having nothing, they could not be legally punished by being deprived of their possessions: some of them grew to hold lawful behaviour in disdain, and became a headache to the authorities.

From England in the eleventh century there is a good deal of evidence, which has recently been studied by Lawson (1984), about the collection of danegeld and heregeld in the reigns of Æthelred II and Cnut.

What is the implication if a large sum took an unexpectedly long time to collect? – That people simply had not got the cash when it was demanded of them, but that over the following twelve or eighteen months they managed to lay hands on it? – If so, was that because many people had assets which they could sell for cash, given time, or because they enjoyed a cash income from which they could set resources aside? That may well be part of the implication. But when one recalls that worthy folk today delay until the last possible moment before paying their rates or their gas bill, usually on the grounds that they don't see why the council should have the interest (!), one can imagine that part of the delay, in the ninth to eleventh centuries, might have resulted merely from brinkmanship and what one may politely call sturdy individualism. For all the difficulties of collection, it seems self-evident that there was a general prior expectation that the sums agreed upon would eventually be found; and we ought to try to understand the situation from the point of view of the kings or rulers who made the decisions, and who hoped to be able to live with the consequences.

Did the collection of danegeld require increased activity at the mints?

Another theme which recurs in historical consideration of the uses of money for the payment of danegeld is that of the activity of the mints. Did the need to collect and hand over a heavy tribute provoke the striking of coinage over and above the normal output? Were mints, even, brought into commission sometimes specifically in order to meet the requirements of danegeld? The former hypothesis has often been assumed to apply to England in the late tenth and early eleventh centuries, the latter to Francia in the ninth. The problem in both cases is to see where the silver would have come from, other than from existing coinage; and to see what the point would be of reminting existing coin, when the

Vikings (to judge by their acceptance of a medley of coin-types in the currency of Scandinavia) were quite unconcerned by anything beyond the bullion value of the payments. The theory is, presumably, that in normal times there were considerable stocks of silver (and gold?) in private possession in the form of foreign or obsolete coins or plate or whatever, which the owners did not wish or need to turn into current coin, because they had built up a reserve of wealth, but which could be wrung out of them in desperate times. The major obstacle to this theory is that some danegelds certainly, and most as seems likely, were collected very widely through the country and through the ranks of society. Danegeld was a political response to an emergency of state, and all men were expected to contribute, either uniformly or according to their means. The numbers of the powerful were limited, and one does not imagine that ordinary farmers up and down the land were eating off silver dishes. So where could the silver have come from, to create a greater than usual amount of coinage – other than from existing coinage? A certain number of pilgrim churches may be assumed to have accumulated great treasures in precious metal: Peterborough's losses are described in the *Chronicle* s.a. 1070 when 'the king had all the monasteries in England plundered'. But this would seem to have been exceptional.

The supposed link between danegelds and minting probably only makes sense in the context of a very restricted money economy, supplied by a small currency. It rests upon a failure to take account of the different orders of magnitude of danegelds and of the currency at large, and upon a general historical conviction that the estate economy, throughout the countryside, operated largely without benefit of monetary exchanges. Again, the division of the currency between town and country could be invoked.

One remaining possibility however is that, although the Vikings did not mind what sort of coin or bullion they were paid in, the king saw fit in the interests of good administration to collect the tax in current coin. This thought seems to lie behind the theory, advanced by Dr Ian Stewart, that the periodic type-changes in England from *c.* 973 onwards were not as thorough as the hoard-evidence implies. Hoards from the time of Æthelred and Cnut are normally one-type or at least contain only a few obsolete coins. (Under Edward the Confessor some multi-type hoards occur.) It may be, on this view, that various official payments were required to be made in current coin, but that because of the fee payable for reminting, people would hold their long-term savings in obsolete coin until they needed to draw on them, at which point they would take them to the mint. This could very well explain a link between danegelds and unusually heavy minting, and would involve only the assumption that many people were sufficiently comfortably off to have long-term savings. The weaknesses of the theory are, first, that it requires us to disregard or depreciate the hoard-evidence (hoards are sums that people unexpectedly failed to recover, and at least a few of them might be expected to include obsolete coins if such were widely hoarded), and secondly that it is historically not very plausible that there was widespread surplus capital which people left untouched for substantially longer than a validity-period of e.g. six years.

Glittering prizes. Attitudes in the time of Charles the Bald

Viking leaders and the western rulers whose territories they attacked in the ninth century had more ideas and assumptions in common than the chronicling of their conflicts usually reveals. One such shared assumption seems to have been that the winner in a trial of military strength was entitled to huge rewards – glittering prizes, both in plunder from the regions he swept through, and also in the form of a negotiated tribute. Warfare was like a gambling game, in which the outcome was uncertain, and which was played for high stakes, that were well understood as belonging to the rules of the game. 'They see nothing wrong in the rule that to the victors belong the spoils of the enemy':[2] to the winners belonged the glittering prizes. These same prizes, viewed by those who were contributing them, were monstrous impositions. The sums of money involved bore no relationship to the sums paid in customary taxation. Gelds were incommensurately larger. Where the rulers of two adjacent territories were at war, the expectation of winning plunder and/or a geld was understood on both sides. The final part of the struggle – the end-game, so to speak – consisted of conceding, and then negotiating the size of the geld or 'penalty'.

There must have been some rancour, especially when much-esteemed leaders had been killed, but neither side regarded the other as unspeakable. In the next round of the struggle, a different set of alliances might be formed, with former opponents now on the same side. Undertakings given were, for the most part, honourably kept: honour in the midst of death and destruction. War was indeed akin to a game, and at the end of the day the two sides might, so to speak, have tea together in the pavilion. What made the Viking assaults upon England different was that there was no effective possibility of the English carrying the war back into enemy territory. But winning prizes was not, in principle, something that only heathens did at the expense of Christians. The boot was sometimes on the other foot; and heathens might exact gelds from heathens, and Christians from Christians. Christian rulers were, in the jargon of the present day, equal opportunity employers, readily hiring mercenaries without regard to race or religion. All these points are lavishly illustrated by the Annals of St Bertin's in the 860s.[3]

The annal for 861 describes the Danes sailing up the River Seine with 200 ships and besieging the fort built by the Northmen on the island of Oscelle: dog bites dog. Charles the Bald ordered a levy on his own realm in order to give the Danes 5000 lb of silver and a large amount of livestock and corn: Christian hand in glove with heathen (admittedly with the realistic purpose of forestalling looting). Another group of Danes with 60 ships next sailed up the Seine, and joined forces with their compatriots. The besieged Northmen were compelled by starvation to pay the besiegers £6000 in gold and silver (which they happened to have with them!) and entered into an alliance. Having repaired their ships during the winter, most of the Danes in the spring of 862 adjourned to Brittany, in the expectation that the (Christian) Breton ruler Salomon would hire them to attack Robert, duke of Neustria. But Robert made a preemptive alliance with the Danes (to prevent Salomon doing the same), and paid them 6,000 pieces of silver.

The annal then interposes the remark that the Danish leader Weland *with his wife and sons* came to Charles (for tea in the pavilion?), and he and his family became Christians. This may strike us as carrying a policy of no hard feelings to the extreme. But before we pass over it as an astonishing piece of ninth-century eccentricity, we should remember that something exactly similar happened in Wessex sixteen years later. After the battle of Edington and the siege of Chippenham in 878, Guthrum capitulated to Alfred and, a few weeks later, received baptism. It seems that what the events of 862 and 878 have in common is that the Viking leaders on both occasions were challenging and being inwardly challenged by a Christian culture which was both materially very prosperous (that is why they had come) and morally superior. In the skein of Weland's and Guthrum's thoughts there may have been a strand of religious dread: kings were upheld by unseen forces. For Charles and Alfred, the God of the first and second books of Samuel was undoubtedly an ever-present reality in their daily lives; and they probably judged that their opponents were rather more likely to keep their treaty promises if they were brought within the fold of the true religion, and within the bonds of spiritual kinship. In all the prior fighting and negotiating, the Vikings had had this tactical advantage, namely that they were the ruffians.

After this digression we return to Francia in 862, where the next event was that Louis, Charles's own son, outrageously offered his services to Salomon and, leading a strong contingent of Bretons, attacked Robert, his own father's liege man, and plundered Anjou. Robert, however, ambushed the Bretons and prised their booty out of them.

Two years later at Pîtres, Charles held a general assembly, at which he received not only the annual gifts but also the tribute from Brittany, sent by Salomon, 'following the customs of his ancestors, and amounting to 50lb of silver'. The contrast between the £11,000 which the Danes managed to extract from both sides at Oscelle, and £50 as the tribute from a region as large as Brittany, could not be more pointed. This figure of £50 throws into relief the element of duresse inherent in gelds. One sum was obtained under the rules of war, the other under the conventions of peace. Geld was extorted with threats, by hard men, whose threats would if necessary be backed up by exemplary retribution. The obvious modern equivalent is not reparations but the sums demanded by blackmailers or terrorists – demands sometimes running into millions of pounds or dollars. Such demands are not peaceable, but we should hesitate to say that they are not reasonable. In some black and selfish sense they are, at least by intention, measured in terms of what is reasonable, even if they bear no psychological comparison with the sums that honest citizens grudgingly pay in rates and taxes. Danegeld was, in short, war continued by other means.

Large danegelds under Æthelred II. The credibility of the chronicler's figures

The English experience of danegeld is dominated by a sequence of events in the reign of Æthelred the Unready, or (to be more precise) by a version of those events: a version that is coloured by hindsight, by old-testament styles of narrative, by a underlying conviction (which we may find hard to share) that God intervenes directly in the fates of nations in order to punish secret sins, by lack of political information, and by a Benedictine horror of the ways of the world.

> 991. In this year Ipswich was ravaged and very soon afterwards Ealdorman Brihtnoth was killed at Maldon. And in that year it was determined that tribute should first be paid to the Danish men because of the great terror they were causing along the coast. The first payment was 10,000 pounds. Archbishop Sigeric first advised that course.

There is a touch of ecclesiastical bitterness here: the church was implicated from the start. And then the story rolls on in a crescendo of disaster, with mounting payments of 16,000 pounds, 24,000, 36,000, 48,000; and in 1018 'the tribute was paid all over England, namely 72,000 pounds in all, apart from what the citizens of London paid, which was 10,500 pounds.' That is the sequence we all remember, and indeed that is the story-line. To be fair to the writer, he does mention other payments, in general terms, usually without figures (perhaps because that would detract from the dramatic force of the story), and he does set them all in the context of a blow-by-blow account of the long marches, the burning and harrying, the reaching of positions where realistically it seemed better to settle, the giving of hostages, the swearing of oaths of peace, demands for provisions for the army, for the procurement of horses, the building of warships, and so on. But his general moral is that paying the heathen only increased their rapacity, and made them ask for more next time, and that in the end it did no good, it was all a waste.

I have argued elsewhere that the 'Quatrefoil' type of coinage (Cnut's first issue in England) reveals unusual and intense minting activity at small and small-to-medium sized mints in the south-west, the west midlands, and to a lesser extent elsewhere; that special die-cutting arrangements had to be made in order to cope with a very large and unforeseen demand for the moneyer's services; and in short that there is positive evidence, from the coinage itself, that the geld paid to Cnut in 1018 was quite exceptionally large (Metcalf 1988). The chronicler's figure of £72,000 is credible enough, I have suggested, provided we understand that it was indeed a geld or exaction, and not taxation in the 'normal' sense. It differed, admittedly, from the danegelds collected in Æthelred's reign in that it was not a tribute collected in an orderly manner by the king in order to be handed over to a menacing foreign power. Cnut did not hand it over to anyone, but used it at his own discretion. It that sense it was a hybrid demand, which can be seen as geld or tax. If it was allocated by hides, it was a staggeringly heavy imposition, of about a pound per hide, and we might well be surprised that it did not provoke insurrection. The point was, however, that it was imposed while Cnut and the English were still technically at war. It was the end-game, understood (I suggest) according to the same rules as had governed war and its spoils in the ninth century. The geld was quickly followed by a national assembly at Oxford, at which the English and the Danes agreed a *modus vivendi*. The agreement was reached 'as soon as King Cnut with the advice of his councillors completely established peace and friendship [!] between the Danes and English and put an end to all their former strife.' (Whitelock 1979). The geld was the final act of the hostilities, before good faith was pledged on both sides. It was the heavy penalty that Cnut was entitled to exact under the rules of the game – a far heavier burden than would have been found tolerable had it been seen as taxation.

Lawson has suggested that the geld of 1018 was that which Edmund Ironside had agreed to pay after the battle of Ashingdon, late in 1016. Blackburn and Lyon (1986) take the same view, and say (more specifically) that it took Cnut two years to collect the very large amount that had been agreed. The Chronicle does indeed say, s.a. 1018, 'In this year the tribute was paid', rather than 'In this year Cnut levied a tribute', or something similar: the form of words might imply knowledge that the tribute had been decided before 1018. But there are still some difficulties in construing the annal for 1016 accordingly. After the battle, Cnut and Edmund met, became sworn brothers (tea in the pavilion again?), and fixed the amount of money to be paid to the host. They then separated, sharing England between them: Edmund was to hold Wessex, and Cnut the more northerly parts of the country. The host then went to the ships with what they had taken (this is presumable booty rather than tribute, unless Edmund paid out of the royal coffers), and the citizens of London came to terms with the host and bought peace from them. – If the geld collected in 1018 had been agreed in 1016, would it have been intended at that point to collect it uniformly all over England, or would it not rather have taken account of the division of the country between the two kings? If the sum agreed had been as huge as £72,000, would not the annalist have commented on it in some way at this point in his narrative? Was there one payment from the citizens of London, or were there two, one in 1016 to buy peace, and the other as Stenton suggested originating only in 1018 to cover the costs of paying the crews when the fleet in the spring of that year dealt for the last time with the Londoners' old enemies, by destroying thirty ships' companies of Vikings, which had ventured into English waters?

It is, arguably, the case that the need for cash throughout England to pay the geld in 1018 caused a special surge of activity at the mints, which is reflected in the very large scale and unusual geographical distribution of the 'Quatrefoil' type. (For detailed statistical estimates see Metcalf 1980 & 1981.) But this seems to have been the only occasion, except in Æthelred's 'Crux' type (*c.* 991–7) in East Anglia, when the existing arrangements for minting could not take a geld in their stride (Lyon 1970 & 1976; Stafford 1978). The volume of English mint-output was normally far in excess of the sums that had to be collected.

Quatrefoil pennies were mostly very light in weight – much lighter than the immediately preceding Last Small Cross type. We do not know whether payment of the geld was accepted in pence at face value or only by weight, and equally we do not know what sort of a charge was levied on reminting old coins into the Quatrefoil type – whether, in percentage terms, it was less than the average weight difference. We cannot judge, therefore, whether the light weight of the new coins was a kind of leniency. But the die-cutting arrangements and the scale and geographical distribution of minting strongly imply that new coins were needed in unprecedented quantities and as a matter of urgency at about the date when the geld was being collected.

Quatrefoil is the exception that proves the rule, and it does not entitle us to assume that the pattern of Carolingian minting was governed by the need to pay gelds. One should respond very cautiously to the superficially attractive idea that large numbers of mints were opened in north-eastern Francia in the 860s specifically in order to cope with the Danegeld of 866 (Grievson 1981, 5). It may be, for example, that the decline and by 863 the effective ruin of Dorestad (which had for so long been a major commercial centre with a prolific mint) coupled with a continuing demand for currency, led to a realignment of minting, pushing it back into the hinterland of the Meuse valley and the surrounding regions. One should also remember that the XPISTIANA RELIGIO coins which preceded those of the Edict of Pîtres were not mint-signed, and may have been struck more widely than we are in a position to demonstrate (Gelder 1965); and also that the mints of north-eastern Francia did not close again as soon as the danegeld was paid.

Likewise there is the clearest possible evidence that the English monetary system in the same years proved remarkably resilient to the ravages of the great army and the frequent buying of peace. Debasement under Burgred and Alfred was *not* a symptom of the country's financial exhaustion, for it was accompanied by a significant increase in the amount of silver passing through the mints (Metcalf & Northover 1985).

Harthacnut's exaction of 1041

'With the best intentions', says the Abingdon *Chronicle* (Version C), after the death of Harold I, 'they sent to Bruges for Harthacnut, and he came then to this country with sixty ships before midsummer, and then imposed a severe tax which was borne with difficulty'. The Laud *Chronicle* tells us that it amounted to £21,099, 'and £11,048 was afterwards paid to 32 ships'. The charitable view of this heavy taxation is that Harthacnut was simply presenting his English subjects with the bill for the expenses incurred in his taking possession of what was rightfully his own. Because of the delay before Harthacnut could safely leave Denmark to come to England, Harold's regency had been converted into kingship over the whole of England. Even during the regency, he was king enough to strike coins in his own name and with the title REX, in Mercia and throughout the eastern Danelaw. The numismatic evidence, recently very ably established by Talvio (1986), shows that through the operation of local loyalties (no doubt along the lines of the ealdormanries) England was in effect partitioned by agreement (thus confirming what Florence of Worcester seems to be saying, but about which the Chronicle is silent). The southern mints struck 'Jewel Cross' coins in the name of Cnut (for Harthacnut), and the more northerly mints struck matching coins in the name of Harold, from an early stage – probably in virtue of the agreement reached at the *witan* at Oxford in 1036. By a nice touch, Harthacnut's coins have a right-facing bust, and Harold's a left-facing bust. As 'portraits' they are otherwise indistinguishable. Very soon, however, Harthacnut's issues were terminated. By *c.* 1037 Harold had abrogated the agreement, had driven the queen-mother Emma out of Winchester, and had seized power throughout the country: almost all the mints now struck in his name. The coins of this second phase of the Jewel Cross type can be recognized by the simpler style of their dies. Harold then introduced a new design, the Fleur-de-lis type, which again was struck virtually in his name alone. It was current from *c.* 1038 until Harold's death, and was continued for a time, (probably only a few months) by Harthacnut before the next periodic type, Arm-and-Sceptre, was introduced. (This is an interesting example of the degree to which minting was outside the political arena, and also of the continuous need for the services of the minters.) Perhaps the ship tax was collected largely in Fleur-de-lis pennies, for the Arm-and-Sceptre issue is not prolific.

From Harthacnut's point of view, therefore, Harold was a usurper, whose position had become so strongly entrenched that it was necessary to raise an army against him. Harthacnut was in due course invited to England, after Harold's death, and it is perhaps just as well that some semblance of peace and harmony could be presented, for Harthacnut's treatment of Harold's corpse, and his punishment of the city of Worcester for disloyalty suggest that his wrath would have been unbridled. The ship tax was not claimed under the same 'rules of the game' as earlier danegelds, but it seems to have belonged in the same spectrum of ideas.

William I's 'heavy and severe tax' of 1084

Can we detect a parallel between the heavy geld paid in 1018, concurrently with unusually active minting of the 'Quatrefoil' type, and followed by the peace agreement at Oxford, and the 'heavy and severe' tax levied by William the Conqueror in 1084, concurrently perhaps with the unusually plentiful 'PAXS' type, and followed by oaths of homage and fealty at Salisbury in 1086? The correct answer would seem to be a guarded negative. At most, the later events are reminiscent of earlier procedures. William was not negotiating terms with a defeated enemy, but asserting his hold over men who were already committed to him (Holt 1987). If we ask whether there was a link between the scale of the 'PAXS' issue and the needs generated by the heavy tax of 1084, we plunge into detailed and inconclusive controversy on almost every aspect of the equation. When was the 'PAXS' type introduced? How long did it take to collect the tax of 1084? Was there another unusually heavy tax in 1085/6, or was it the same one still being slowly collected? (Galbraith 1961; Holt 1987). Was the 'PAXS' type struck on a larger scale than William's preceding issues? Was the geographical distribution of minting different? As the tax was not, in any case, danegeld, and as it would be a lengthy matter to set out the evidence, it will not be discussed here, except to say that a single tax of six shillings per hide in relation to an estimated total mintage for the 'PAXS' type of 880 'equivalent reverse dies', say roughly 8.8 million pence, or £36,000, would indeed involve a substantial proportion of the currency if the king gathered it all in and kept it in his coffers (Metcalf 1988). The corresponding figures for 1018 were very much higher at about one pound per hide (£72,000), and 47 million pence, or approaching £200,000 (Metcalf 1988).

Twelfth-century 'danegeld' was radically different

Words can change their meanings, even if originally the institutions they described remain the same. *Geldum* in medieval Latin is merely tax, whereas geld in modern English carries the connotation of a heavy exaction. Danegeld survived the Conquest in name at least, but changed its nature radically to become merely an annual levy (Green 1981). Comparisons with the amounts raised in the time of Æthelred would be irrelevant.

What became of the coins collected as danegeld? The Cuerdale hoard

Where did danegelds disappear to? It is a well-known puzzle that few Carolingian coins have been found in Scandinavia, in spite of all the raiding of the later ninth century. Some of the money handed over to the Vikings was no doubt spent locally, and will thus quickly have found its way back into the currency of the region where it was levied. Much of it may have been melted down into ingots and arm-rings and the like, in Scandinavia or elsewhere. Without a major programme of lead isotope analysis, of both coins and artefacts, and perhaps even with it, this will remain difficult to demonstrate. There are hints of regional transfers of coin, e.g. from Aquitaine to the lower Rhinelands (Metcalf 1981). The famous Cuerdale hoard, concealed *c.* 905 in Lancashire, included (as well as ingots) a thousand Carolingian coins, which may reflect the transfer of plunder from one region of western Europe to another (but in value they are only £4!). The silver pennies of the Vikings of York, which suddenly replaced the brass stycas of the Anglian kings, may similarly have been boosted by the expulsion of the Vikings from Dublin, or by the reminting of Carolingian coinage acquired by raiding (Stewart 1987).[4] The York coinage, however, has been estimated to have amounted, altogether, to as much as nine or ten tonnes of coinage-silver – whereas a £5,000 geld in the 860s amounted to only about two tonnes.

In the nature of the case, danegelds were conspicuous in their collection, but they were then shared out or dispersed in various lower-profile ways, about which it seems fruitless to speculate further. Almost every farm on Gotland had its buried treasure; and perhaps a few of those sums originated in the spoils of raiding. But because English danegelds were (so far as one can judge) always paid in coins from a medley of mints, there is nothing regionally distinctive about the composition of the treasures found in Scandinavia. Kenneth Jonsson has recently claimed that the famous Igelösa hoard from Skåne consists of 'several parcels of which two large ones may be associated with danegelds, which makes it foremost among the (surprisingly few) hoards that can be said to consist of danegeld payments.' (Jonsson 1987). Even in these few instances, the eye of faith is needed.

Notes

1. Its force is much reduced by the need to envisage the commodities which were traded: if there was a money economy in ordinary small towns (say, in the upwards of fifty places where there was a mint in the eleventh century), it almost certainly drew on a trade which reached out into the surrounding countryside. Town and country should be assumed to have been commercially integrated.
2. W. Mercy, in a speech to the United States Senate in 1832.
3. I am indebted to Dr J.L. Nelson for the opportunity to study her translation of the *Annales Bertiniani*.
4. The idea that Carolingian coinage obtained as booty was straightforwardly melted down and turned into Viking pennies at York runs into the difficulty, however, that the trace-element patterns of the silver are different (Metcalf and Northover 1988).

References

Blackburn, M. and Lyon, S. 1986: Regional die-production in Cnut's *Quatrefoil* issue, in *Anglo-Saxon Monetary History*, ed. M.A.S. Blackburn (Leicester), 223–72.

Galbraith, V. H. 1961: *The Making of Domesday Book*, 87ff.

Gelder, H. Enno van 1965: Le trésor carolingien d'Ide, *Revue Numismatique* 7, 241–61, esp. at p. 245.

Green, J.A. 1981: The last century of Danegeld, *English Historical Review* 96, 241–58.

Grierson, P. 1981: The 'Gratia Dei Rex' coinage of Charles the Bald, in M. Gibson and J. Nelson (eds.), *Charles the Bald: Court and Kingdom* (BAR International Series, 101. Oxford), 39–51.

Holt, J.C. 1987: 1086, in *Domesday Studies*, ed. J.C. Holt, 41–64.

Jonsson, K. 1987: *Viking-Age Hoards and Late Anglo-Saxon Coins. A Study in Honour of Bror Emil Hildebrand's Anglosachsiska mynt*, (Stockholm).

Lawson, M. K. 1984: The collection of Danegeld and heregeld in the reigns of Æthelred II and Cnut, *English Historical Review* 99, 721–38.

Lyon, S. 1970: Historical problems of Anglo-Saxon coinage – (4). The Viking Age, *British Numismatic Journal* 39, 200

Lyon, S. 1976: Some problems in interpreting Anglo-Saxon coinage, *Anglo-Saxon England* 5, 173–224, at p. 197 and n. 4.

Metcalf, D.M. 1980 & 1981: Continuity and change in English monetary history, c. 973–1086, *British Numismatic Journal* 50, 20–49; *ibid.* 51, 52–90.

Metcalf, D.M. 1981: A sketch of the currency in the time of Charles the Bald, in *Charles the Bald: Court and Kingdom* (BAR International Series, 101. Oxford), 53–84.

Metcalf, D.M. 1988: Can we believe the very large figure of £72,000 for the geld levied by Cnut in 1018?, *Studies in Memory of B.E. Hildebrand* (Stockholm), forthcoming.

Metcalf, D.M. and Northover, J.P. 1985: Debasement of the coinage in southern England in the age of King Alfred, *Numismatic Chronicle* 145, 150–76.

Metcalf, D.M. and Northover, J. P. 1988: Carolingian and Viking coins from the Cuerdale hoard: an interpretation and comparison of their metal contents, *Numismatic Chronicle* 158, forthcoming.

Stafford, P. 1978: Historical implications of the regional production of dies under Æthelred II, *British Numismatic Journal* 48, 35–51.

Stewart, I. 1987: CVNNETTI reconsidered, in *Coinage in Ninth-Century Northumbria: The Tenth Oxford Symposium on Coinage and Monetary History* (BAR. Oxford), 345–54.

Talvio, T. 1986: Harold I and Harthacnut's *Jewel Cross* type reconsidered, in *Anglo-Saxon Monetary History*, ed. M.A.S. Blackburn (Leicester), 273–90.

Whitelock, D. 1979: *English Historical Documents*, vol. 1, 2nd edn., p. 452, no. 47.

Chapter 13

The Anglo-Saxons at War

Nicholas Hooper

The subject of war and the Anglo-Saxons is a curiously neglected one. The author of the only lengthy survey described it as an 'institutional history rather than military history' (Hollister 1962, p. vii). This is quite understandable. It is reasonable to think that the study of the institutions of a society will result in important insights. Moreover, the study of medieval war has generally taken the sterile form of the quest for the 'Holy Grail' of decisive battles. It has been the preserve of retired soldiers with a firm conviction in their experience and 'IMP', inherent military probability. But if the study of battles alone tells little about the societies we seek to understand, the historian of war can uncover valuable insights to set beside those gleaned by the institutional historian. In recent years an increasing number of works have appeared devoted to aspects of medieval warfare which have begun to revise the damming conclusions of Oman (1924), but on the whole they have still tended to concentrate on institutions – military obligations, recruitment etc. – to the detriment of practical studies of how war was waged. Yet this was of overriding importance to kings, magnates and the church, for successful war was essential to stable kingship and society.

Two important works, Smail on crusading warfare and Gillingham on Richard I have paid more attention to the practicalities of waging war and have shown how important it is to put it into a broader context (Smail 1956, Gillingham 1984). This paper is inspired by these and other recent work on the practice of war by the Carolingians, in the twelfth century and in the fourteenth and fifteenth centuries, too many to mention here. My intention is to see what can be said about how the Anglo-Saxons went to war and what they did while they were away from home. There is desperately little to work from, particularly when we consider the length of the period and the degree of change which can only be perceived dimly. A study of this nature is heavily dependent on literary sources which cluster around a few periods: Bede and the roughly contemporary authors of Saints' lives provide material for the 7th and early 8th centuries; the Anglo-Saxon chronicle and Asser shine the spotlight on Alfred and the relative abundance of material continues through the reign of his son; then obscurity until the time of Æthelred II and the detailed account in the Chronicle, the *Battle of Maldon* poem and the Laws (disappointingly thin on going to war); lastly, the accounts of 1066 yield important information. There are obvious dangers in interpreting such materials, not least the need to generalize from isolated fragments of evidence. It has recently been pointed out that Bede owed a significant debt to the Books of Samuel and Kings in his descriptions of war, that they had taught him 'to ask the pertinent questions about significant military encounters in the history of his own people' (McClure 1983, p. 88). Does this mean that his testimony is to be rejected? My approach to the episodes quoted below is that they are accurate descriptions of what happened, or at least what was thought could reasonably have happened.

Firstly, the mustering of armies. For both offensive and defensive war, and whether armies consisted essentially of household bands, as seems to have been characteristic of the earlier period, or were recruited on a territorial basis, soldiers had to be summoned. The mustering of an army, annually at times, occupied an important place in Frankish history, both military and constitutional. The English kingdoms appear to have known no institution similar to the 'Field of Mars'. It would be useful to know three things: how men were summoned, where they mustered and how long it took. Were they inspected before they set off and what were they expected to take with them? The earliest reference is Bede's story of the overthrow of the Northumbrian Æthelfrith by Redwald overlord of the southern English. Redwald raised a large army, presumably from among the kings who accepted his overlordship, and 'not giving him time to summon and assemble his whole army, Redwald met him with a much greater force and slew him on the Mercian border on the east bank of the river Idle' (HE ii.12). The geographical description is not precise, although the battle may have taken place where the Roman road from Lincoln to Castleford crosses the Idle. Nevertheless, it does indicate that whether or no his army was complete, Æthelfrith advanced to the southern border of Northumbria to meet the invader. How did he know of Redwald's approach and route? It is much easier, of course to raise questions than to answer them, but the event as Bede describes it suggests a degree of intelligence and planning on both sides. If it did not happen like this, it is nonetheless significant that Bede believed it possible.

There is a more detailed account of raising an army in 878, when the Danes made a surprise attack on Alfred at Chippenham after Twelfth Night. Alfred retreated to Athelney 'after Easter' and then seven weeks after Easter mustered an army at "Egbert's stone" (ASC 878, Asser c. 55). It is not difficult to imagine that Alfred sent out word to the ealdormen of Somerset, Wiltshire and Hampshire, and to the reeves, to call his men to arms. This may explain the delay, and it is probably no more than coincidence that the army mustered at the beginning of May, a time when there would have been sufficient grass for the horses and one often chosen for the Field of Mars. It is a unique reference to both the time and place of assembly for an English army, yet the way in which it was achieved must have been commonplace and well-practised. However, the information given in the Chronicle contradicts the general impression of crisis which had been built up, for the rendez-vous was only a few miles from the Danish base at Chippenham and suggests the Danish army was not widely dispersed over Wessex.

We are rather better informed, in fact, about the mustering of fleets in the eleventh century. From 992 to 1066 fleets were assembled at London, or returned to the city at the end of their service, on several occasions. Where they took up station depended on the quarter from which a threat was expected: Sandwich if invasion was expected from the north, or the Isle of Wight if it was from Normandy. Today Sandwich is a quiet backwater and the eleventh-century description of it as 'the most famous of all the ports of the English' comes as a surprise (Campbell 1949, pp. 20–1).[1] In the eleventh century it occupied a strategic site: it's now silted-up bay formed a safe anchorage in the sheltered lee of Thanet from which ships could move north, along the channel of the Stour, into the Thames estuary; move south and west along the coast of Wessex; or stay put to intercept fleets from Scandinavia. At the same time there is some evidence that London may have been the naval base at which ships were laid up, perhaps upstream of the protection provided by London Bridge with its twin fortresses.

Eleventh-century events indicate more clearly how long it might take to raise an army. In 1004 Ulfcetel found it politic to pay tribute when a Danish fleet came to Norwich, because he was taken by surprise and 'had not had time to gather his army'. Within three weeks, however, he was able to confront King Swein at Thetford, but although the battle was hard-fought it ended in defeat for Ulfcetel. He had been unable to assemble his full strength in something under three weeks, although this was partly due to the need for secrecy to avoid warning the Danes (ASC 1004). There is a further clue from 1066 when Harold raised two armies from a rather larger area. On 8 September he disbanded the fleet and army which was watching the south coast against Norman invasion, only to hear a few days later of the Norwegian landing near York. He rode north 'day and night as quickly as he could assemble his force', pausing at Tadcaster on Sunday 24 September to marshal his troops. He marched on through York to fall on the Norwegian camp the next day. Harold repeated the feat in an even shorter time after the Norman landing, news of which reached him in early October, when he rode rapidly to London, raising more men and advanced to Battle in Sussex. There he was intercepted and forced to fight. The different versions in the Chronicle and Florence of Worcester agree that Harold advanced from London before all his troops had assembled, and that he fought the battle before his men were all drawn up. As these accounts post-date 1066 by some time it is possible that this is nothing more than an apology, but it at least sounds feasible (ASC 1066, Douglas 1953, pp. 213–4). In the space of about a month, then, the English government was able to muster two armies for major battles fought some 240 miles apart. Information about which areas sent contingents to the two battles is sparse. It refers to one man each from Essex and Worcestershire at Stamford Bridge, and the more numerous references to men who were present at Hastings show they came from an area which corresponds, not surprisingly, to the centre of Harold's Wessex, the earldoms of his brothers Gyrth and Leofwine (who fell with him), and also Waltheof's east Midland earldom. Flimsy as it is, this evidence suggests that by the early eleventh century an army could be summoned within two or three weeks by using the network of royal officials and arranging muster points. It is no surprise to find this in a kingdom as intensively governed as late Anglo-Saxon England, but it is also a further demonstration of the power of its rulers. For a prepared campaign or to meet a determined invader this might have been adequate. Against a mobile raider it was perhaps too slow moving unless advance information was available, or the threat could be dealt with by magnates with their retinues.

Once they left home these armies and fleets had to be supplied, not only with food and clothing for the men but also forage for the horses which gave them mobility and were fitting to their station. As Campbell has observed, the distances over which seventh century campaigns were fought shows that armies almost certainly rode to war and the English had no need to learn this from the Danes (Campbell 1982, p. 59; Clapham 1910). Small armies in hostile territory could live off the land, so long as it was fertile enough, but there would not be much chance of this in most of Wales or Scotland, or even parts of Northumbria. Foraging and plundering of course played a central role in medieval warfare and had several purposes. Apart from the collection of provisions, ravaging served to enrich those taking part as they seized valuable objects, captives and livestock. In thus serving their own interests they also did damage to the enemy, both physical and to the reputation of a king who failed to prevent it. There was no need then, for a campaign to end in battle if sufficient plunder was taken or the payment of tribute exacted. The necessity to offer battle lay with the king whose land was under attack. This is no more than summarizing what is well-known about the war of the Merovingian and Carolingian kings, and about twelfth century warfare. As Jordan Fantosme made Count Philip of Flanders say:

> Destroy your foes and lay waste their country
> By fire and burning let all be set alight
> That nothing be left for them outside, either in wood or meadow
> Of which in the morning they could have a dinner

> Thus should war be begun; such is my advice,
> First destroy the land, then one's foe.
> (Howlett 1886, iii. 241–3, 11.439–50)

This is a lesson Anglo-Saxon historians do not seem to have taken to heart. It is what Penda and Cadwallon did in seventh century Northumbria and what the Vikings did, or threatened to do until they were paid, in the ninth century.[2]

But there were circumstances in which living off the land was inappropriate. The most obvious is where an army fought on its home ground. For English armies this became increasingly the case as the West Saxon kingdom expanded in the tenth century, although in 1016 friend and foe were not easy to differentiate (ASC 1016). A king who wished to win hearts and minds might also wish to put a curb on ravaging, as Swein did in 1013 after the people north of Watling Street had submitted to him. Anyway, large or relatively large armies could not support themselves by foraging without dispersing and thereby losing their advantage in numbers and making themselves more vulnerable to attack. This is what happened in the campaign of 903 when Edward summoned an army 'as soon as he could' to pursue raiders from East Anglia who had been active in the upper Thames valley. He went to Cambridgeshire and ravaged, and what happened next shows the army dispersed to do this more effectively. Edward announced his intention of withdrawing but the men of Kent lingered – in spite of receiving seven messengers. They were isolated by the army of East Anglia and heavily defeated (ASC 903).

It was necessary, then, to arrange for armies to carry supplies with them so that a reasonable amount could be achieved before they had to disperse. Charlemagne, the most successful warleader of the early middle ages, paid particular attention to this problem of logistics, indeed to many aspects of calling out armies, in several capitularies. Men summoned to the host were to bring with them provisions for three months in carts, together with other necessaries for war, and there is also evidence of the collection of supplies for the use of armies on the march. Fresh meat could be provided by taking beasts on the hoof. This sort of supply train required, as well as an escort of the type which was mauled in the pass of Roncesvalles, a great deal of labour which was drawn from the poor. If the only specific references to it come from the time of Charlemagne it was, nevertheless, a common requirement of armies (Ganshof 1970, pp. 66–7; the capitularies in King 1987, pp. 260–3, 266 8; Leyser 1968, p. 21).

The evidence that English kings paid similar attention to the question of supply is less full, as usual, but it is there. Bede's miracle story about the loosing of the thegn Imma, taken prisoner at the battle of the Trent (679), is the first clue. In order to avoid being killed in vengeance for his captor's kinsmen, Imma masqueraded as 'a peasant and a poor man and married; and declared that he had come on that campaign with others of his kind to bring provisions to the troops' (HE iv.22). The whole tale is a fascinating one, and seems to suggest that the supply train of the Northumbrian army was made up of married, poor peasants. His Mercian captors did not find his tale in the least surprising. There is no reason to doubt that there were men whose duties required them to go with the army but not to fight in the front line. It is difficult to imagine the noble Anglo-Saxon warrior going to war without a groom for his horses and a valet for his personal needs, and the 'fyrd-work' of the common obligations could well have provided men for logistical services as well as for the shield-wall.

Yet if armies of the seventh and eighth centuries were accompanied by servants and a supply train of lesser free men, Alfred found these arrangements insufficient to defeat the Vikings. One of his reforms, if he was responsible for them, was to divide his military resources into three. One part manned the burhs and found the permanent garrisons which would make it impossible for the Danes to overrun Wessex, although they would also take to the field when extra soldiers were needed. The remaining two would take it in turns to serve. They were allocated a fixed term of service and brought the necessary provisions with them. This arrangement did not always function perfectly. On one occasion a division on service went home in the middle of blockading a Danish army on Thorney island, its provisions consumed and its term expired, before the king came to relieve them (ASC 893; also Asser c. 100 for the organisation of the royal household).[3]

This method of division and rotation remained in force right up to 1066. In 917, when armies from Wessex and Mercia were in the field from early April until November, one division went home and another took over. Again, in 1052 when Edward's fleet was waiting at Sandwich to intercept Godwine's return, the ships returned to London to take on new earls and crews. And in 1066 Harold's fleet disbanded on the Feast of the Nativity of St. Mary (8 Sept) after holding station at the Isle of Wight 'all the summer', and appears first to have been summoned in late April or early May. That is to say, it had been out for about 4 months altogether. Now, the Domesday account of Berkshire (Domesday Book i f.56v, Douglas 1953, p. 929) says that men summoned to the host took with them 20s for victuals and payment for two months. It would seem that Harold maintained his watch on the south coast by calling out one part of the host for two months, and a second part for a further two months. When the second division had served its term he gave up, either because after four months of inaction he could no longer keep up the effort, or because he decided the Normans were not coming that year. It was a considerable achievement, if in the end it was not good enough (ASC 917, 1052, 1066).

Of this evidence, only the tale in the Ecclesiastical History explains how the army in the field was supplied. It is possible that the men in the later examples carried their own provisions but more likely that they were accompanied by servants with pack-horses or wagons, as Charlemagne's capitulary envisaged. It meant that the later Old English kings were able, on the whole, to overcome the problem of keeping armies in the field for quite long periods. The distances over which they fought do not compare with the campaigns of Charlemagne, but so far as aggressive wars are concerned they achieved success over Scots, Welsh and Danes. They were not invincible, but the distances over which they fought is comparable with post-conquest campaigns. In military, as in political terms, the West Saxon monarchs of the tenth century went a long way to solving the problems of ruling their enlarged kingdom.

Military training and strategy are two important matters on which the sources are more than usually silent. There are no references in literature or laws to men training, and so it is necessary to fall back on inference. For the noble warrior, his childhood was of first importance in learning both individual military skills and the teamwork essential for success in battle. Perhaps the games the youthful Cuthbert played ('wrestling, jumping, running, and every other exercise') had some military significance (Webb and Farmer 1965, pp. 43–4). As Roger of Howden said of the military training the sons of Henry II received

> they realised that without practice the art of war did not come naturally when it was needed. No athlete can fight tenaciously who has never received any blows: he must see his blood flow and hear his teeth crack under the fist of his adversary...The oftener he falls the more determinedly he must spring to his feet again. Anyone who can do that can engage in battle confidently...The price of sweat is well paid where the Temples of Victory stand (Verbruggen 1977, p. 29).

This is a text which will do for budding warriors of any age. The most important part of the young warrior's military experience came when he was fostered in another household. Beowulf went to the household of King Hrethel when he was seven. Bede, in the life of Cuthbert, described the change of life: the eighth year was 'the end of infancy and the threshold of boyhood' (Beowulf, 11.2425–36, Webb and Farmer 1965, pp. 43–4). The young man graduated at the age of thirteen or fourteen. This was the age at which Wilfrid chose to leave his father's estates. He went to the queen, armed and mounted, accompanied by his servants (Webb and Farmer 1965, p. 107). Guthlac was about the same age when

> his youthful strength had increased, and a noble desire for command burned in his young breast...he changed his disposition and gathering bands of followers took up arms' (Colgrave 1956, pp. 80–1).

Athelstan, according to William of Malmesbury,

> clad in the flower of young manhood, practised the pursuit of arms at his father's orders

after being sent to school in his childhood (Whitelock 1979, p. 306). If the young warrior survived the rigours of a decade of the military life, in another man's household or leading his own war-band, he might expect when he reached his mid-twenties the reward in land which was his due, unless he underwent a spiritual conversion or the land was not forthcoming from his lord (Webb and Farmer 1965, p. 185 (Benedict Biscop), Bede's Letter to Egbert in Whitelock 1979, p. 805, Alfred in Keynes and Lapidge 1983, pp. 132, 139). Of course this scheme is a cliché, and the young Ceolfrith entered Gilling when he was eighteen (Whitelock 1979, p. 759), but clichés frequently reflect reality.

An important and informal way of acquiring familiarity with weapons and horses was hunting which

> taught boys and youths how to move in company across the countryside, instilled in them the arts of scouting and selecting a line of advance, and gave excellent training in arms, the bow against many running animals and the sword and spear against the wild boar (Barlow 1983, pp. 119f).

This was as true of the seventh as the twelfth century. The nearest parallel I can find in an Anglo-Saxon source is the horse-racing indulged in by the young laymen in the retinue of John of Beverley (HE v.6). There is one more possible hint to training, if it is not stretching credibility too far. What was Beorhtnoth doing at Maldon when he 'rode and gave counsel and taught his warriors how they should stand and keep their ground, bade them hold their shields aright, firm with their hands and fear not at all?' (Whitelock 1979, p. 320). Was he drilling them in something they were unaware of, or was he reminding them of something they knew well? The Ottonian historian Liutprand of Cremona has a similar story in his account of the battle of Riade (933), in which Henry the Fowler advised his men on how to approach the Magyars. It is a literary story, but we need not believe that these men were ignorant of how to use their arms or to form ranks. In each case the author was directing an explanation to the audience. To use Leyser's words, 'it is as if their drill-master was reminding them not to forget the important lessons just at the moment they were about to be put to the test' (Leyser 1968, p. 33). These 'important lessons' were learned as the prospective warrior grew up and practised in the household of father or lord.

Turning to strategy, on the whole the descriptions of warfare are too bald to permit much to be said. Of the period before Alfred the evidence gives the impression that Anglo-Saxon armies fought battles frequently. If this is not solely due to the deficiencies of the sources, it would make England a special case. Battle was risky and best avoided unless all the factors were on your side. But if you were in a position so advantageous that you were willing to take the chance, it is likely that your enemy would be in such a weak position that he would avoid battle and pay tribute. Unless, of course, he was Bede's Oswald and trusted in God. Anyway, battle put the princes' lives at risk, as is demonstrated by the Northumbrian and Mercian overlordships brought to an end by a defeat in the field.

Gillingham has shown how few pitched battles successful warrior-kings like Charlemagne and Richard I chose to fight: 'in European medieval history as a whole battles are rare and making war did not normally involve seeking battle' (Gillingham 1984, pp. 90–1). Strategic objectives could usually be achieved in other ways, one of which was ravaging. In the wars of the seventh, eighth and ninth centuries a high number of battles appear to have been fought in England, and few recorded campaigns finished without battle.[4] The reason for this is obscure. Where battles were rare it was usually because war was dominated by fortified points, and it is no coincidence that before the 9th century there are almost no references to sieges in English campaigns. The paradox is that from the middle of the previous century the Mercian kings had reserved labour on fortresses when they granted bookland free of most royal burdens (Brooks 1971). The works on which Mercian peasant laboured have so far proved difficult to identify, with the exception of a rampart at Hereford and the monumental Offa's Dyke. Yet the activities of the Vikings show there were towns worth sacking and taking shelter in. For what reason they played little part in earlier warfare, then, is a mystery, although the probability that trading centres like Southampton and London were undefended is suggestive.

A defensive strategy becomes more apparent in the later part of Alfred's reign. It was built around the possession of fortified places and the close pursuit of the Danes to harass them and impede their preferred occupation of plundering. Alfred and his lieutenants were able to fight the Danes to a standstill by their repeated ability to pursue and closely besiege them in fortified camps at Nottingham, Wareham, Exeter, Chippenham, Rochester, Milton, Appledore, Thorney, Buttington, Chester and Hertford. At Chester they besieged them for some two days, and seized all the cattle that was outside, and killed the men whom they could cut off outside the fortress, and burnt all the corn, or consumed it by means of their horses, in all the surrounding district...the Danish army...could not stay there...because they were deprived both of the cattle and the corn...'.[5]

It was only in the later part of Edward the Elder's reign that we see a type of war which a twelfth century soldier would have recognised. In this phase of the war the West Saxons conquered land by building and holding burhs from which to threaten and dominate Danish territory. The fortification of sites at Witham, Buckingham, Towcester and Colchester persuaded the Danes of the surrounding regions to submit (ASC 912, 914, 917). The key to this warfare was sieges and the control of fortified places. It is clear that the new fortresses had permanent garrisons, and that they were supported by the inhabitants of the existing burhs when danger threatened. This is brought out most clearly in the description of the campaigns of 917 in the Chronicle, but throughout the conquest of the Danelaw by Edward and Æthelflæd it is clear that a sophisticated and coordinated strategy was being applied. It is possible that it was the Danes who had introduced the idea to England, but when they were on the receiving end they found that the West Saxons were far more proficient at this new strategy than their teachers had been. Indeed, when the Danes attempted to capture the new burhs which threatened them, for example at Towcester, *Wigingamere* and Maldon, they were incapable of breaking in.

In some cases Anglo-Saxon strategies resemble those of later times. For example, on two occasions invasions of Scotland were mounted by a land army supported by a fleet. In the late thirteenth and fourteenth centuries the fleet was required partly to provision the land forces, which may have been one of its roles in the campaigns of Athelstan and Siward (ASC 934, 1054 (D only)). In 1063 the same combination of land force and fleet was sent against Wales, the ships from Harold's earldom and the army from Tostig's. Again, fleets played a significant role in post-conquest operations against Gwynedd. We can also say that Harold's fast movement in 1066, whatever its advisability, conformed to a pattern of making war which was later common. Although he has been accused of 'reckless and impulsive' haste (Brown 1969, p. 158, 1981, p. 8) this is chiefly because he failed. The strategy of moving quickly was widely used by later commanders to achieve surprise. The ability to 'pop up as through a trap-door, with the suddenness of a demon-king' (Warren 1961, p. 94, on Henry II and Richard I) was an asset in war. Harold had used it with success against Griffith in Wales in 1063 and against the Norwegians in September 1066. His intention may have been to prevent William's 'foraging' rather than to force battle, but if so he went too close (Gillingham 1984, p. 85). He was undone not by reckless and impulsive haste, but by William's superior generalship which forced him to fight in unsuitable circumstances. What is clear from these few examples is that Anglo-Saxon commanders could adopt and follow effective strategies.

Finally, battle tactics. The tactics of the Anglo-Saxons have been the subject of frequent criticism: 'the stationary tactics of a phalanx of axemen' was Oman's slighting opinion; to H.W.C. Davis 'on any field and in an engagement on any scale nothing short of the most desparate odds could have prevented the superiority of Norman tactics and equipment from taking their natural effect'; to Stenton, Harold's army was 'confined by its nature to a type of warfare which was already obsolete in the greater part of Western Europe' (references collected by Glover 1952, p. 1). Indeed their tactics have found few defenders, apart from Glover and Hollister, and his defence took the form of a misguided and unsuccessful attempt to belittle Norman tactics. Evidence of how the Anglo-Saxons fought is limited to two battles, Maldon in 991 and Hastings in 1066, although there are a few details to be gleaned from other fights (Ashdown (871), Sherston and Ashingdon (1016)). The battle of Brunanburh was also described in a tenth century poem which consists entirely of heroic formulae and is of limited use here. It tells, for example, that

> Edward's sons clove the shield-wall, hewed the linden-wood shields with hammered swords...there lay many a man destroyed by the spears, many a northern warrior shot over his shield...The whole day long the West Saxons with mounted companies kept in pursuit of the hostile peoples, grievously they cut down the fugitives from behind with their whetted swords (ASC 937).

It is glorious stuff, but difficult to draw any clear picture from. In many respects the Maldon poem resembles it, consisting largely of a catalogue of single combats and epic speeches, but it does give more indication of how the English fought. Its narrative portions may not have the status of an eye-witness account, but as a vernacular poem it was written for an audience who knew what war and battle were like and so its details can be seen as an authentic setting. The same may be said of Hastings. William of Poitiers, if not present at the battle, had been a soldier, and although his account is not objective its circumstantial details are probably accurate. This gives very little to work from, but there are some conclusions which may be drawn.

In both battles the English are made to dismount and send their horses to the rear. As they are unlikely to have been turned loose they were most likely held by the non-combatants who accompanied the army but took no place in the battle-line. At Maldon Beorhtnoth next handed out coaching tips on how his men should stand in the "war-hedge". William of Poitiers, duke William's chaplain described the English formation at Hastings as so dense that the dead could scarcely fall, and the Bayeux Tapestry shows men standing shoulder-to-shoulder. While William may have been describing the constricted position of the English army he wrote in terms which later writers might have used to denote a solid and disciplined formation (Smail 1956, p. 128). There may be an element of exaggeration in these portrayals of the shieldwall. Common sense, and the sort of demonstrations put on at the conference, suggest that each warrior must have had some space in which to wield his weapons, especially the two-handed axes. On both occasions the two leaders would have occupied a position near the centre of the line, not in the front rank, with their military households around them. The rest of the line would have consisted of the retinues of landowners and the contingents led by sheriffs.

At Maldon as at Hastings the foe made the initial advance, and both sides shot spears and other missiles. The *Battle of Maldon* contains the enigmatic statement that 'bows were busy' and may also refer to the hostage Æscferth using a bow (the difficulty is that *flan* and *fysan* in 1.269 can refer either to arrows or throwing spears). The sole reference to English archers at Hastings is the solitary figure on the Bayeux Tapestry. This at least makes it unlikely that the English were ignorant of the use of the bow in war, contrary to the twelfth century Henry of Huntingdon (Arnold 1879, p. 202). Glover suggested that in 1066 the English archers, drawn from the poorer element of free society, were left behind in the rush from York to Battle and so played no part in the battle. This makes the mistake of assuming

that armies which included men on horseback moved about at a gallop. No satisfactory
answer seems possible, but if the late testimony of Snorre Sturlason's account of the battle of
Stamford Bridge (Magnusson and Palsson 1966, p. 162) is rejected, the limited evidence
suggests that English archers played no decisive role in battle. This is rather different to
concluding that there were no English archers. Rather, it means they were not used in
significant concentrations.

In these two battles the English stood on the defensive, but there is evidence that the
shield-wall was capable of limited manoeuvre. At Ashdown (878) and again at Sherston
and Ashingdon in 1016 we are told that the English advanced to engage the Danes. In
battles which involved two infantry armies the shieldwalls locked in combat and hewed
away at each other until the nerve of one or other side broke and it fled. This was
particularly prone to happen when a leader fell – or was rumoured to have fallen, as
happened to William in 1066. At Hastings Harold's army stood as if rooted to the spot
either because they chose to, or more likely because forced to by William's rapid advance.
Nevertheless, it occupied a strong position with its flanks protected, and could afford to let
William launch attacks and suffer casualties. After all, he needed a victory, while a draw
would do for Harold. This meant that William launched a series of assaults with the
different arms of his host in various combinations. The permutations are interesting and
demonstrate a flexibility which the English probably lacked. Nevertheless, the battle was
long and hard-fought, and it was only the death of Harold towards the end of the day
which brought English resistance to an end. It is by no means inconceivable that Hastings
could have been an English victory. This may seem far-fetched, but if William had indeed
fallen or been gravely wounded, or if a general English charge had been launched from the
brow of the hill, the outcome might well have been different. The English were out-
generalled at Hastings, not overrun. Certainly, though, it must be concluded from this
evidence that English tactics were less sophisticated and flexible than those employed by
William at Hastings. But this is very different to saying that their infantry tactics were
becoming obsolete. Indeed, the role of infantry was never to be neglected in medieval
warfare (Gillingham 1984, p. 91, Bradbury 1985, pp. 39–57).

The evidence of battles we do know about is that the English habitually fought on foot,
and that was the twelfth century tradition:

> The English do not know how to joust, nor how to bear arms on horseback, they carry
> axes and guisarmes, and with such arms they fight (Holden 1970–3, p. 206,
> 11.8603–4).

The thirteenth-century Scandinavian account of the battle of Stamford Bridge with its
English cavalry charges is rather flimsy evidence to the contrary.[6] Yet the English nobility
and 'gentry' were very used to riding horses, and the equipment of the English and Norman
warriors was very similar. In a skirmish or in a pursuit, as in that which followed the battle
of Brunanburh, it is likely that the English were capable of fighting on horseback. What set
them apart from the Franks and the Normans was their lack of specific cavalry tactics.
Since at least the end of the eighth century the Franks had possessed specific cavalry tactics
which consisted of a close order charge with spear and sword, one which the Ottonians
imitated in the tenth century. In the later part of the eleventh century a new cavalry tactic
was adopted, that of fighting with the lance couched. To argue that the English could on
occasion fight from horseback is not the same as saying they were trained in the tactics of
specialised horse soldiers.

The evidence for the Anglo-Saxon practice of war permits few firm conclusions to be drawn. It may be felt already that too much of what has been said relies on inference. And yet the all too few detailed episodes in the literary sources do demonstrate that the English were capable of more than gang warfare. The importance of supply, vital to military success, was appreciated even if it was taken for granted and features only incidentally in the sources. Although campaigns are usually too badly documented to discern it, a sense of strategy was not absent. If English tactics in battle appear to have been relatively simple, they brought victory over the other inhabitants of Britain and Scandinavian invaders. It is possible to conclude with confidence, then, that the Anglo-Saxons were not ignorant of the science of war and that their methods were adaptable.

* I am particularly grateful to Jinty Nelson, John Gillingham and Alfred Smyth for their comments on earlier versions of this paper.

Notes

1. ASC 992, 1009, 1044, 1045, 1049, 1052, 1066. For Viking fleets making land at Sandwich, 1006, 1013, 1014, 1015, 1040, 1048. The unexplained statement that Cnut took his ships to the Isle of Wight in 1022 may indicate hostilities with Normandy. Hill 1981, p. 14 shows the 11th century coastline.

2. Specific references to plundering are in ASC 903, 909, 1013, 1016; Roger of Wendover in Whitelock 1979, p. 281; it is graphically depicted in the Bayeux Tapestry during the Norman sojourn at Hastings. According to Bede, HE iii.24, in 655 Penda refused payment to cease ravaging Northumbria, although the Historia Brittonum (Whitelock 1979, p. 263) claims the payment was accepted and the treasure distributed to the kings with him. The latter may well be right, for there was a point to Bede's version.

3. For the way the rotation may have worked see Keynes and Lapidge 1983, pp. 285–6 n. 4; ASC 893, 917 (bis) refers to armies collected from men stationed in burhs. Æthelweard's version of the ASC appears to have had a rather different account of the outcome of the siege of Thorney island: Æthelred, king of the Mercians, sent reinforcements from London to help prince Edward bring the blockade to a successful conclusion (Keynes and Lapidge 1983, pp. 189–90).

4. Campaigns concluded without battles: Simeon of Durham sub anno 798, 801, 934, Roger of Wendover s.a. 829, ASC 868 (at Nottingham, where 'there occurred no serious battle'), 934 (Whitelock 1979, pp. 275–6, 278, 281, 192, 219).

5. ASC 868, 876, 877, 878, 885, 893, 895.

6. It is generally suspected that Snorre Sturlason transposed the events of Hastings to Stamford Bridge, although Glover 1952 did trust in his account.

References

Arnold, T. (ed.) 1879: *Henry of Huntingdon, Historia Anglorum* (London).

ASC, Anglo-Saxon Chronicle in Whitelock 1979.

Asser, Life of Alfred, in Keynes and Lapidge 1983.

Barlow, Frank 1983: *William Rufus* (London).

Bradbury, J. 1985: *The Medieval Archer* (Woodbridge).

Brooks, N.P.1971: The Development of Military Obligations in Eighth-and Ninth-century England, in Clemoes, P. and Hughes, K. (ed.), *England Before the Conquest* (Cambridge) pp. 69–84.

Brown, R.A. 1969: *The Normans and the Norman Conquest* (London).

Brown, R.A. 1981: *Proceedings of the Battle Conference iii 1980* (Woodbridge).

Campbell, A. (ed.) 1949: *Encomium Emmae Reginae* (Camden Soc. 3rd series).

Campbell, J. 1981: *The Anglo-Saxons* (Oxford).

Clapham, J.H. 1910: The Horsing of the Danes, *EHR* xxv, 287–93.

Colgrave, B. (ed.) 1956: *Felix, Life of Guthlac* (Cambridge).

Douglas, D.C. (ed.) 1953: *English Historical Documents ii* (London).

Ganshof, F.L. 1970: *Frankish Institutions under Charlemagne* (pbk ed. New York).

Gillingham, J. 1984: Richard I and the Science of War in the Middle Ages, in J. Holt and J. Gillingham (eds.), *War and Government in the Middle Ages* (Woodbridge).

Glover, R. 1952: English Warfare in 1066, *EHR* lxvii, pp. 1–18.

HE. Bede, *Ecclesiastical History of the English People*, quoted from the ed. by B. Colgrave and R.A.B. Mynors (Oxford, 1969).

Hill, D. 1981: *An Atlas of Anglo-Saxon England* (Oxford).

Holden, A. J. (ed.) 1970–3: *Wace, Roman de Rou* (Paris).

Hollister, C.W. 1962: *Anglo-Saxon Military Institutions* (Oxford).

Howlett, R. (ed.) 1886: *Chronicles of the Reigns of Stephen, Henry II and Richard I* (London).

Keynes, S. and Lapidge, M. (eds.) 1983: *Alfred the Great* (Harmondsworth).

King, P.D. (ed.) 1987: *Charlemagne. Translated Sources* (Lancaster).

Leyser, K., 1968. Henry I and the Beginnings of the Saxon Empire, *EHR* lxxxiii, 1–32.

Magnusson, M. and Palsson, H. (eds.) 1966: *King Harald's Saga* (Harmondsworth).

McClure, J. 1983: Bede's Old Testament Kings, in *Ideal and Reality in Frankish and Anglo-Saxon Society*, ed. P. Wormald (ed.) (Oxford), pp. 7698.

Oman, C. 1924: *A History of the Art of War in the Middle Ages* (London).

Smail, R.C. 1956: *Crusading Warfare 1097–1193* (Cambridge)

Verbruggen, J.F. 1977: *The Art of Warfare in Western Europe during the Middle Ages* (Amsterdam).

Warren, W.L. 1961: *King John* (London).

Webb, J.F. and Farmer, D.H. 1965: *The Age of Bede* (Harmondsworth).

Whitelock, D. (ed.) 1979: *English Historical Documents* i (2nd ed. London).

Index of People and Places

Compiled by Sonia Chadwick Hawkes

Select Subject Index

Compiled by Sonia Chadwick Hawkes

Contributors

Barry Ager
    Department of Medieval and Later Antiquities, British Museum, London WC1 3DG

Peter Bone
    35 St Margarets, Broadwater, Stevenage, Herts SE12 8RQ

Hilda R. Ellis Davidson
    23 Eltisley Avenue, Cambridge CB3 9JG

R. H. C. Davis
    349 Banbury Road, Oxford OX2 7PL

David A. Gale
    1 Wychdell, Stevenage, Herts

Margaret Gelling
    31 Pereira Road, Harborne, Birmingham B17 9JG

Guy Halsall
    Department of Archaeology, The University, Micklegate House, York YO1 1JZ

Heinrich Härke
    Department of Archaeology, The Queen's University, Belfast BT7 1NN

Sonia Chadwick Hawkes
    Institute of Archaeology, University of Oxford, 36 Beaumont Street, Oxford OX1 2PG

John Hines
    Department of English, University College, PO Box 78, Cardiff CF1 1XL

Nicholas Hooper
    14 Cambridge Terrace, Otley LS21 1JS

Janet Lang
    Research Laboratory, British Museum, London WC1 3DG

D. M. Metcalf
    Heberden Coin Room, Ashmolean Museum, Oxford OX1 2PH

S. J. Wenham
    University of Leicester, Medical Sciences Building, Department of Anatomy, University Road, Leicester LE1 7RH